MAPPING THE MODERN MIND:

READINGS FOR WORLD CULTURES III

SEVENTH EDITION

Compiled by
The Interdisciplinary Faculty
of World Cultures III

David Longfellow, History, Coordinator
Robert Baird, Philosophy
Frieda Blackwell, Spanish Literature
Scott E. Bryant, Religion
Ray Cannon, Mathematics
Jay Losey, English Literature
Robin Wallace, Musicology
Lenore Wright, Baylor Interdisciplinary Core

BAYLOR
UNIVERSITY

Copley Custom Textbooks

An imprint of XanEdu Publishing, Inc.

ISBN 13: 978-158152-712-4
ISBN 10: 1-58152-712-8

Cover art:

Matsuo Bashō (1644–1694) Japanese poet. Painted portrait. Osaka, Japan. Photo credit: Snark/Art Resource, NY.

Mary Godwin née Wollstonecraft (1759–1797). British writer and feminist. Oil on canvas by John Opie, 76.8 x 64.1 cm. Inv. 1237 Photo: Jochen Remmer. National Portrait Gallery, London. Photo credit: Bildarchiv Preussicher Kulturbesitz/Art Resource, NY.

Friedrich Nietzsche. Oil on canvas by Curt Stoeving, 1894. Stiflung Weimarer Klassik und Kunstsammlungen, Weimar, Germany. Photo credit: Bildarchiv Preussicher Kulturbesitz/Art Resource, NY.

Voltaire (1694–1778). Portrait by Jacques-Augustin Pajou. Comedie Francaise, Paris, France. Photo Credit: Scala/White Images/Art Resource, NY.

Acknowledgments:

pp. 1–3: From *A Lateral View: Essays on Culture and Style in Contemporary Japan* by Donald Ritchie. Copyright © 1987, 1991, 1992 by Stone Bridge Press. Reprinted by permission.

pp. 4–11: From *Lost Japan* by Alex Kerr. Copyright © 1996 by Lonely Planet Publications. Reprinted by permission.

pp. 12–17: From *The Japanese Today: Change and Community* by Edwin O. Reischauer and Marius B. Jansen, pp. 203–210, 212–215. Cambridge, Mass.: The Belknap Press, of Harvard University Press. Copyright © 1977, 1988, 1995 by the President and Fellows of Harvard College. Reprinted by permission of the publisher.

pp. 18–31: From *Matsuo Bashō* by Makoto Ueda. Copyright © 1970 by Kodansha International. Reprinted by permission of the publisher.

pp. 32–39: From *Narrow Road to the Interior* by Matsuo Bashō, translated by Sam Hamill. Copyright © 1991 by Sam Hamill. Reprinted by arrangement with Shambhala Publications, Inc., Boston, www.shambhala.com.

pp. 40–47: From *Rembrandt's Biblical Roles* by H. Perry Chapman. Copyright © 1990 by Princeton University Press, 1992 paperback edition. Reprinted by permission of the publisher.

pp. 48–52: From *Text and Act: Essays on Music and Performance* by Richard Taruskin. Copyright © 1995 by Oxford University Press. Reprinted by permission of the publisher via the Copyright Clearance Center.

pp. 53–56: From *Foundations of the Metaphysics of Morals and What Is Enlightenment?* by Immanuel Kant, translated by Lewis White Beck. Copyright © 1959. Published by Liberal Arts Press.

pp. 66–75: From *The Critical Reception of Beethoven's Compositions by His German Contemporaries* Vol. 2, edited by Wayne Senner and Robin Wallace, translated by Robin Wallace. Copyright © 2001 by University of Nebraska Press. Reprinted by permission of the publisher.

Copley Custom Textbooks
An imprint of XanEdu Custom Publishing
138 Great Road
Acton, MA 01720
800-562-2147

Contents

Japan: A Description

Donald Richie

Japan is entered; the event is marked, as when one enters a Shinto shrine, by passing beneath the *torii* gateway. There is an outside; then, there is an inside. And once inside—inside the shrine, inside Japan— the experience begins with a new awareness, a way of looking, a way of seeing.

You must truly observe. Go to the garden and look at the rock, the tree. Ah, nature, you say and turn—then stop. You have just observed that rock and tree have been placed there, placed by the hand of man, the Japanese hand. A new thought occurs: Nature does not happen; it is wrought. A new rule offers itself: Nothing is natural until it has been so created.

This comes as a surprise to us of a different culture. The Japanese view is anthropomorphic, unashamedly, triumphantly so. The gods here are human, and their mysteries are on display. If we occasionally find the Japanese scene mysterious, it is only because we find such simplicity mysterious—in the West, cause and effect this clear tend to be invisible. Look again at the torii—the support, the supported, and that is all.

Observation, appreciation and, through these, understanding. Not only in Japan, of course, but everywhere, naturally. But in Japan the invitation to observe is strongest because the apparent is so plain.

Look at the architecture. The floor defines the space; from it the pillars hold the beams; on them the roof contains the whole. Nothing is hidden. Traditionally there is no façade. Take the shrines at Ise. Cut wood, sedge, air—that is all they are made of.

The spatial simplicity extends temporally as well. The shrines have been destroyed and identically rebuilt every twenty years since antiquity. This cycle is an alternative to the Pyramids—a simpler answer to the claims of immortality. Rebuild precisely, and time is obliterated. Ise embodies the recipe for infinity: 100 cubits and two decades. That is all. Such simplicity, such economy suggest the metaphysical:

the ostensible is the actual, the apparent is the real. We see what is there, and behind it we glimpse a principle.

Universal principles make up nature, but nature does not reveal these principles, in Japan, until one has observed nature by shaping it oneself. The garden is not natural until everything in it has been shifted. And flowers are not natural either until so arranged to be. God, man, earth—these are the traditional strata in the flower arrangement, but it is man that is operative, acting as the medium through which earth and heaven meet.

And the arrangement is not only in the branches, the leaves, the flowers. It is also in the spaces in between. Negative space is calculated, too—in the architecture, in the gardens, in the etiquette, in the language itself. The Japanese observe the spaces in between the branches, the pillars; he knows too when to leave out pronouns and when to be silent. Negative space has its own weight, and it is through knowing both negative and positive (yin and yang), the specific gravity of each, that one may understand the completed whole, that seamless garment that is life. There are, one sees, no opposites. The ancient Greek Heraclitus knew this, but we in the Western world forgot and are only now remembering. Asia never forgot; Japan always remembered.

If there are no true opposites, then man and nature are properly a part of one another. Seen from the garden, the house is another section of the landscape. The traditional roof is sedge, the stuff that flourishes in the fields. The house itself is wood, and the mats are reed—the outside brought inside.

The garden is an extension of the house. The grove outside is an extension of the flower arrangement in the alcove. Even now, when land prices make private gardens rare, the impulse continues. The pocket of earth outside the door contains a hand-reared tree, a flowering bush. Or, if that too is impossible, then the alcove in the single matted room contains a tiny tree, a flowering branch, a solitary bloom. Even now that sedge and reed are rarely used, the shapes they took continue—the Japanese reticulation of space insists on inside, outside, man-made nature made a part of nature, a continuing symbiosis. Even now, the ideal is that the opposites are one.

A garden is not a wilderness. It is only the romantics who find wildness beautiful, and the Japanese are too pragmatic to be romantic. At the same time, a garden is not a geometrical abstraction. It is only the classicists who would find that attractive, and the Japanese are too much creatures of their feelings to be so cerebrally classic. Rather, then, a garden is created to reveal nature. Raw nature is simply never there.

Paradigm: In Japan, at the old-fashioned inn, you get up, go to take your morning bath, and you are invisible—no one greets you. Only when you are dressed, combed, ready—only then comes the morning greeting. Unkempt nature, unkempt you, both are equally nonexistent. The garden prepared is acknowledged as natural. What was invisible is now revealed, and everything in it is in "natural" alignment.

Thus, too, the materials of nature, once invisible, are now truly seen. Formerly mute, they are now "heard." The rock, the stone, are placed in view; textures—bark, leaf, flower—are suddenly there. From this worked-over nature emerge the natural elements. Wood is carved with the grain so that the natural shape can assert itself. In the way the master sculptor Michelangelo said he worked, the Japanese carpenter finds the shape within the tree. Or, within the rock, for stone too has grain, and this the Mason finds, chipping away to reveal the form beneath.

Made in Japan is a slogan we know, and one we now see has extensions—like silicon chips and transistors. Not the same as carved wood or stone, but created by a similar impulse. And with such an un-formulated national philosophy—nature is for use—this is not surprising. Everything is raw material, inanimate and animate as well.

Not only is nature so shaped, but human nature, too, is molded. We of the West may approve of the hand-dwarfed trees, the arranged flowers and the massaged beef, but we disapprove when people are given the same attention. Our tradition is against such control. Japan's, however, is not. It welcomes it. Society is supposed to form. Such is its function. We are (they would say) all of one family, all more or less alike. So we have our duties, our obligations. If we are to live contentedly, if society (our own

construct) is to serve, then we must subject ourselves to its guiding pressures.

As the single finger bends the branch, so the social hand inclines the individual. If the unkempt tree is not considered natural, then the unkempt life is equally out of bounds. So, the Japanese do not struggle against the inevitable. And, as they say, alas, things cannot be helped, even when they can be. This simplified life allows them to follow their pursuits. These may be flower arranging, or Zen, or *kendo* fencing. Or, on the other hand, working at Sony, Toyota, Honda. Or *is* it the other hand?

The support, the supported. The structure of Japanese society is visible, little is hidden. The unit is among those things most apparent. The module—*tatami* mats are all of a size, as are *fusuma* sliding doors and *shoji* paper panes. Mine fits your house, yours fits mine.

Socially, the module unit is the group. It is called the *nakama*. Each individual has many: family, school, club, company. Those inside (*naka*) form the group. This basic unit, the nakama, in its myriad forms, makes all of society. The wilderness, nature unformed and hence invisible, is outside the nakama of Japan, and that wilderness includes all non-members, among them, of course, us, the *gaijin* (foreigners). The West also has its family, its school, its company, but how flaccid, how lax. They lack the Japanese cohesion, the structural denseness, and at the same time the utter simplicity of design.

Land of the robot? Home of the bee and the ant? Given this functional and pragmatic structure, given this lack of dialectic (no active dichotomies—no good, no bad, no Platonic ideals at all), one might think so. But, no—it is something else. Let the Westerner sincerely try to live by Japanese custom, says Kurt Singer, Japan's most perspicacious observer, "and he will instantly feel what a cell endowed with rudiments of human sensibility must be supposed to feel in a well-coordinated body."

Does this not sound familiar? It is something we once all knew, we in the West as well. It is something like a balance between the individual and his society. One lives within social limitations to be sure. And if you do not have limitations, how do you define freedom? In Japan, the result is individual conformity: Each city, each house and each person is different from all the others yet essentially the same. The hand may shape the flower, but it is still a flower.

If one answer to the ambitions of immortality is to tear down and reconstruct exactly the Ise shrines, then one answer to the external problem of the one and the many (a Western dichotomy), to reconciling the demands of the individual and those of society, is the Japanese self in which the two selves become one. They are not, Japan proves, incompatible. The individual and that individual playing his social role are the same. As the house and the garden are the same. The nakama dissolves fast enough when not wanted—and freezes just as fast when desired. To see Japan then is to see an alternate way of thinking, to entertain thoughts we deem contradictory. Having defined nature to his satisfaction, the Japanese may now lead what is for him a natural life.

This natural life consists of forming nature, of making reality. Intensely anthropomorphic, the Japanese are, consequently, intensely human. This also means curious, acquisitive, superstitious, conscious of self. There is an old garden concept (still to be seen at Kyoto's Entsu-ji temple) that is called *shakkei*. We translate it as "borrowed scenery." The garden stops at a hedge. Beyond that hedge, space. Then in the distance—the mountain, Mount Hiei. It does not belong to the temple, but it is a part of its garden. The hand of the Japanese reaches out and enhances (appropriates) that which is most distant. Anything out there can become nature. The world is one, a seamless whole, for those who can see it; for those who can learn to observe, to regard, to understand.

—1984

Kabuki:

Only the Salt Remains

Alex Kerr

In the summer of 1977 my long college years end-ed, and I returned to Japan to work at a Shinto foundation called Oomoto, based in the small town of Kameoka, west of Kyoto. The founder of Oomo-to had said, 'Art is the mother of religion,' and in keeping with his philosophy, Oomoto sponsors a summer seminar in traditional Japanese arts (tea cer-emony, Noh drama, etc.), which I had attended in 1976. My job at Oomoto was to help with arts-relat-ed international activities.

However, my first months in Kameoka were ex-tremely lonely. Although Oomoto provided the op-portunity to study tea ceremony and Noh drama, their world of ritual failed to interest me. For a per-son of serious temperament, the quiet of the tea-room and the formality of Noh should be an inspiration. But with some feelings of guilt, I had to admit to myself that I did not have a serious tem-perament. I tried to distract myself by making the rounds of Kyoto's temples, but soon reached my limit of raked sand. It was very frustrating. There had to be more than this zestless, ritualized Kyoto, with every tree pruned, every gesture a formula.

That summer, the old Mother Goddess of Oomoto had a visit from an important guest—the Tibetan lama Tomo Geshe Rinpoche, abbot of a monastery in Sikkim. He was famed for his psychic powers. At the end of the summer, we met one day in a beer garden in Kameoka. Knowing Tomo Geshe's repu-tation as a psychic, I came straight to the point and blurted, "What should I do?" He looked me over and said, "You must seek out another world. If not on this earth, then the moon. If not the moon, then somewhere else. Without fail you will find that world by the end of the year."

Tomo Geshe went on to America, leaving his secre-tary, Gail, to take care of odds and ends in Kyoto. One day in December, Gail invited me to go and see a Kabuki play. I had been dragged to Kabuki as a child, but my only memory was of ugly old wom-en with harsh croaking voices—the *onnagata* (male actors who play women's roles). I was not very en-thusiastic about the invitation, but having nothing better to do I accompanied Gail into Kyoto to see the play at the Minamiza Theater.

It was Kyoto's *kaomise* (literally, 'face showing'), when leading Kabuki actors come down from To-kyo to act in the gala performance of the year. Gei-sha dressed in their finery sit in the boxes that line the theater, and the refined matrons of Kyoto throng the lobby exchanging cruel politenesses with each other. But we were too poor to be a part of all that. We bought the cheapest tickets available and climbed to our seats high in the rafters.

As the dance 'Fuji Musume' ('Wisteria Maiden') began, I saw that the *onnagata* playing the maiden was not one of the ugly old women of my child-hood memory, but was truly picture lovely. The flute and drums were fast flowing; the sliding feet and impossible turns of the neck and wrists of the dancer were playful and sensuous—everything I had been missing. I was stagestruck.

After the dance, Gail informed me to my surprise that the *onnagata*, whom I had thought to be about twenty-five years old, was the veteran actor Naka-mura Jakuemon, aged sixty at the time. On leaving the theater, Gail took me to a nearby teahouse called Kaika. The master of the teahouse asked me what I had thought of *kaomise*, and I replied, "Jakuemon was amazing. His sixty-year-old body managed to be totally sensuous." The master gestured to the woman sitting next to me, and said, "She has an appointment with Jakuemon right now. Why don't you go along?" So before I knew it, I was backstage at the Minamiza Theater. One minute, Jakuemon was a vision dancing on a stage miles below me, someone I could only view from afar with no hope of ever meeting; the next, I was backstage talking to him.

Jakuemon, still in make-up, looked fortyish, like a refined Kyoto matron. But he had a sly grin, and a coquettish sideways glance flashed from eyes lined with red and black. This sideways glance, called *nagashime* (literally, 'flowing eyes'), was a hallmark of beautiful women in old Japan, and is found in countless woodblock prints of courtesans and *onnagata*. I was seeing it at close range. An attendant dressed in black brought out a small saucer, in which Jakuemon blended white face powder and crimson lipstick with a gentle hand. Dipping a brush in the resulting '*onnagata* pink,' he wrote the character *hana* (flower) for me on a square *shikishi* (calligraphic plaque). Then, with the removal of wig, robes and make-up, there emerged a tanned, short-haired man, who looked like a tough Osaka businessman. With a brusque "See ya," spoken in a gravelly voice, he strolled out of the room in white suit and shades.

In my case, the secret door to the world of Kabuki was the Kaika teahouse. *Kaika*, which means 'transformation,' refers to the Bunmei Kaika (Transformation of Civilization) which took place in Japan after the Meiji Restoration in 1868. The master of Kaika was a former Kabuki *onnagata*, and the interior of the teashop was covered with Meiji and Taisho-period theater decorations. As it was close to the Minamiza Theater, Kaika was a meeting place for actors and teachers of traditional Japanese music and dance.

After my audience with Jakuemon, I was taken to see various other actors, among them Kawarazaki Kunitaro, a childhood friend of the Kaika master. Kunitaro, who was in his sixties, was a true child of the Meiji 'transformation,' his father having founded Tokyo's first coffee house on the Ginza at the turn of the century. As a young man, Kunitaro joined a group of leftist intellectuals who broke away from traditional Kabuki and co-founded a theater troupe called Zenshinza (Progressive Theater). Kunitaro was especially adept at *akuba* roles—sharp-tongued townswomen. Other actors would come to him to study his distinctive technique of *sute-serifu*—catty quips 'tossed' at the audience.

I found it curious that the Progressive Theater featured something so retrograde as *onnagata*. Kabuki was founded by a troupe of women in the early 1600s, but during the Edo period, women were banned from the Kabuki stage because they were considered conducive to immoral behavior. The *onnagata* took their place. There was a brief attempt in early Meiji to replace *onnagata* with real women but the audience rejected them. By that point, Kabuki was so thoroughly imbued with the art of *onnagata* that real women did not play the roles properly. After Meiji, women found their place in modern theater. However, in certain unexpected pockets, such as Zenshinza and in Japanese dance, *onnagata* continue to exist even outside of Kabuki.

I soon heard of a particular *onnagata* called Tamasaburo. Unlike the others, he had achieved fame outside of Kabuki as his face was everywhere—on TV, on posters, in advertisements. In 1967, at the age of seventeen, Tamasaburo had caught the eye of the public with his appearance in the play *Azuma Bunsho Sakurahime (The Scarlet Princess of Edo)*. Yukio Mishima wrote a play for him; teenage girls besieged the theaters. For the first time in a century, a Kabuki *onnagata* had become a popular star.

The February after the Minamiza *kaomise*, I saw Tamasaburo perform for the first time, at the Shinbashi Enbujo Theater in Tokyo, in the dance 'Sagi Musume' ('Heron Maiden')—Kabuki's *Swan Lake*. In it, a young maiden dances as a white heron in the snow. Through successive costume changes, from white, to purple, to red, she passes through the stages of girlhood, young adulthood and first love. Then comes heartbreak: her wing (or sleeve) is wounded. She becomes deranged and whirls madly through the snow. At the end, mounting a red felt-covered platform, her face distorted with suffering and rage, she strikes a final pose.

The beginning of the dance was quiet. Sagi Musume, dressed in a pure white kimono, a white hood over her head, turned slowly at the center of the stage, her movement so smooth and perfectly controlled that she seemed like a marble statue. Though Tamasaburo had yet to show his face, he had already conjured up a quiet, twilit, snow-covered world. The hood fell, revealing the pure face of an angel, radiantly white. The audience gasped; this was not the usual *onnagata*. Impossible to describe, the beauty of Tamasaburo is almost a natural phenomenon, like a rainbow or a waterfall. At the end, when, her long black hair disheveled, Sagi Musume mounted the red platform brandishing a magic staff, she was like a shaman of ancient times, evoking the wrath of heaven. The audience around me wept.

Afterwards, a friend of the Kaika master took me to Tamasaburo's dressing room backstage. Out of make-up, Tamasaburo was a tall, thin young man, who looked not much different from somebody one might sit next to on the subway. In contrast with his sadness-tinged femininity of the stage, he was no-nonsense, cheerful, funny. He was then aged twenty-seven, two years older than me.

Kabuki, an almost perfectly preserved remnant of Japan's feudal past, is dominated by a handful of old families. Actors are ranked according to the importance of their hereditary names, like barons and dukes in the peerage. Actors not born into a Kabuki family are doomed to spend their whole lives as *kuroko*—the black-clad attendants, supposedly invisible to the audience, who appear onstage to supply a prop and remove or adjust a piece of costume. At best, they might appear in a row of maids or retainers. But occasionally someone manages to gain entrance to the hierarchy from outside, and Tamasaburo was one of these.

Although not born into the Kabuki world, Tamasaburo began dancing when he was four. At the age of six he was adopted by the Kabuki actor Morita Kanya XIV, and appeared as a child actor under the name of Bando Kinoji. From then on, his entire life was devoted to the stage; he never went beyond high school. When I met him, he had just returned from his first trip to Europe and was dying to talk to someone about world culture. Fresh from Oxford, I seemed to him to be the ideal candidate. For my part, having just watched Sagi Musume, I was still marveling at his genius, and had a host of questions to ask about Japanese theater. We hit it off at once, and soon became fast friends.

From then on, I neglected Oomoto and stole every opportunity to take the train to Tokyo to see Kabuki. Jakuemon and Tamasaburo gave me free run of the backstage, and Tamasaburo's adoptive mother, Kanshie, was a master of Nihon Buyo (Japanese dance), so I would often watch her classes. For five years I more or less lived inside the Kabuki theater.

Kabuki seems to me to have the perfect balance between the sensuality and ritual which are the two poles of Japanese culture. On one hand, there is Japan's free-wheeling sexuality, out of which was born the riotous *ukiyo* (floating world) of Edo: courtesans, colorful woodblock prints, men dressed as women, women dressed as men, 'naked festivals,' brilliantly decorated kimonos, etc. This is a remnant of ancient Southeast Asian influence on Japan, and is more akin to Bangkok than to Beijing or Seoul. In fact, early Jesuits traveling from Beijing to Nagasaki at the end of the sixteenth century wrote letters in which they contrasted the colorful costumes of the Japanese with the drab gowns of the common people of Beijing.

At the same time, there is a tendency in Japan towards over-decoration, towards cheap sensuality too overt to be art. Recognizing this, the Japanese turn against the sensual. They polish, refine, slow down, trying to reduce art and life to its pure essentials. From this reaction were born the rituals of tea ceremony, Noh drama and Zen. In the history of Japanese art you can see these two tendencies warring against each other. In the late Muromachi period, gorgeous gold screens were in the ascendant; along came the tea masters, and suddenly the aesthetic was misshapen brown tea bowls. By late Edo the emphasis had swung back to courtesans and the pleasure quarters.

Today, this war goes on. There are garish *pachinko* parlors and late-night pornographic TV, and there is a reaction against all that, which I call the 'process of sterilization': the tendency to fill every garden with raked sand and every modern structure with flat concrete and granite. Kabuki, however, has the right balance. It began as a popular art, and is rich in humor, raw emotion and sexual appeal. At the same time, after hundreds of years, it has been slowed and refined to the point where, within the sensuality, there is that timeless 'stop'—the meditational calm which is Japan's special achievement.

Kabuki, like all theater, is a world of illusion. With its extreme elaboration of costumes, make-up and the *kata* (prescribed 'forms' of movement), it may be the most illusionistic of all: when the elegant court lady removes her make-up, one is left facing an Osaka businessman. Once, I was translating for Tamasaburo when an Englishman asked him, "Why did you want to become an actor?" Tamasaburo answered, "Because I longed for a world of beauty beyond my reach." I, too, was bewitched by this elusive world of illusion.

In the play *Iriya*, there is a scene where the woman Michitose is about to meet her lover after a long separation. Her samurai is being hunted by the police but has crept through the snow to see her. He waits in front of some *fusuma* sliding doors. Hearing of his arrival, she bursts into the room and the lovers are reunited. When Tamasaburo was once playing the part of Michitose, we were sitting together backstage, next to the *fusuma* doors and more or less on the stage itself, just prior to Michitose's dramatic entrance. Tamasaburo was chatting casually and was not the least bit feminine—very much an average man, although he was in full costume. When the time came for his entrance, he stood up, laughed, said, "OK, here I go!", and walked over to the *fusuma*. He adjusted his robe, flung open the *fusuma*, and in that instant was transformed into a beauty straight out of an Ukiyoe print. In a silvery voice fit to melt the audience's heart, he cried out, "*Aitakatta, aitakatta, aitakatta wai na!*—I've missed you, I've missed you, I've missed you so much!" A world of illusion had sprung up from one side of a *fusuma* to the other.

The illusion is achieved by Kabuki stagecraft, probably the most highly developed in the world. The *hanamichi* (flower path) through the audience is a particularly famous example. Actors enter and leave the stage via this walkway; separated from the action on the main stage, the actor on the *hanamichi* enters a solitary realm where he is free to reveal the inner depths of his role. For instance, the play *Kumagai Jinya (Kumagai's Battlecamp)* is a traditional tale of *giri-ninjo* (the conflict between love and duty): Kumagai must kill his own son and substitute the boy's severed head for the son of his lord. His ruse is successful, but in remorse Kumagai shaves off his hair to enter a life of asceticism, and exits down the *hanamichi*. When the late Kanzaburo XVIII played Kumagai, he imparted such a sense of personal desolation as he exited down the *hanamichi* that *Kumagai Jinya* seemed not a tale of *giri-ninjo*, but an antiwar play.

Kabuki stagecraft sometimes seems symbolic of life itself. An example of this is *danmari*, or pantomime scenes, in which all the lead characters come silently out onto the stage at the same time. As though walking in pitch darkness, they move about in slow motion, oblivious to each other's existence; they run into each other or drop things which are retrieved by others. There is an eerie quality about *danmari* which has nothing to do with any specific play. Watching scenes of *danmari*, where a man picks up a letter his lover has dropped, or two people looking for each other pass by unawares, one senses the blindness of human existence. What begins as just another bit of eccentric Kabuki stagecraft ends up symbolizing a deeper truth.

Why did stagecraft develop to such a level in Japan? At the risk of oversimplification, I would say it was because Japan is a country where the exterior is more often valued over the interior. One may see the negative effects of this in many aspects of Japanese life. For instance, the fruits and vegetables in a Japanese supermarket are all flawless in color and shape as if made made from wax, but they are flavorless. The importance of the exterior may be seen in the conflict between *tatemae* (officially stated position) and *honne* (real intent), which is a staple of books written about Japan. Listening to the debates in Japan's Diet, it is abundantly clear that *tatemae* is given precedence over *honne*. Nevertheless, this emphasis on the surface is not without its positive side, for Kabuki's unparalleled stagecraft is a direct result of such prizing of the outward.

Though I learned many things from Kabuki stagecraft, the aspect I found most fascinating was the artistry used to capture and accentuate the emotion of a single fleeting moment. The *mié*, when actors pose dramatically with eyes crossed and arms flung out, is an obvious example of this. But it may be said of many other Kabuki *kata* as well. For example, there might be a scene where two people are casually talking; then, from some detail of the conversation, the characters suddenly comprehend each other's true feelings. In that instant, action stops, actors freeze, and from stage left wooden clappers go 'battari!.' The two characters resume speaking as though nothing has happened; however, in the instant of that 'battari!,' everything has changed. While most forms of theater try to preserve a narrative continuity, Kabuki focuses around such crucial instants of stop and start, start and stop.

This can also be said of Kabuki audiences' expressions of appreciation. At a Western play or concert, the audience waits politely until the very end before applauding; nothing could be more déclassé than to clap between movements of a symphony. In contrast, during highlights of a Kabuki play, audience members will show their appreciation by shouting out the *yago* (house names) of the actors. When the play is over, they just get up and leave.

The shouting of *yago* is an art in itself. One doesn't shout at any time, but only at certain moments of dramatic tension. You can recognise the amateurs in the audience by their poorly timed shouts. There is a group of knowledgeable old men, called the *omuko* (literally, 'men in the back'), who are the masters of this art form; they frequent the upper rafters, where I sat at my first *kaomise*. From there, they shout *yago* such as *Yamatoya!* for Tamasaburo or *Nakamuraya!* for Kanzaburo. Or they will vary their repertoire with *Godaime!* ('fifth generation!'), *Goryonin!* ('the pair of you!') or *Mattemashita!* ('I've been waiting for this!'), I remember watching the legendary *onnagata* Utaemon, then aged seventy, appearing as the grand courtesan Yatsuhashi. At the climactic moment, when Yatsuhashi turns to the peasant following her and bestows upon him the smile which is going to destroy his life, there was a shout from the *omuko*: "Hyakuman doru!"—'a million dollars!.'

I have only shouted once in my life; it was in the early days, for Kunitaro. His yago was *Yamazakiya!*. I practiced and practiced, and then at the right moment I shouted "*Yamazakiya!*" from the rafters as best as I could. It wasn't easy. The timing is so important that the actors depend on the shouts to sustain the rhythm of the performance. I once saw Tamasaburo in rehearsal pause at a critical moment, whisper "*Yamatoya!*," and then glide into the next movement of the dance.

Focus on the 'instant' is characteristic of Japanese culture as a whole. In Chinese poetry, the poet's imagination might begin with flowers and rivers, and then suddenly leap up into the Nine Heavens to ride a dragon to Mt. K'un-lun and frolic with the immortals. Japanese haiku focus on the mundane moment, as in Basho's well-known poem: 'The old pond, a frog leaps in, the sound of water.' The frog leaps into the pond, not up to heaven. There are no immortals, just 'the sound of water.' In the concision of haiku and *waka*, Japan created unparalleled literary forms. On the other hand, long poems of narrative or ideas are almost completely absent from the history of Japanese literature. Long verse was created by stringing pearls together into longer chains, as in *renga* (linked *waka* poems).

This 'instantaneous culture' is something I also noticed in the real-estate world, where I was later to work in Tokyo. There are innumerable detailed building codes, but the overall design of a building and its aesthetic relation to street and skyline are ignored; the result is careless, disjointed, ugly. The sorry state of the highway system is also the result of *renga* thinking: there is no master plan, just a stringing together of annual budgets to build highways piecemeal.

Kabuki is no exception. The arrangement of a play's elements are ambiguous, and sudden narrative leaps are often made. For anyone expecting dramatic unity, Kabuki seems weak. My friends who value logic invariably dislike Kabuki. However, with its emphasis on the depth of a single instant, Kabuki creates an atmosphere of intense excitement which is rare in other theater. Tamasaburo once told me, "In ordinary drama, the story proceeds step-by-step. What a bore! Kabuki's fascination lies in its outrageous leaps of logic."

Kabuki, like everything else in Japan, is torn between the poles of refinement and hedonism—hedonism being represented by *keren* (acrobatic tricks), refinement by the actors' measured grace. These days, plays featuring multiple costume changes, actors attached to cables flying through the air, and waterfalls onstage are all the rage. The popularity of *keren* is a sign of the sickness currently plaguing the traditional Japanese arts in general. When one looks at Japan's wilderness breathing its dying gasps, the traditional arts seem comparatively healthy. Kabuki has actually experienced a box-office resurgence over the last twenty years, and the theaters are often sold out. But trouble is brewing because of Kabuki's irrelevance to any life a modern audience can now experience. There is hardly a single object on the Kabuki stage recognizable to young people today. When stage chanters sing of

fireflies or autumn maples, such things are now almost mythical subjects in this land of vast cedar plantations.

Actors such as Jakuemon or Tamasaburo spend hours with the kimono dyers discussing the precise shade of purple a certain kimono should be, what color the great actor Kikugoro VI ('the Great Sixth') used, what is chic or not chic by standards of the Edo period. Certain older attendants, who came in from outside and therefore can never achieve major roles, have amassed incredible knowledge about such Kabuki arcana. In many cases, these men, not the actors you see onstage, are the true standard-bearers of the tradition; they know by heart not only what Kikugoro VI used, but what was used before him.

An example is Tamasaburo's old retainer Yagoro, now in his eighties, whom Tamasaburo inherited from his adoptive father Kanya. Yagoro performed major roles in his youth as a member of the small troupes that used to travel the countryside. As the tide of Westernization swept Japan after World War II, these smaller troupes disappeared or were gradually absorbed into one large troupe. The 'Grand Kabuki' we see today consists of several hundred actors (and their assistants), all based in Tokyo. 'Grand' though it is called, it is actually the shrunken remnant of a larger Kabuki world which once numbered thousands of performers spread throughout the provinces. Yagoro belongs to the last generation who knew that larger Kabuki world.

Yagoro will come into the room backstage after a show and sit there with a smile on his face. Then Tamasaburo will say, "What do you think, Father?" (actors address each other as 'elder brother,' 'uncle,' 'father'). Yagoro will say, "The Great Sixth used a silver fan, but that was because he was short and it accentuated his height. For you it would be inappropriate. Use gold, like the former Baiko did." This is how their knowledge is passed down.

But what use are all these refinements when you are performing to an audience whose familiarity with the kimono is about on a par with that of Americans? Fine details tend to be lost, and the audience goes for the obvious crowd-pleasers, like *keren*.

Another problem is the generation gap. The training of actors, including those of Tamasaburo's generation, used to be fierce. Intense dedication was required. Jakuemon told me how he used to memorize *nagauta* (long narrative lyrics) by chanting them on the train on his way to the theater; one day, the train suddenly stopped and he found all the other passengers staring at him as he chanted loudly in the ensuing silence. In those days, Kabuki was more of a popular form, and less of a formalized 'traditional art,' so audiences were more knowledgeable and demanding. A bad actor would find the *omuko* shouting, "*Daikon!*" ('big radish!'), to his everlasting humiliation. Now there are no calls of *Daikon!*, and audiences sit reverently with their hands in their laps, no matter how good or bad the actor might be. The younger actors, born in privilege because of their family names, have it easy. Tamasaburo once said, "Communism in Russia was a terrible thing, but it produced great ballet dancers. In order to be great you need a Moscow in your background."

After I began watching Kabuki, I discovered Nihon Buyo (Japanese dance) and Shinpa (Meiji-style drama) as well. I realized that 'Grand Kabuki' is just the tip of the iceberg—the arts connected to Kabuki are vigorously active in their own right. There is a constant round of recitals, called *kai* (gatherings), of Nihon Buyo, flute, *nagauta* (long lyrics), *kouta* (short lyrics), *samisen*, and more.

While one invariably sees foreigners at Kabuki theater, I have found it extremely rare to see another foreigner at any of these recitals. But given the diversity of Nihon Buyo, which includes dozens of styles, tens of thousands of teachers and millions of students, it is a broader world than Kabuki. Many of the finest dancers are women, which is a return to Kabuki's pre-*onnagata* roots. Some of them are legends such as Takehara Han, who began as a geisha in Osaka and ended up as the premier master of Zashiki-mai (sitting-room dance), a subtle form of dance which originated in the intimate quarters of the geisha house. If you included classical Kabuki dance styles such as Fujima-ryu, as well as the numerous varieties of Zashiki-mai, Kyo-mai (Kyoto dance) and even *enka* (modern pop dancing), you could spend your life watching Nihon Buyo.

When the Fates were planning my introduction into the world of Kabuki, they arranged not only the Kaika teahouse and my meeting with Tamasaburo, but also that I should become friends with a man named Faubion Bowers. Faubion traveled to Japan as a student before World War II, and had become enamored of Kabuki, sitting up in the rafters night after night learning from the *omuko*. He was especially a fan of the prewar actor Uzaemon.

During the war he was a translator and ended up as General Douglas MacArthur's aide-de-camp, and at war's end MacArthur dispatched Faubion a few days in advance of his arrival to make arrangements. So, when Faubion and his group arrived at Atsugi air base, they were the first enemy soldiers to set foot in Japan. A contingent of Japanese officials and press nervously awaited them, fearful of what the Americans' first move would be. But Faubion approached the press and asked, "Is Uzaemon still alive?" The tension instantly relaxed.

Following the war, all 'feudalistic' customs were banned by the U.S. Occupation, and Kabuki, with its subject matter of samurai loyalty, was banned as well. However, Faubion managed to get himself appointed as censor of the theater, and so was able to revive Kabuki. He later received an award from the Emperor in recognition of his historic role. Having seen Kabuki's prewar greats, and having been close to postwar leaders Baiko, Shoroku and Utaemon when they were still young, Faubion has an unparalleled knowledge of Kabuki.

During our lifetimes, Kabuki has undergone a critical transformation. The art form will of course continue, but we will never see the likes of actors such as Utaemon and Tamasaburo again. As foreigners, Faubion and I both had access to Kabuki in a way which is unlikely to be repeated. We hope to put our knowledge together in a book some day for future generations.

However, Faubion and I disagree about everything. For instance, I am not partial to Kabuki's historical plays such as *Chushingura (The Forty-Seven Samurai)*; most of them involve tales of *giri-ninjo*, and for me there are more interesting themes. For an earlier audience, trained fanatically to obey their superiors, these plays about sacrificing oneself for one's lord were truly heart-rending; it was what all Japanese did every day of their lives, at the office or in the army. There is a moment in *Chushingura* when the lord has committed *hara-kiri* and is dying, but his favorite retainer, Yuranosuke, is late. Finally, Yuranosuke arrives, only to see his master expire with the words, "You were late, Yuranosuke." Yuranosuke looks into his master's eyes and silently understands that he is to wreak vengeance for his lord's martyrdom. I have seen older audiences weeping uncontrollably at this scene. But for people who have grown up in soft, affluent, modern Japan—including myself—resonances of personal sacrifice are growing faint. Faubion, however, insists that these historical plays embody the essence of Kabuki. He also contends that the ugly old ladies I remember from my youth epitomize the true *onnagata* art, and that the beauty of Tamasaburo and Jakuemon is far too striking, even 'heretical.'

On no point do Faubion and I disagree so much as on the subject of *onnagata*, which brings me to the difficult question of what *onnagata* really are. Obviously, they have something in common with a drag show. From English pantomime to traveling performers in India, the desire to see male actors dressed up as women seems to be universal. In

China and Japan the primeval drag show developed into art. The *dan* (Chinese *onnagata*) have largely disappeared (although they may be making something of a comeback), not because the public gradually lost interest, but because the Cultural Revolution dealt such a blow to traditional theater; once a tradition like *dan* is weakened, it is difficult to reconstruct. Japan, however, escaped the turmoil of the Cultural Revolution, and so it is only here that the tradition survives in healthy form.

Development into high art meant that *onnagata* concentrated on the romantic rather than the comic, the essential feminine rather than the physical body. This is why Faubion values older *onnagata*: the fact that they are old and unattractive allows their art to shine unalloyed with common sensual appeal. According to him, "The art of old Kabuki actors is like sea water which has been sitting in the sun. As actors get older, more and more water evaporates, and it gets more and more salty. In the end, only essential salt remains."

Due to their exact preservation of details of the old lifestyle, Kabuki plays may be seen as a 'living museum.' How to light an *andon* (paper floor lantern), open a *fubako* (lacquered letter case), arrange hair with *kanzashi* (hairpins), handle a scroll—these and countless other techniques live on in Kabuki's use of stage properties. Kimono fashions, shops and houses, prescribed movements of hands and feet, the ways to bow, the ways to laugh, samurai etiquette and many other aspects of Japan that existed prior to the arrival of Western culture are all reflected in Kabuki's mirror. Kabuki is one giant nostalgia for the past; I cannot think of any other theatrical art form which preserves ancient daily life so thoroughly.

Especially in the light of the modernization which has swept over Japan in recent years, the world of Kabuki seems particularly poignant. There are, of course, no longer any *fubako* or *kanzashi*, but the disappearance of these things is no more significant than the disappearance in the West of the bustle and fringed parasol. In the West, modernization, while drastic, did not wipe away every single reminder of what life once was. But in Japan, cities and countryside alike have been bulldozed. Even the trees and rice paddies painted on backdrops are fast vanishing from day-to-day surroundings. Only in Kabuki does the dream world of the past live on.

Over eighteen years have passed since I first went to meet Jakuemon, and since then I have entered the backstage door countless times. Yet even now I get butterflies in my stomach every time I approach it. I live in fear of the doorman, I wonder if I am

neglecting some bit of backstage punctilio. Kabuki's window into Japan's traditional lifestyle does not end on the stage.

Lesser actors make the rounds of greater actors' rooms, entering on their knees to make official greetings and to ask for good wishes before they go onstage. Actors are addressed by titles which sound strange to modern ears, such as 'Wakadanna' ('Young Master') for an *onnagata* like Tamasaburo. ('Danna,' or 'Master,' is the title for an important male-role player, but *onnagata*, no matter how old they get, remain 'Young Master.') Each backstage room is decorated with banners carrying the distinctive emblems of the actors, just like aristocratic heraldry. There is a constant exchange of gifts: fans, hand towels or rolls of fabric, all of which carry symbolic significance. It is a truly feudalistic world, far removed from that of ordinary mortals. Once, when I told Tamasaburo about my trepidation on going backstage, I was surprised when he answered, "I feel exactly the same way!"

I sometimes think that what bewitched me about Kabuki was not the plays themselves, but the life behind them. What is so remarkable is the tenuous line between illusion and reality which exists backstage. At the opera, the performance does not continue backstage; the actors don't sing arias at you, and on removing their costumes they become just ordinary people, no matter how famous they are as artists. Backstage at Kabuki, however, the illusion continues. Most people wear kimonos, which is rare enough in Japan today, and the kimonos—all black for *kuroko* attendants, printed *yukata* (a cotton kimono) for other attendants and gowns for major actors—clearly indicate social status; the backstage kimonos are sometimes as striking as anything you might see onstage.

Occasionally, an actual play may even continue behind the scenes. For instance, during a performance of *Chushingura*, which is considered Kabuki's supreme play, the actors and attendants maintain a particularly serious demeanor backstage. Another example is *Kagamiyama*. In this play, the court lady Onoe is humiliated by Iwafuji, who is trying to bring ruin to Onoe's house. Onoe exits slowly down the *hanamichi*, deep in thought. When Jakuemon played this part, he remained seated alone, in silence, in the small room behind the curtain at the end of the *hanamichi*, until it came time for Onoe's next entrance; although not onstage, he was still in character. Later, when I asked Jakuemon about this, he replied that it was a *Kagamiyama* tradition, which allows the depths of Onoe's emotional concentration to remain unbroken until she reappears the second time.

Faubion once pointed out that Kabuki actors spend a greater percentage of their life onstage than almost any other actors. First put on the stage at age five or six, they appear in two performances a day, twenty-five days a month, month after month, year after year. In essence, the Kabuki actor spends his entire life onstage. As a result, says Faubion, older actors sometimes find it difficult to differentiate between their stage personas and their real selves.

The actor Utaemon's normal movements, the distinctive turn of hands or neck, bear striking resemblances to his body language onstage. After performing as the character Onoe, Jakuemon remarked to me that he felt very tired; when I asked why, he replied, "Onoe bears a great responsibility. I was very worried about Ohatsu." Ohatsu is Onoe's protégé in the drama, and Ohatsu also happened to be played by Tamasaburo in that performance. In Jakuemon's concern for Ohatsu/Tamasaburo (it was not clear which), the onstage and offstage worlds were so intertwined as to be inseparable.

Kabuki's themes provide much insight into Japanese society. For instance, many plays are about the relationship between a lord and his retainers, or that between lovers, but there are none about friends. Friendship has been a key theme of Chinese culture since ancient times. The second sentence of Confucius's *Analects*—'When a friend comes from afar, is this not a joy?'—demonstrates the Chinese attitude towards the subject. But in Japan such examples are rare. True friendship is not easy here.

Long-term foreign residents complain that after ten or twenty years in the country they are lucky to know one Japanese they consider to be a true friend. Yet the problem goes deeper than the culture gap between foreigners and Japanese. The Japanese often tell me that they can't make friends with each other; they say, "There are the people you knew in high school who remain bosom buddies for life. Everyone you meet after that cannot be trusted."

One reason for this could be that the educational system traditionally discourages the Japanese from speaking their mind. They never quite trust each other, making friendship difficult. Another reason might be that hierarchical structures of society get in the way. In the old society the master-retainer relationship was a familiar one; relationships between equals were not. This is a question for sociologists to ponder, but in any case, the culture of friendship is strikingly absent from Kabuki.

And yet it was through Kabuki that I eventually made my best friends. Over the years, I became close to a number of Kabuki actors; I am still mystified how this came to pass. The world of Kabuki, with its nebulous border between illusion and reality, is at once very Japanese, and not of Japan at all. As Tomo Geshe had predicted, it's a world which is not of this earth, not of the moon—a 'world beyond reach.' That's why when I pass through the scary barrier to the backstage, though it is a world of illusion, I feel at home. My good friends are here.

Religion

Edwin O. Reischauer and Marius B. Jansen

If this book were about a South Asian or Middle Eastern people, it would be unthinkable to have delayed a discussion of religion so long and until after topics such as women and education. Religion in fact might well have been the starting point for these Islamic, Hindu, or Buddhist lands, because of its importance there, but in modern Japan it plays a lesser and more peripheral role. I purposely delayed its presentation to emphasize this point. Before the seventeenth century, religion did play an important role in Japanese society, but the trend toward secularism that has only recently become marked in the West dates back at least three centuries in Japan.

The secularism of Japanese society is the product of the influence of Confucian philosophy, which had the same effect in China beginning in the ninth century and in Korea in the fifteenth. East Asians call this philosophy "the teaching of the scholars" (*jukyo* in Japanese), but in the West it has been named for its first master, Confucius, who lived from approximately 551 to 479 B.C. Confucianism did not take final shape in China until the twelfth century A.D. It stressed a rational natural order, of which man was a harmonious element, and a social order based on strict ethical rules and centering on a unified state, governed by men of education and superior ethical wisdom. It had revered texts but no concept of deity, no priesthood, and very little religious ritual. There was no worship, only right thinking and right living, as shown particularly through loyalty to the ruler, filial piety to one's father, and strict observance of proper social ritual and etiquette.

The Confucian classics, the five basic human relationships, the emphasis on history, and many other features of the Confucian system entered Japan with the first great wave of Chinese influence between the sixth and ninth centuries, but Confucianism tended to be overshadowed by Buddhism until the emergence of the centralized Tokugawa system in the seventeenth century made it seem more relevant than it had before. From then on, Confucian schools of philosophy dominated thought and Confucian attitudes pervaded society, until in the early

nineteenth century the Japanese had become almost as thoroughly Confucian as the Chinese or Koreans, despite their very non-Confucian feudal political system.

Confucianism, however, did not survive the great transition of the late nineteenth century as an organized philosophy. Its concepts of the cosmos were seen to be highly inaccurate when compared with the results of modern Western science, and its moral values appeared to be tied to a type of society and government that had to be abandoned in the face of the Western menace. The government, in reorganizing inherited Tokugawa educational institutions into Tokyo University, dropped the old Confucian academy and concentrated only on the Western scientific and medical aspects of these schools. A few Confucian scholars fought a rearguard action, forcing the old terminology and concepts into the new system wherever they could. The outstanding example of this was the Imperial Rescript on Education, issued in 1890 at the time of the adoption of the constitution. It had very little to say about education but was a purely Confucian statement of the Confucian relationships and the duties of citizens to the throne. Thus some Confucian attitudes survived, though Confucianism as an accepted body of thought died out completely with the passing of the older generation.

Contemporary Japanese obviously are not Confucianists in the sense that their Tokugawa ancestors were, but Confucian ethical values continue to permeate their thinking. Confucianism probably has more influence on them than does any other of the traditional religions or philosophies. Behind the wholehearted Japanese acceptance of modern science, modern concepts of progress and growth, universalistic principles of ethics, and democratic ideals and values, strong Confucian traits persist, such as the belief in the moral basis of government, the emphasis on interpersonal relations and loyalties, and faith in education and hard work. Almost no one considers himself a Confucianist today, but in a sense almost all Japanese are.

Buddhism is the Japanese religion that comes closest to paralleling Christianity, for it too is concerned with the afterlife and the salvation of the individual. In this it shows its non-East Asian origin in India, a region that in religious and philosophical attitudes is more like the premodern West than like East Asia. The historical Buddha, or "enlightened one," who was roughly contemporary with Confucius, started with the basic Indian idea of a never-ending cycle of lives, each determining the next, and added to this the concepts that life is painful, that its suffering derives from human attachment or desires, but that these desires can be overcome by the Buddha's teaching, thus freeing the individual for painless merging with the cosmos in Nirvana, or "nothingness." As the teaching developed, it came to stress reverence for the "Three Treasures," which were the Buddha, the "law" or teachings embodied in an extensive literature, and the religious community, meaning monastic organizations.

The branch of Buddhism that spread throughout East Asia is called Mahayana, or the "greater vehicle," in contrast to Theravada, or the "doctrine of the elders," which survives in Ceylon and much of Southeast Asia. Mahayana taught salvation into a paradise that is closer to the Western concept of heaven than to the original Buddhist Nirvana. It also emphasized the worship, not just of the historical Buddha, but of myriad Buddhalike figures, including Bodhisattvas, who have stayed back one step short of Nirvana and Buddhahood in order to aid in the salvation of others.

In Japan, Mahayana Buddhism developed three major emphases. The first, appearing in the ninth century, was "esoteric" Buddhism, which stressed magic formulas, rituals, and art. The second emphasis, starting a century later, was on salvation through faith, particularly in Amida, the Buddha of the "pure land" of the Western Paradise, or in the Lotus Sutra, a scripture in which the Buddha promised the salvation of "all sentient beings," that is, of all animal life. This emphasis gave rise to the founding in the twelfth and thirteenth centuries of new sects—the Pure Land Sect (Jodoshu), the True (Pure Land) Sect (Shinshu), and Nichiren—which are today the largest Buddhist sects in Japan. The third emphasis was on self-reliance in seeking salvation through self-discipline and meditation. This became embodied in the two Zen, or "meditation," sects, introduced from China in 1191 and 1227. These developed regimens of "sitting in meditation" (zazen) and of intellectual self-discipline through nonsense conundrums (koan), which were supposed to lead to salvation through sudden enlightenment (satori) and also, incidentally, to character building.

Buddhism first came to Japan in the sixth century and played much the same role as Christianity in northern Europe as the vehicle for the transmission of a whole higher culture. A great part of subsequent esthetic expression in architecture, sculpture, and painting was associated with Buddhism, as it was with Christianity in the West. The monastic establishments became rich landowners, as in the West, and at times exercised considerable military and political power. Even congregations of lay believers were politically active in the fifteenth and sixteenth centuries. Indeed Buddhism permeated the whole intellectual, artistic, social, and political life of Japan from the ninth through the sixteenth centuries.

Not much of this survives in contemporary Japan after the savage destruction of the political power of Buddhist institutions by the unifiers of Japan in the late sixteenth century, the three centuries of the progressive secularization of society that followed, and a ruthless attack by the early Meiji government on Buddhism as an element of the discredited past that stood in the way of the creation of an emperor-centered new political system. Buddhist concepts about such things as paradise and the transmigration of the soul linger on in folklore but serve as guiding principles for few people.

Monasteries and temples, both great and small, dot the Japanese landscape but usually play only a subdued background role in the life of the community. The postwar land reform proved a financially crippling blow to many rural temples because it deprived them of the lands that had helped support them. A few people still come to worship and find solace in the Buddhist message of salvation. Temple grounds are often neighborhood playgrounds for children. Most funerals are conducted by Buddhist priests, and burial grounds attached to temples are the place of interment for most people after cremation, a custom learned from India and adopted by all Japanese, probably because of the scarcity of land. Many people return in midsummer to their ancestral homes in the countryside for the Urabon or Bon Festival ("All Saints Day"), a colorful festival of Buddhist origin. At some places on this day they float miniature lighted boats downstream or out to sea in memory of the souls of deceased relatives. Some families have ancestral tablets, which they place in small Buddhist altars on a shelf in the home. The Tokugawa system of requiring the registry of all persons as parishioners of some Buddhist temple—the purpose of this was to ferret out secret Christians—has given all Japanese families a Buddhist sectarian affiliation, though usually this indicates only the sect of the temple where the family burial plot is located.

Most temples and monasteries today maintain their rituals, though often with pathetically small numbers of monks or priests. Some sects took on new intellectual and religious vigor in modern times, in part in response to the Christian missionary movement. They developed publishing ventures, schools, and even a Buddhist missionary movement in East Asia and America. A few modern Japanese, such as some prewar military men and postwar business executives, have practiced Zen, but their numbers are small and their concern is usually less with Buddhist enlightenment than with the development of their own personalities. Contemporary Japanese life thus is full of traces of Buddhism as a sort of background melody, but it is not for many a leitmotif in either their intellectual or emotional lives.

Shinto, the earliest and most distinctive of the Japanese religions, has also slipped into a background role in modern urbanized Japan. Primitive Shinto centered on the animistic worship of natural phenomena—the sun, mountains, trees, water, rocks, and the whole process of fertility. Totemistic ancestors were included among the *kami*, or deities, worshiped, and no line was drawn between man and nature. A mythology concerning the deities, reminiscent of early Greek mythology, explained the creation of the Japanese islands and tied the origins of the imperial line to the sun goddess, the supreme *kami*.

Shrines dedicated to the various *kami* are to be found everywhere. The main one for the sun goddess stands at Ise, east of the old capital district, facing the rising sun across the Pacific Ocean. Thousands of lesser shrines, each marked by a *torii* gateway, were dedicated to imperial ancestors, the mythological forebears of other once-powerful local families, the deity of rice, or some remarkable natural phenomenon, such as a great mountain, a beautiful waterfall, or simply an unusual tree or rock. Deities are worshiped through offerings, prayers, the clapping of one's hands to gain their attention, and, at larger shrines, lighthearted festivals. But original Shinto had no theology or even a concept of ethics, beyond an abhorrence of death and defilement and an emphasis on ritual purity.

Since Shinto was unconcerned with the problem of the afterlife that dominated Buddhist thought, and Mahayana was no exclusive, jealous religion but throughout its spread easily accommodated itself to local faiths, Buddhism and Shinto settled into a comfortable coexistence, with Shinto shrines often becoming administratively linked with Buddhist monasteries. The Japanese never developed the idea, so prevalent in South and West Asia as well as the West, that a person had to adhere exclusively to one religion or another. Premodern Japanese were usually both Buddhists and Shintoists at the same time and often enough Confucianists as well.

For most of the premodern period, Shinto was definitely subordinate to Buddhism, being thought of as representing the locally valid Japanese variants of universal Buddhist truths and deities. But Buddhist fervor waned after the sixteenth century, while the native origins of Shinto and its association with the foundation myths of Japan and with the cult of the imperial ancestors focused new attention on it in a Japan that was becoming more nationalistic and eventually came to seek a new unity under symbolic imperial rule. A sort of Shinto revival centering on reverence for the emperor became part of the movement that led to the overthrow of the Tokugawa and the founding of the new regime in 1868.

The leaders of the Meiji Restoration, being thoroughly anti-Buddhist, brutally cut Buddhism off from Shinto, and they attempted at first to create a Shinto-centered system of government. Although they soon discovered that this concept could not be mixed successfully with their basically Western political patterns, they did create a system of state support for the great historic Shinto shrines and developed new national ones, such as the beautiful Meiji Shrine in Tokyo, dedicated to the first modern emperor, and the Yasukuni Shrine, also in Tokyo, for the souls of military men who had died in defense of the country. In order to maintain the claim that Japanese enjoyed complete religious freedom, this nationalistic "state Shinto" was officially defined by the government as being not a religion but a manifestation of patriotism. In a sense it was not a religion, because, even though it did impinge, at least in form, on the field of religion in its enforced worship at Shinto shrines and the reverential treatment of pictures of the emperor and empress and copies of the Imperial Rescript on Education that was required of all schools throughout the country, it was essentially an artificial creation, far removed from the basic attitudes of Shinto and deriving more from modern nationalism.

"State Shinto" reached its peak in the frenzy of nationalism preceding World War II. The American occupation naturally attacked it with vigor as a dangerous manifestation of xenophobia, and in the general postwar reaction against militarism and patriotism it disappeared almost completely. The occupation also demanded that a sharp line be drawn between government and religion. The great historical shrines were thrown back on their own individual sources of income, and as a result all but the most popular ones fell into dire financial straits. Although a few had wide support, which has enabled them to generate new sources of income, the ban on public funds for institutions connected with religion hit most of them hard and also, incidentally, contributed to the slowness with which the government came to the aid of private universities, many of which have Christian, Buddhist, or even Shinto affiliations.

With "state Shinto" gone, Shintoism has reverted to a more peripheral role in Japanese life. Shrines of all types are scattered everywhere, often in places of great beauty and charm, though usually with signs of quiet decay. They are visited by a few believers in the efficacy of their rituals and prayers to their deities or, if they are historically famous or are known for their natural beauties, by throngs of eager sightseers. Visits in recent years by prime ministers to the Yasukuni Shrine for the war dead and the enshrinement there in 1978 of some of the men executed by the American occupation as "Class A" war criminals have stirred up great opposition among Christians and other religious groups as well as members of the political left. But on the whole the Yasukuni Shrine is regarded as analogous to the Tomb of the Unknown Soldier, and the Meiji Shrine to the Lincoln Memorial in Washington. Children are often taken to shrines at certain prescribed points in their lives—shortly after birth, at special festivals in their third, fifth, and seventh years, and at annual boys' and girls' festivals. Shrines are also the setting for many marriages, and homes frequently have "god shelves" where offerings are made to Shinto deities.

Traditional Shinto seems most alive today in the spirited shrine festivals held annually on specific dates by all shrines of any importance. At these times, scores of booths ply a brisk trade on the shrine grounds, and the shrine deity is boisterously carried about in a portable shrine by somewhat inebriated local youths. These shrine festivals remain a prominent feature of local life, particularly in rural Japan, though some of them are taking on the character of self-conscious, historical pageants, or else are losing out in urbanized areas to more secular community festivals that feature marching bands and drum majorettes.

In these various ways, Shinto continues to be a part of Japanese life, and folklore remains full of Shinto elements. The Japanese love of nature and sense of closeness to it also derive strongly from Shinto concepts. But very few modern Japanese find in traditional Shinto any real focus for their lives or even for their social activities or diversions.

Christianity is usually linked with Shinto and Buddhism as one of the three main religions of Japan, though it is considered a foreign religion in a way Buddhism is not. First introduced by the famous Jesuit missionary, Saint Francis Xavier, in 1549, it spread more rapidly in Japan during the next several decades than in any other Asian country, and Christians came to number close to half a million, a much larger percentage of the population of that time than they are today. But Hideyoshi and the early Tokugawa shoguns came to view Christianity as a threat to political unity and suppressed it ruthlessly, creating in the process a large number of Japanese martyrs but virtually stamping the religion out by 1638. Only a few tiny communities of secret Christians survived, and in time they lost most real knowledge of the tenets of their religion.

The nineteenth-century Japanese remained deeply hostile to Christianity, but they soon learned the strength of Western feelings about the religion and therefore tacitly dropped their prohibition of it in 1873 and subsequently made explicit a policy of complete religious toleration. But Christianity this time spread much more slowly. Even today its adherents number less than 2 percent of the population—divided fairly evenly between Protestants and Catholics.

After the Meiji Restoration, Protestant Christianity, largely brought by American missionaries, was taken up by a number of able young samurai, particularly those from the losing side in the civil war, who sought in Christianity a new ethics and philosophy of life to take the place of discredited Confucianism. These men injected a strong sense of independence into the native church. In fact, under the leadership of Uchimura Kanzo, a leading intellectual of the time, a "No Church" movement was founded in reaction to the sectarian divisions of Protestantism in the West. During World War II the government, for control purposes, forced the various Protestant sects into a United Church, and today some 40 percent of the Protestant movement remains in the United Church of Christ in Japan (Nihon Kirisuto Kyodan).

The influence of Christianity on modern Japanese society is far greater than the small number of its adherents would suggest. Christians are strongly represented among the best-educated, leading elements in society and have therefore exerted a quite disproportionate influence. Another factor is that Christianity, as an important element of Western civilization, has attracted general attention. Most educated Japanese probably have a clearer concept of the history and basic beliefs of Christianity than they do of Buddhism. A superficial example of the general Japanese familiarity with Christianity is the enthusiasm with which Christmas decorations are displayed by department stores and Christmas carols are blared out along the shopping streets at Christmas time.

During the Meiji period, Christians played a major role in education, particularly at the secondary level and in schools for girls. Even today a large percentage of the private secondary schools and women's universities and some of the other private universities are of Christian origin, though the role of Christianity in education is much less important now than it once was. In the early twentieth century Christians also led in the development of social work for underprivileged and handicapped persons, and Protestant Christians were also prominent in the founding of the Socialist movement. In fact, they remained an important element in the movement throughout the prewar period, and they continued even into postwar days as a significant, moderate branch of the Socialist Party. But perhaps the largest area of Christian influence is in ethics. As modern Japanese turned increasingly to universalistic values, they adopted many ethical attitudes that both historically in the West and in the Japanese mind today are associated with Christianity. The Christian influence on contemporary Japanese ethical values is at least more recognizable if not actually greater than the influence of either Buddhism or Shinto. Moreover, many Japanese look upon Christians as people of high moral principles, and they often envy the apparent firmness of Christian beliefs, though they find themselves unable to accept the accompanying theology.

Christianity, though intellectually influential, is numerically only a tiny religion in Japan, and Shinto and Buddhism are for most people more a matter of custom and convention than of meaningful belief. Many if not most Japanese who feel strong religious needs today look elsewhere, turning instead to superstitious folk beliefs, prevalent especially in rural Japan and among the less educated, or to a great variety of popular religious movements, which are normally lumped together under the name of the "new religions." The popular superstitious beliefs are usually an amalgam of concepts derived from Shinto, Buddhism, and Chinese folk superstitions. There are numerous local cults of all sorts, and many people pay serious attention to lucky and unlucky days, astrology, and fortune-tellers.

The new religions have grown in part out of an old Japanese tendency to form special groups for pilgrimages or other religious activities, outside the formal organization of the established religions, but a more important reason for their development is that they have been responsive to the social needs of Japanese, as the movement of people to the cities

broke their ties with rural religious bodies or left them without a suitable social group to which to belong. The new religions, thus, do not cater to the common Western religious need for individual strength through the establishment of a personal bond with God, but rather to the typical Japanese need for a supportive social environment.

The new religions tend to be highly syncretic, combining Shinto, Buddhist, and sometimes even Christian or Western philosophic influences. Most, however, are basically Shinto in their leanings, though the largest, Soka Gakkai (the "Value Creating Association"), is a lay association supporting a branch of the Nichiren sect of Buddhism. The new religions usually stress this-worldly values rather than the afterlife, emphasizing the achievement of health, prosperity, self-improvement, and happiness through faith or through magical practices. Some were founded by individuals, particularly women, who felt themselves to be possessed by the deities in a shamanistic way. Other founders merely claimed to have discovered the true way. Leadership in these religions frequently becomes hereditary, and their organization tends to be hierarchical, made up of typically Japanese groups of leaders and followers. This makes them highly susceptible to fissions, and in many there is also a relatively rapid turnover of members.

The officially recognized new religions number in the hundreds, and there are many more small groups lacking official recognition. The total membership is in the tens of millions. Soka Gakkai alone claims 16 million, though 6 million would probably be a better estimate of its actual membership at any one time. Some of these new religions are by now quite old. Tenrikyo ("Teaching of the Heavenly Truth"), which today claims a membership of almost 2 million, was founded by a peasant woman in 1838. Others, like Soka Gakkai, were either founded or had their major growth after World War II. The large new religions tend to have grandiose headquarters and to hold numerous elaborate mass festivals and rallies. Only Soka Gakkai has attempted to play a direct role in politics by founding a party, the Komeito, which later separated at least in theory from Soka Gakkai. All the new religions, however, provide their participants with a tightly organized, protective community, with study groups and social activities that minister perhaps more to their social than their spiritual needs.

All in all, religion in Japan offers a confused and indistinct picture. Shinto shrines and Buddhist temples are found everywhere. The lives of most Japanese are intertwined with religious observances—shrine festivals, "god shelves" and Buddhist altars in the homes, and Shinto or Christian marriages, Buddhist funerals, and other religious rites of passage. But the majority of Japanese—some 70 to 80 percent—even though carried on the rolls of one or more religious body, do not consider themselves believers in any religion. The ethics of the Japanese for the most part are derived from Confucianism, to which none now "belongs," and from Christianity, which is the faith of less than 2 percent. Popular religious customs are derived mostly from traditional Shinto and Buddhism, in which few really believe. And most religious life among the few who are religiously active is devoted to folk religious beliefs or new religions that have little prestige or general influence. Clearly religion in contemporary Japan is not central to society and culture.

Matsuo Bashō

Makoto Ueda

Chronology

1644	Matsuo Bashō born at or near Ueno in Iga Province.
1656	His father's death. Probably by this time Bashō had entered the service of Tōdō Yoshitada, a young relative of the feudal lord ruling the area.
1662	Wrote his earliest verse extant today.
1666	Yoshitada's death. Bashō resigned and entered a long period of unsettled life. He may have gone to live in Kyoto for a time.
1672	Dedicated *The Seashell Game* to a shrine in Ueno. Later moved to Edo in search of a new career.
1676	Wrote a pair of hundred-verse renku with another poet in Edo. Paid a brief visit to Ueno in the summer.
1678	Wrote critical commentaries for *Haiku Contests in Eighteen Rounds*.
1680	*Best Poems of Tōsei's Twenty Disciples* published. Judged "The Rustic Haiku Contest" and "The Evergreen Haiku Contest." Settled in the initial Bashō Hut.
1682	The Bashō Hut destroyed by fire. He took refuge in Kai Province for a few months.
1683	*Shriveled Chestnuts* compiled. His mother died in Ueno. New Bashō Hut built.
1684–1685	Went on a journey that resulted in *The Records of a Weather-Exposed Skeleton*. In Nagoya he led a team of poets to produce *The Winter Sun*.
1686	Wrote what is now known as *Critical Notes on the New Year's Renku*.
1687	Traveled to Kashima and wrote *A Visit to Kashima Shrine*. Judged one of the haiku contests published in *The Extending Plain*.
1687	Undertook a journey which produced *The Records of a Travel-Worn Satchel* and *A Visit to Sarashina Village*. Returned to Edo in the autumn of 1688.
1689	Journeyed in northern provinces of Honshu. The journey provided material for *The Narrow Road to the Deep North*, which he completed some time later.
1690	Visited friends and disciples in the Kyoto area. Stayed at the Unreal Hut near Lake Biwa for several months during the summer.
1691	Stayed at the House of Fallen Persimmons for a couple of weeks in the summer and wrote *The Saga Diary*. *The Monkey's Cloak* published. Returned to Edo toward the end of the year.
1692	The third Bashō Hut built. Wrote a haibun about the transplanting of banana trees.

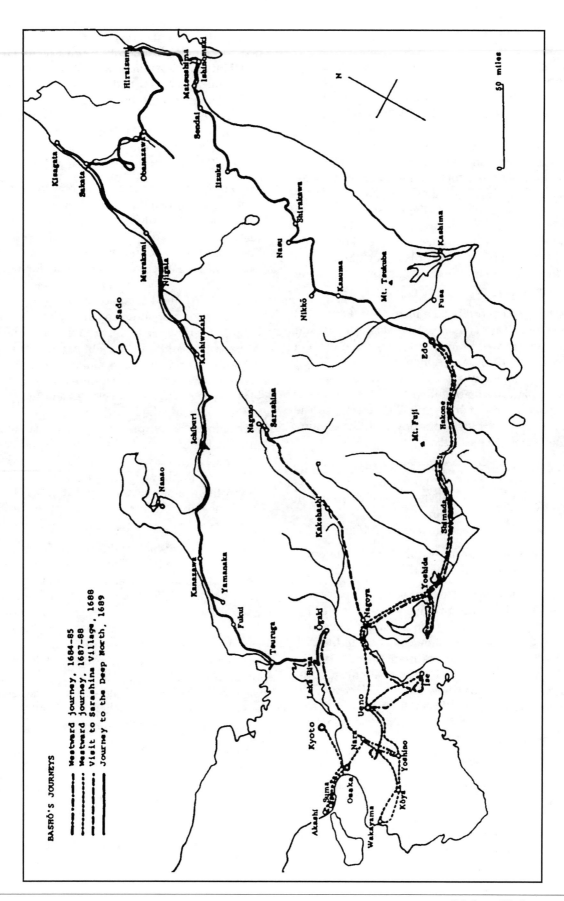

BASHŌ'S JOURNEYS

-·-·-·- Westward journey, 1684-85
·········· Westward journey, 1687-88
-··-··- Visit to Sarashina Village, 1688
————— Journey to the Deep North, 1689

Chapter 1 Life

One day in the spring of 1681 a banana tree was seen being planted alongside a modest hut in a rustic area of Edo, a city now known as Tokyo. It was a gift from a local resident to his teacher of poetry, who had moved into the hut several months earlier. The teacher, a man about thirty-six years of age, was delighted with the gift. He loved the banana plant because it was somewhat like him in the way it stood there. Its large leaves were soft and sensitive and were easily torn when gusty winds blew from the sea. Its flowers were small and unobtrusive; they looked lonesome, as if they knew they could bear no fruit in the cool climate of Japan. Its stalks were long and fresh-looking, yet they were of no practical use.

The teacher lived all alone in the hut. On nights when he had no visitor, he would sit quietly and listen to the wind blowing through the banana leaves. The lonely atmosphere would deepen on rainy nights. Rainwater leaking through the roof dripped intermittently into a basin. To the ears of the poet sitting in the dimly lighted room, the sound made a strange harmony with the rustling of the banana leaves outside.

Bashō nowaki shite	A banana plant in the autumn gale—
Tarai ni ame o	I listen to the dripping of rain
Kiku yo kana	Into a basin at night.

The haiku seems to suggest the poet's awareness of his spiritual affinity with the banana plant.

Some people who visited this teacher of poetry may have noticed the affinity. Others may have seen the banana plant as nothing more than a convenient landmark. At any rate, they came to call the residence the Bashō ("banana plant") Hut, and the name was soon applied to its resident, too: the teacher came to be known as the Master of the Bashō Hut, or Master Bashō. It goes without saying that he was happy to accept the nickname. He used it for the rest of his life.

I *First Metamorphosis: From Wanderer to Poet*

Little material is available to recreate Bashō's life prior to his settlement in the Bashō Hut. It is believed that he was born in 1644 at or near Ueno in Iga Province, about thirty miles southeast of Kyoto and two hundred miles west of Edo. He was called Kinsaku and several other names as a child; he had an elder brother and four sisters. His father, Matsuo Yozaemon, was probably a low-ranking samurai who farmed in peacetime. Little is known about his mother except that her parents were not natives of Ueno. The social status of the family, while respectable, was not of the kind that promised a bright future for young Bashō if he were to follow an ordinary course of life.

Yet Bashō's career began in an ordinary enough way. It is presumed that as a youngster he entered the service of a youthful master, Tōdō Yoshitada, a relative of the feudal lord ruling the province. Young Bashō first served as a page or in some such capacity. His master, two years his senior, was apparently fond of Bashō, and the two seem to have become fairly good companions as they grew older. Their strongest bond was the haikai, one of the favorite pastimes of sophisticated men of the day. Apparently Yoshitada had a liking for verse writing and even acquired a haikai name, Sengin. Whether or not the initial stimulation came from his master, Bashō also developed a taste for writing haikai, using the pseudonym Sōbō. The earliest poem by Bashō preserved today was written in 1662. In 1664, two haiku by Bashō and one by Yoshitada appeared in a verse anthology published in Kyoto. The following year Bashō, Yoshitada, and three others joined together and composed a renku of one hundred verses. Bashō contributed eighteen verses, his first remaining verses of this type.

Bashō's life seems to have been peaceful so far, and he might for the rest of his life have been a satisfied, low-ranking samurai who spent his spare time verse writing. He had already come of age and had assumed a samurai's name, Matsuo Munefusa. But in the summer of 1666 a series of incidents completely changed the course of his life. Yoshitada suddenly died a premature death. His younger brother succeeded him as the head of the clan and also as the husband of his widow. It is believed that Bashō left his native home and embarked on a wandering life shortly afterward.

Various surmises have been made as to the reasons for Bashō's decision to leave home, a decision that meant forsaking his samurai status. One reason which can be easily imagined is Bashō's deep grief at the death of his master, to whom he had been especially close. One early biography even has it that he thought of killing himself to accompany the master in the world beyond, but this was forbidden by the current law against self-immolation. Another and more convincing reason is that Bashō became extremely pessimistic about his future under the new master, whom he had never served before. As Yoshitada had Bashō, the new master must have had around him favored companions with whom he had been brought up. They may have tried to prevent Bashō from joining their circle, or even if they did not Bashō could have sensed some vague animosity in their attitudes toward him. Whatever the truth may have been, there seems to be no doubt that Bashō's future as a samurai became exceedingly clouded upon the sudden death of his master.

Other surmises about Bashō's decision to leave home have to do with his love affairs. Several early biographies claim that he had an affair with his elder brother's wife, with one of Yoshitada's waiting ladies, or with Yoshitada's wife herself. These are most likely the fabrications of biographers who felt the need for some sensational incident in the famous poet's youth. But there is one theory that may contain some truth. It maintains that Bashō had a secret mistress, who later became a nun called Jutei. She may even have had a child, or several children, by Bashō. At any rate, these accounts seem to point toward one fact: Bashō, still in his early twenties, experienced his share of the joys and griefs that most young men go through at one time or another.

Bashō's life for the next few years is very obscure. It has traditionally been held that he went to Kyoto, then the capital of Japan, where he studied philosophy, poetry, and calligraphy under well-known experts. It is not likely, however, that he was in Kyoto all during this time; he must often have returned to his home town for lengthy visits. It might even be that he still lived in Ueno or in that vicinity and made occasional trips to Kyoto. In all likelihood he was not yet determined to become a poet at this time. Later in his own writing he was to recall "At one time I coveted an official post with a tenure of land." He was still young and ambitious, confident of his potential. He must have wished, above all, to get a good education that would secure him some kind of respectable position later on. Perhaps he wanted to see the wide world outside his native town and to mix with a wide variety of people. With the curiosity of youth he may have tried to do all sorts of things fashionable

among the young libertines of the day. Afterward he even wrote, "There was a time when I was fascinated with the ways of homosexual love."

One indisputable fact is that Bashō had not lost his interest in verse writing. A haikai anthology published in 1667 contained as many as thirty-one of his verses, and his work was included in three other anthologies compiled between 1669 and 1671. His name was gradually becoming known to a limited number of poets in the capital. That must have earned him considerable respect from the poets in his home town, too. Thus when Bashō made his first attempt to compile a book of haikai, about thirty poets were willing to contribute verses to it. The book, called *The Seashell Game* (*Kai Ōi*), was dedicated to a shrine in Ueno early in 1672.

The Seashell Game represents a haiku contest in thirty rounds. Pairs of haiku, each one composed by a different poet, are matched and judged by Bashō. Although he himself contributed two haiku to the contest, the main value of the book lies in his critical comments and the way he refereed the matches. On the whole, the book reveals him to be a man of brilliant wit and colorful imagination, who had a good knowledge of popular songs, fashionable expressions, and the new ways of the world in general. It appears he compiled the book in a lighthearted mood, but his poetic talent was evident.

Then, probably in the spring of 1672, Bashō set out on a journey to Edo, apparently with no intention of returning in the immediate future. On parting he sent a haiku to one of his friends in Ueno:

Kumo to hedatsu	Clouds will separate
Tomo ka ya kari no	The two friends, after the migrating
Ikiwakare	Wild goose's departure.

His motive for going to Edo cannot be ascertained. Now that he had some education, he perhaps wanted to find a promising post in Edo, then a fast-expanding city which offered a number of career opportunities. Or perhaps, encouraged by the good reception that *The Seashell Game* enjoyed locally, he had already made up his mind to become a professional poet and wanted his name known in Edo, too. Most likely Bashō had multiple motives, being yet a young man with plenty of ambition. Whether he wanted to be a government official or a haikai master, Edo seemed to be an easier place than Kyoto to realize his dreams. He was anxious to try out his potential in a different, freer environment.

Bashō's life for the next eight years is somewhat obscure again. It is said that in his early days in Edo he stayed at the home of one or another of his patrons. That is perhaps true, but it is doubtful that he could remain a dependent for long. Various theories, none of them with convincing evidence, argue that he became a physician's assistant, a town clerk, or a poet's scribe. The theory generally considered to be closest to the truth is that for some time he was employed by the local waterworks department. Whatever the truth, his early years in Edo were not easy. He was probably recalling those days when he later wrote: "At one time I was weary of verse writing and wanted to give it up, and at another time I was determined to be a poet until I could establish a proud name over others. The alternatives battled in my mind and made my life restless."

Though he may have been in a dilemma Bashō continued to write verses in the new city. In the summer of 1675 he was one of several writers who joined a distinguished poet of the time in composing a renku of one hundred verses; Bashō, now using the pseudonym Tōsei, contributed eight. The following spring he and another poet wrote two renku, each consisting of one hundred verses. After a brief visit to his native town later in the year, he began devoting more and more time to verse writing. He must have made up his mind to become a professional poet around this time, if he had not done so earlier. His work began appearing in various haikai anthologies more and more frequently, indicating his increasing renown. When the New Year came he apparently distributed a small book of verses among his acquaintances, a practice permitted only to a recognized haikai master. In the winter of that year he judged two haiku contests, and when they were published as *Haiku Contests in Eighteen Rounds (Jūhachiban Hokku Awase)*, he wrote a commentary on each match. In the summer of 1680 *The Best Poems of Tōsei's Twenty Disciples (Tōsei Montei Dokugin Nijikkasen)* appeared, which suggests that Bashō already had a sizable group of talented students. Later in the same year two of his leading disciples matched their own verses in two contests, "The Rustic Haiku Contest" ("Inaka no Kuawase") and "The Evergreen Haiku Contest" ("Tokiwaya no Kuaswase"), and Bashō served as the judge. That winter his

students built a small house in a quiet, rustic part of Edo and presented it to their teacher. Several months later a banana tree was planted in the yard, giving the hut its famous name. Bashō, firmly established as a poet, now had his own home for the first time in his life.

II *Second Metamorphosis: From Poet to Wanderer*

Bashō was thankful to have a permanent home, but he was not to be cozily settled there. With all his increasing poetic fame and material comfort, he seemed to become more dissatisfied with himself. In his early days of struggle he had had a concrete aim in life, a purpose to strive for. That aim, now virtually attained, did not seem to be worthy of all his effort. He had many friends, disciples, and patrons, and yet he was lonelier than ever. One of the first he wrote after moving into the Bashō Hut was:

Shiba no to ni	Against the brushwood gate
Cha o konoha kaku	Dead tea leaves swirl
Arashi kana	In the stormy wind.

Many other poems written at this time, including the haiku about the banana tree, also have pensive overtones. In a headnote to one of them he even wrote: "I feel lonely as I gaze at the moon, I feel lonely as I think about myself, and I feel lonely as I ponder upon this wretched life of mine. I want to cry out that I am lonely, but no one asks me how I feel."

It was probably out of such spiritual ambivalence that Bashō began practicing Zen meditation under Priest Butchō (1642–1715), who happened to be staying near his home. He must have been zealous and resolute in this attempt, for he was later to recall: ". . . and at another time I was anxious to confine myself within the walls of a monastery." Loneliness, melancholy, disillusion, ennui—whatever his problem may have been, his suffering was real.

A couple of events that occurred in the following two years further increased his suffering. In the winter of 1682 the Bashō Hut was destroyed in a fire that swept through the whole neighborhood. He was homeless again, and probably the idea that man is eternally homeless began haunting his mind more and more frequently. A few months later he received news from his family home that his mother had died. Since his father had died already in

1656, he was now not only without a home but without a parent to return to.

As far as poetic fame was concerned, Bashō and his disciples were thriving. In the summer of 1683 they published *Shriveled Chestnuts (Minashiguri)*, an anthology of haikai verses which, in its stern rejection of crudity and vulgarity in theme and in its highly articulate, Chinese-flavored diction, set them distinctly apart from other poets. In that winter, when the homeless Bashō returned from a stay in Kai Province, his friends and disciples again gathered together and presented him with a new Bashō Hut. He was pleased, but it was not enough to do away with his melancholy. His poem on entering the new hut was:

Arare kiku ya	The sound of hail—
Kono mi wa moto no	I am the same as before
Furugashiwa	Like that aging oak.

Neither poetic success nor the security of a home seemed to offer him much consolation. He was already a wanderer in spirit, and he had to follow that impulse in actual life.

Thus in the fall of 1684 Bashō set out on his first significant journey. He had made journeys before, but not for the sake of spiritual and poetic discipline. Through the journey he wanted, among other things, to face death and thereby to help temper his mind and his poetry. He called it "the journey of a weather-beaten skeleton," meaning that he was prepared to perish alone and leave his corpse to the mercies of the wilderness if that was his destiny. If this seems to us a bit extreme, we should remember that Bashō was of a delicate constitution and suffered from several chronic diseases, and that travel in seventeenth-century Japan was immensely more hazardous than it is today.

It was a long journey, taking him to a dozen provinces that lay between Edo and Kyoto. From Edo he went westward along a main road that more or less followed the Pacific coastline. He passed by the foot of Mount Fuji, crossed several large rivers, and visited the Grand Shinto Shrines in Ise. He then arrived at his native town, Ueno, and was reunited with his relatives and friends. His elder brother opened a memento bag and showed him a small tuft of gray hair from the head of his late mother.

Te ni toraba	Should I hold it in my hand
Kien namida zo atsuki	It would melt in my burning tears—
Aki no shimo	Autumnal frost.

This is one of the rare cases in which a poem bares his emotion, no doubt because the grief he felt was uncontrollably intense.

After only a few days' sojourn in Ueno, Bashō traveled farther on, now visiting a temple among the mountains, now composing verses with local poets. It was at this time that *The Winter Sun (Fuyu no Hi)*, a collection of five renku which with their less pedantic vocabulary and more lyrical tone marked the beginning of Bashō's mature poetic style, was produced. He then celebrated the New Year at his native town for the first time in years. He spent some more time visiting Nara and Kyoto, and when he finally returned to Edo it was already the summer of 1685.

The journey was a rewarding one. Bashō met numerous friends, old and new, on the way. He produced a number of haiku and renku on his experiences during the journey, including those collected in *The Winter Sun*. He wrote his first travel journal, *The Records of a Weather-Exposed Skeleton (Nozarashi Kikō)*, too. Through all these experiences, Bashō was gradually changing. In the latter part of the journal there appears, for instance, the following haiku which he wrote at the year's end:

Toshi kurenu	Another year is gone—
Kasa kite waraji	A travel hat on my head,
Hakinagara	Straw sandals on my feet.

The poem seems to show Bashō at ease in travel. The uneasiness that made him assume a strained attitude toward the journey disappeared as his trip progressed. He could now look at his wandering self more objectively, without heroism or sentimentalism.

He spent the next two years enjoying a quiet life at the Bashō Hut. It was a modest but leisurely existence, and he could afford to call himself "an idle old man." He contemplated the beauty of nature as it changed with the seasons and wrote verses whenever he was inspired to do so. Friends and disciples who visited him shared his taste, and they often gathered to enjoy the beauty of the moon, the snow, or the blossoms. The following composition, a short prose piece written in the winter of 1686, seems typical of his life at this time:

> A man named Sora has his temporary residence near my hut, so I often drop in at his place, and he at mine. When I cook something to eat he helps to feed the fire, and when I make tea at night he comes over for company. A quiet, leisurely person, he has become a most congenial friend of mine. One evening after a snowfall, he dropped in for a visit, whereupon I composed a haiku:

Kimi hi o take	Will you start a fire?
Yoki mono misen	I'll show you something nice—
Yukimaroge	A huge snowball.

The fire in the poem is to boil water for tea. Sora would prepare tea in the kitchen, while Bashō, returning to the pleasures of a little boy, would make a big snowball in the yard. When the tea was ready, they would sit down and sip it together, humorously enjoying the view of the snowball outside. The poem, an unusually cheerful one for Bashō, seems to suggest his relaxed, carefree frame of mind of those years.

The same sort of casual poetic mood led Bashō to undertake a short trip to Kashima, a town about fifty miles east of Edo and well known for its Shinto shrine, to see the harvest moon. Sora and a certain Zen monk accompanied him in the trip in the autumn of 1687. Unfortunately it rained on the night of the full moon, and they had only a few glimpses of the moon toward dawn. Bashō, however, took advantage of the chance to visit his former Zen master, Priest Butchō, who had retired to Kashima. The trip resulted in another of Bashō's travel journals, *A Visit to the Kashima Shrine (Kashima Kikō)*.

Then, just two months later, Bashō set out on another long westward journey. He was far more at ease as he took leave than he had been at the outset of his first such journey three years earlier. He was a famous poet now, with a large circle of friends and disciples. They gave him many farewell presents, invited him to picnics and dinners, and arranged several verse-writing parties in his honor. Those who could not attend sent their poems. These verses, totaling nearly three hundred and fifty, were later collected and published under the title *Farewell Verses (Kusenbetsu)*. There were so many festivities that to Basho "the occasion looked like

some dignitary's departure—very imposing indeed."

He followed roughly the same route as on his journey of 1684, again visiting friends and writing verses here and there on the way. He reached Ueno at the year's end and was heartily welcomed as a leading poet in Edo. Even the young head of his former master's family, whose service he had left in his youth, invited him for a visit. In the garden a cherry tree which Yoshitada had loved was in full bloom.

Samazama no	Myriads of things past
Koto omoidasu	Are brought to my mind—
Sakura kana	These cherry blossoms!

In the middle of the spring Bashō left Ueno, accompanied by one of his students, going first to Mount Yoshino to see the famous cherry blossoms. He traveled on to Wakanoura to enjoy the spring scenes of the Pacific coast, and then came to Nara at the time of fresh green leaves. On he went to Osaka, and then to Suma and Akashi on the coast of Seto Inland Sea, two famous places which often appeared in old Japanese classics.

From Akashi Bashō turned back to the east, and by way of Kyoto arrived at Nagoya in midsummer. After resting there for awhile, he headed for the mountains of central Honshu, an area now popularly known as the Japanese Alps. An old friend of his and a servant, loaned to him by someone who worried about the steep roads ahead, accompanied Bashō. His immediate purpose was to see the harvest moon in the rustic Sarashina district. As expected, the trip was a rugged one, but he did see the full moon at that place celebrated in Japanese literature. He then traveled eastward among the mountains and returned to Edo in late autumn after nearly a year of traveling.

This was probably the happiest of all Bashō's journeys. He had been familiar with the route much of the way, and where he had not, a friend and a servant had been there to help him. His fame as a poet was fairly widespread, and people he met on the way always treated him with courtesy. It was a productive journey, too. In addition to a number of haiku and renku, he wrote two journals: *The Records of a Travel-Worn Satchel (Oi no Kobumi)*, which covers his travel from Edo to Akashi, and *A Visit to Sarashina Village (Sarashina Kikō)*, which focuses on his moon-viewing trip to Sarashina. The former has an especially significant place in the Bashō canon, including among other things a passage that declares the haikai to be among the major forms of Japanese art. He was now clearly aware of the significance of haikai writing; he was confident that the haikai, as a serious form of art, could point toward an invaluable way of life.

It was no wonder, then, that Bashō began preparing for the next journey almost immediately. As he described it, it was as if the God of Travel were beckoning him. Obsessed with the charms of a traveler's life, he now wanted to go beyond his previous journeys; he wanted to be a truer wanderer than ever before. In a letter written around this time, he says he admired the life of a monk who wanders about with only a begging bowl in his hand. Bashō now wanted to travel, not as a renowned poet, but as a self-disciplining monk. Thus in the pilgrimage to come he decided to visit the northern part of Honshu, a mostly rustic and in places even wild region where he had never been and had hardly an acquaintance. He was to cover about fifteen hundred miles on the way. Of course, it was going to be the longest journey of his life.

Accompanied by Sora, Bashō left Edo in the late spring of 1689. Probably because of his more stern and ascetic attitude toward the journey, farewell festivities were fewer and quieter this time. He proceeded northward along the main road, stopping at places of interest such as the Tōshō Shrine at Nikkō, the hot spa at Nasu, and an historic castle site at Iizuka. He then came close to the Pacific coast near Sendai and admired the scenic beauty of Matsushima. From Hiraizumi, a town well known as the site of a medieval battle, Bashō turned west and reached the coast of the Sea of Japan at Sakata. After a short trip to Kisagata in the north, he turned southwest and followed the main road along the coast. It was from this coast that he saw the island of Sado in the distance and wrote one of his most celebrated poems:

Araumi ya	The rough sea—
Sado ni yokotau	Extending toward Sado Isle,
Amanogawa	The Milky Way.

Because of the rains, the heat, and the rugged road, this part of the journey was very hard for Bashō and Sora, and they were both exhausted when they finally arrived at Kanazawa. They rested at the famous hot spring at Yamanaka for a few days, but

Sora, apparently because of prolonged ill-health, decided to give up the journey and left his master there. Bashō continued alone until he reached Fukui. There he met an old acquaintance, who accompanied him as far as Tsuruga, where another old friend had come to meet Bashō, and the two traveled south until they arrived at Ōgaki, a town Bashō knew well. A number of Bashō's friends and disciples were there, and the long journey through unfamiliar areas was finally over. One hundred and fifty-six days had passed since he left Edo.

The travel marked a climax in Bashō's literary career. He wrote some of his finest haiku during the journey. The resulting journal, *The Narrow Road to the Deep North (Oku no Hosomichi)*, is one of the highest attainments in the history of poetic diaries in Japan. His literary achievement was no doubt a result of his deepening maturity as a man. He had come to perceive a mode of life by which to resolve some deep dilemmas and to gain peace of mind. It was based on the idea of *sabi*, the concept that one attains perfect spiritual serenity by immersing oneself in the egoless, impersonal life of nature. The complete absorption of one's petty ego into the vast, powerful, magnificent universe—this was the underlying theme of many poems by Bashō at this time, including the haiku on the Milky Way we have just seen. This momentary identification of man with inanimate nature was, in his view, essential to poetic creation. Though he never wrote a treatise on the subject, there is no doubt that Bashō conceived some unique ideas about poetry in his later years. Apparently it was during this journey that he began thinking about poetry in more serious, philosophical terms. The two earliest books known to record Bashō's thoughts on poetry, *Records of the Seven Days (Kikigaki Nanukagusa)* and *Conversations at Yamanaka (Yamanaka Mondo)*, resulted from it.

Bashō spent the next two years visiting his old friends and disciples in Ueno, Kyoto, and towns on the southern coast of Lake Biwa. With one or another of them he often paid a brief visit to other places such as Ise and Nara. Of numerous houses he stayed at during this period Bashō seems to have especially enjoyed two: the Unreal Hut and the House of Fallen Persimmons, as they were called. The Unreal Hut, located in the woods off the southernmost tip of Lake Biwa, was a quiet, hidden place where Bashō rested from early summer to mid-autumn in 1690. He thoroughly enjoyed the idle, secluded life there, and described it in a short but superb piece of prose. Here is one of the passages:

> In the daytime an old watchman from the local shrine or some villager from the foot of the hill comes along and chats with me about things I rarely hear of, such as a wild boar's looting the rice paddies or a hare's haunting the bean farms. When the sun sets under the edge of the hill and night falls, I quietly sit and wait for the moon. With the moonrise I begin roaming about, casting my shadow on the ground. When the night deepens I return to the hut and meditate on right and wrong, gazing at the dim margin of a shadow in the lamplight.

Bashō had another chance to live a similarly secluded life later at the House of Fallen Persimmons in Saga, a northwestern suburb of Kyoto. The house, owned by one of his disciples, Mukai Kyorai (1651–1704), was so called because persimmon trees grew around it. There were also a number of bamboo groves, which provided the setting for a well-known poem by Bashō:

Hototogisu	The cuckoo—
Ōtakeyabu o	Through the dense bamboo grove,
Moru tsukiyo	Moonlight seeping.

Bashō stayed at this house for seventeen days in the summer of 1691. The sojourn resulted in *The Saga Diary (Saga Nikki)*, the last of his longer prose works.

All during this period at the two hideaways and elsewhere in the Kyoto-Lake Biwa area, Bashō was visited by many people who shared his interest in poetry. Especially close to him were two of his leading disciples, Kyorai and Nozawa Bonchō (16?–1714), partly because they were compiling a haikai anthology under Bashō's guidance. The anthology, entitled *The Monkey's Cloak (Sarumino)* and published in the early summer of 1691, represented a peak in the haikai of the Bashō style. Bashō's idea of sabi and other principles of verse writing that evolved during his journey to the far north were clearly there. Through actual examples the new anthology showed that the haikai could be a serious art form capable of embodying mature comments on man and his environment.

Bashō returned to Edo in the winter of 1691. His friends and disciples there, who had not seen him for more than two years, welcomed him warmly. For the third time they combined their efforts to build a hut for their master, who had given up the old one before his latest journey. In this third Bashō

Hut, however, he could not enjoy the peaceful life he desired. For one thing, he now had a few people to look after. An invalid nephew had come to live with Bashō, who took care of him until his death in the spring of 1693. A woman by the name of Jutei, with whom Bashō apparently had had some special relationship in his youth, also seems to have come under his care at this time. She too was in poor health, and had several young children besides. Even apart from these involvements, Bashō was becoming extremely busy, no doubt due to his great fame as a poet. Many people wanted to visit him, or invited him for visits. For instance, in a letter presumed to have been written on the eighth of the twelfth month, 1693, he told one prospective visitor that he would not be at home on the ninth, tenth, eleventh, twelfth, fourteenth, fifteenth, and sixteenth, suggesting that the visitor come either on the thirteenth or the eighteenth. In another letter written about the same time, he bluntly said: "Disturbed by others, I have no peace of mind." That New Year he composed this haiku:

Toshidoshi ya	Year after year
Saru ni kisetaru	On the monkey's face,
Saru no men	A monkey's mask.

The poem has a touch of bitterness unusual for Bashō. He was dissatisfied with the progress that he (and possibly some of his students) was making.

As these responsibilities pressed on him, Bashō gradually became somewhat nihilistic. He had become a poet in order to transcend worldly involvements, but now he found himself deeply involved in worldly affairs precisely because of his poetic fame. The solution was either to renounce being a poet or to stop seeing people altogether. Bashō first tried the former, but to no avail. "I have tried to give up poetry and remain silent," he said, "but every time I did so a poetic sentiment would solicit my heart and something would flicker in my mind. Such is the magic spell of poetry." He had become too much of a poet. Thus he had to resort to the second alternative: to stop seeing people altogether. This he did in the autumn of 1693, declaring:

> Whenever people come, there is useless talk. Whenever I go and visit, I have the unpleasant feeling of interfering with other men's business. Now I can do nothing better than follow the examples of Sun Ching and Tu Wu-lang, who confined themselves within

locked doors. Friendlessness will become my friend, and poverty my wealth. A stubborn man at fifty years of age, I thus write to discipline myself.

Asagao ya	The morning-glory—
Hiru wa jō orosu	In the daytime, a bolt is fastened
Mon no kaki	On the frontyard gate.

Obviously, Bashō wished to admire the beauty of the morning-glory without having to keep a bolt on his gate. How to manage to do this must have been the subject of many hours of meditation within the locked house. He solved the problem, at least to his own satisfaction, and reopened the gate about a month after closing it.

Bashō's solution was based on the principle of "lightness," a dialectic transcendence of sabi. Sabi urges man to detach himself from wordly involvements; "lightness" makes it possible for him, after attaining that detachment, to return to the mundane world. Man lives amid the mire as a spiritual bystander. He does not escape the grievances of living; standing apart, he just smiles them away. Bashō began writing under this principle and advised his students to emulate him. The effort later came to fruition in several haikai anthologies, such as *A Sack of Charcoal (Sumidawara)*, *The Detached Room (Betsuzashiki)*, and *The Monkey's Cloak, Continued (Zoku Sarumino)*. Characteristic verses in these collections reject sentimentalism and take a calm, carefree attitude to the things of daily life. They often exude lighthearted humor.

Having thus restored his mental equilibrium, Bashō began thinking of another journey. He may have been anxious to carry his new poetic principle, "lightness," to poets outside of Edo, too. Thus in the summer of 1694 he traveled westward on the familiar road along the Pacific coast, taking with him one of Jutei's children, Jirōbei. He rested at Ueno for a while, and then visited his students in Kyoto and in towns near the southern coast of Lake Biwa. Jutei, who had been struggling against ill health at the Bashō Hut, died at this time and Jirōbei temporarily returned to Edo. Much saddened, Bashō went back to Ueno in early autumn for about a month's rest. He then left for Osaka with a few friends and relatives including his elder brother's son Mataemon as well as Jirōbei. But Bashō's health was rapidly failing, even though he continued to write some excellent verses. One of his haiku in Osaka was:

Kono aki wa	This autumn
Nan de toshiyoru	Why am I aging so?
Kumo ni tori	Flying towards the clouds, a bird.

The poem indicates Bashō's awareness of approaching death. Shortly afterward he took to his bed with a stomach ailment, from which he was not to recover. Numerous disciples hurried to Osaka and gathered at his bedside. He seems to have remained calm in his last days. He scribbled a deathbed note to his elder brother, which in part read: "I am sorry to have to leave you now. I hope you will live a happy life under Mataemon's care and reach a ripe old age. There is nothing more I have to say." The only thing that disturbed his mind was poetry. According to a disciple's record, Bashō fully knew that it was time for prayers, not for verse writing, and yet he thought of the latter day and night. Poetry was now an obsession—"a sinful attachment," as he himself called it. His last poem was:

Tabi ni yande	On a journey, ailing—
Yume wa kareno o	My dreams roam about
Kakemeguru	Over a withered moor.

[Note to the reader: The next selection is taken from Chapter 4 entitled "Prose." It focuses on the journey of Bashō that resulted in his writing The Narrow Road to the Interior.]

Chapter 4 Prose

Bashō's next journey was to the most undeveloped part of Japan and that the resulting journal was called *The Narrow Road to the Deep North*. The "narrow road" in the title is more metaphorical than literal, and so is the "deep north." On the surface the journal, by far the longest of Bashō's works in this genre, records the events of his journey of 1689 to the northern part of Honshu. Yet at the metaphorical level it is a record of Bashō's spiritual quest, a quest for the ultimate beauty of nature and of man which had been lost in the contemporary "floating world." The journal appropriately comes to its close when Bashō reaches Ōgaki and is surrounded by a host of admirers. He has reached the floating world there; he no longer finds sense in continuing the journal.

Thus *The Narrow Road to the Deep North* abounds with descriptions of people and things whose unobtrusive beauty is rarely found outside of rugged, primitive nature. For instance, this passage appears early in the journal:

> In the shade of a large chestnut tree near this post town, a Buddhist monk was living a secluded life. It seemed a quiet life, indeed, like that of an ancient poet-recluse who picked horse chestnuts in the depths of the mountains. I wrote down on a piece of paper: "The Chinese ideogram Chestnut consists of two letters that signify West and Tree respectively. Hence Bodhisattva Gyōki is said to have associated a chestnut tree with Western Paradise and used it both for his cane and for the pillars of his house."

Yo no hito no	Few in this world
Mitsukenu hana ya	Notice those blossoms:
Noki no kuri	Chestnut by the eaves.

The poem can be interpreted literally and metaphorically. Chestnut blossoms are small and unostentatious, and bloom in the rainy season; they are an apt metaphor for the life of this retired monk. "This world" in the poem means the floating world. The haiku recalls the chestnuts of Kiso we saw in the poem at the end of *A Visit to Sarashina Village*.

Another early passage praises an individual keeping his distance from the floating world. This man is not a monk; he is an innkeeper living amidst the people:

> On the thirtieth day we stopped at the foot of Mount Nikkō. The master of the inn we stayed at said, "I am called Buddha Gozaemon. People honor me with this name because I try to be honest in everything I do. So please make yourselves at home and have a good rest tonight." That set me to wondering what sort of Buddha he could be to reveal himself in this earthly mire and to help beggarly pilgrims like ourselves. I watched the innkeeper closely and found him a ruggedly honest man who had no worldly wisdom or shrewdness. Confucius once remarked that a man of sturdy simple mind approaches Perfect Virtue. Such innate purity as this innkeeper's should be most highly valued.

Instead of wildly primitive nature here is a stubbornly honest man, the sort rarely found in an urban, sophisticated society. He is artless, almost naive; he can tell his guests he is called Buddha, without suspecting that they may consider him presumptuous. Bashō suspected and watched him closely; he found in him not a Buddha but the sort of man so simplehearted as to precede both Buddhism and Confucianism. Bashō saw an image of primeval man unspoiled by the evils of civilization.

Of course, not all the people Bashō encountered were like these two people. Inevitably, some were unenlightened and earthy. But to write about them would be of no help to the presentation of the central theme; better to omit them altogether. This is precisely what Bashō did. According to Sora, who accompanied Bashō and who wrote his own more factual diary, Bashō was entertained by high-ranking samurai and well-to-do merchants at various towns. When he was in Sakata, for instance, he was given hospitality by one of the wealthiest merchants in that commercial city on the coast of the Sea of Japan. In Murakami, a town near Sakata, he was invited to the castle of a local lord and was presented with a substantial amount of money. In Kashiwazaki, another town on the coast, he visited a millionaire's mansion for an overnight stay, but he was somehow treated discourteously and left at once, though it was raining and people at the mansion rushed out to stop him. These people and events would have been memorable enough for the average person to record in his diary, if he kept a diary at all. Bashō makes no mention of them whatsoever. *The Narrow Road to the Deep North* is a literary journal with a deliberate choice of facts.

Not only did Bashō freely choose to omit material, but he changed the facts as he saw fit. *The Narrow Road to the Deep North* is fictional to some degree. The purpose is again the same: Bashō wanted to present his theme more effectively. The following, for instance, describes what occurred when Bashō and Sora left Matsushima:

> On the twelfth day, we set out for Hiraizumi. Having heard that such famous places as the pine of Aneha and the bridge of Odae were near, we chose to take a lonely path that only hunters and woodcutters would use. But soon we lost our way completely and stepped onto the wrong trail, and eventually we found ourselves at a harbor called Ishinomaki. Kinkazan, the island where an ancient poem says flowers of gold blossomed, was seen far out on the sea. In the bay hundreds of barges were anchored, and on the shore numerous houses were clustered, from which the smoke of cooking rose incessantly. We had never expected to come to a town like this! We sought a place to stay for the night, but no one was willing to offer us one. We ended up spending the night at a bleak little house. Next day we again continued to wander along a road totally

unknown to us. Looking at the ford of Sode, the meadow of Obuchi and the heath of Mano in the distance, we traveled over an embankment that stretched endlessly. We then plodded along a long marsh in a desolate area, finally coming to a place named Toima. After a night's stay there, we arrived at Hiraizumi. I think we had covered more than twenty leagues by then.

The passage successfully conveys the lonely, help-less feeling of the two travelers who blundered into a remote area completely unknown to them. It also dramatizes their unexpected joy upon coming to Ishinomaki and its vicinity, which were famous in classical poetry. But the truth seems to be that Bashō and Sora never lost their way. The pine of Ancha and the bridge of Odae were located to the west of Matsushima, and Ishinomaki was to the east; it is highly unlikely that such experienced travelers would unknowingly take a road to Ishi-nomaki when they intended to reach Aneha and Odae. Sora's diary makes no mention of their get-ting lost here; it sounds as if they had planned to go to Ishinomaki from the beginning. As a matter of fact, Ishinomaki is frequently mentioned in an itinerary Sora had prepared for Bashō before the whole journey began. Furthermore, Bashō's words "We sought a place to stay for the night, but no one was willing to offer us one" are not true to the facts. A kind person Bashō and Sora met on the way guided them to an inn (not "a bleak little house") in Ishinomaki; they had no difficulty find-ing accommodations there. The sentence "Next day we again continued to wander along a road total-ly unknown to us" is not quite factual either, for in reality two Ishinomaki residents, who must have known the road very well, accompanied them as they left.

There are similar instances elsewhere in *The Nar-row Road to the Deep North*. To mention just a few, at Iizuka the journal says that Bashō had a severe attack of his chronic illness and almost fainted, but Sora's diary, which is especially detailed on that day, has no record of it. In Matsushima Bashō's journal implies he was too overwhelmed by the beautiful scenery to compose a poem; yet, as we have seen, he did write a haiku. In Kisagata the journal states: "That morning the sky was very clear. When the bright morning sun came out, we went boating on the sea." Yet Sora's diary confirms that it drizzled all that morning, and that they went boat riding only after supper. To explain these

discrepancies, it may be argued that Bashō's memory of events had become fuzzy by the time he wrote the journal. That may be true in some cases, but Bashō's alterations of fact point too uni-formly in one direction to be attributed to mere failure of memory. In almost every case they beau-tify and dramatize the writer's experience in that lonely pilgrimage through the rugged north. The writer seems more interested in giving us the same sort of spiritual experience than in the prosaic re-cording of facts. This is expected of any literary journal. Though to a lesser degree, Bāsho did it in his earlier journals. And he was not original here, either. Ancient Japanese court diaries, beginning with Tsurayuki's, were fictional to varying degrees. Many of them seemed to be based on the assump-tion that it was more important to record inner experience than outward events.

It does not surprise us, then, that for Bashō this was an exploration not only in space but also in time. While he traveled through the wild north and met sturdy unsophisticated men, he also wandered into a bygone age and had imaginary talks with its inhabitants. In some passages of *The Narrow Road to the Deep North* he minimizes description of a place in order to write more about the past event connected with the place. The following was writ-ten on the occasion of his visit to a Shinto shrine near Kanazawa:

> We visited Tada Shrine here and saw Sanemori's hel-met as well as a remnant of the robe he wore under his armor. According to the legend, these had been given him by Lord Yoshitomo, his master in his youth. Indeed, they did not look like an ordinary soldier's. The helmet was inlaid with an arabesque of gold chrysanthemums from the frontlet to the ear-plates, with a dragon's head and two curved horns adorning the crown. The legend vividly told how after Sanemori was killed the enemy general Kiso Yoshinaka sent his deputy Higuchi Jirō to this shrine to offer a letter of prayer along with these memen-toes.

Muzan ya na	How pitiful!
Kabuto no shita no	Underneath the helmet
Kirigirisu	A cricket chirping.

Sanemori was a heroic warrior of medieval times who appears in several masterpieces of Japanese literature, including a nō play by that name. When more than seventy years of age, after dyeing his gray hair black, he fought his last battle among an army of young soldiers. Gazing at the helmet and brocade robe on display at the shrine, Bashō wanders into the twelfth century, a century of war and disorder which demanded the utmost heroism from every person of integrity. Sanemori was a samurai who lived heroically and died heroically; in his own way he too proceeded along the "narrow road to the deep north." The first line of Bashō's haiku, "How pitiful!", is taken from the nō play *Sanemori*, and refers not only to the mournful chirp of an autumn cricket but also to the aged samurai's last battle. It is pitiful and ennobling to see the warrior following the course of his destiny with determination and courage.

Such excursions into the past occur throughout *The Narrow Road to the Deep North*. The passage about Yashima, a place near Nikkō, dwells on the legend of a mythological princess who dared to stay in a burning house to prove her chastity to her husband. In the section on Hiraizumi Bashō mainly reminisces about the glory it enjoyed in the twelfth century. In Shiogoshi, a village some distance west of Kanazawa, he leaves out the scenery altogether, preferring to quote a tanka which Priest Saigyō had written when he was there several centuries earlier. Reading through all these passages we get the impression that Bashō was just as interested in meeting the ghosts of men who had lived there long ago as in meeting his contemporaries. In this sense the writer of *The Narrow Road to the Deep North* can be compared to the deuteragonist of the nō drama, in many cases an itinerant monk who invokes the ghost of a past local resident wherever he goes. Bashō, traveling not only geographically but also historically, is a medium who conjures up bygone persons and events for his readers. And, of course, these visions point in one direction: they all reveal the beauty and sadness of primitive nature and of premodern men steadfastly following their courses of life.

As the language of the nō play must necessarily be poetic and evocative in order to help the audience visualize a world beyond the tomb, the language of *The Narrow Road to the Deep North* is concise, allusive, and figurative to induce the reader to share the author's experiences, actual and emotional. The passages are loaded with sensory images. Most of the sentences are short and crisp, seldom with a conjunction between them. Occasionally two more or less unrelated phrases or clauses are juxtaposed, connected by nothing more than a nominal "and." Often a haiku appears in the middle or at the end of a prose passage, without much explanation but with perfect emotional logic. In brief, the language of *The Narrow Road to the Deep North* has the same qualities as Bashō's finest haibun. The journal can be described as a collection of about fifty superb haibun.

The "leap" method used in haibun seems to have been developed into a structural method unifying the whole journal. On the surface, the structural unity of *The Narrow Road to the Deep North* is attained chronologically: passages describing places and people are arranged in the order in which Bashō visited them. Yet, as we have seen, he took a good deal of liberty in the choice of what and whom he wrote about. While the primary criterion of choice was thematic, the author also seems to have considered structural factors. In selecting material, he carefully studied the nature of each passage and tried to make its successor harmonious and complementary. As a consequence, between two passages which apparently are contiguous because of the time sequence, a "leap" occurs.

To mention just a few examples, early in the journal a passage on Yashima is followed by a paragraph on Mount Nikkō. The first is the one about a mythological princess who braved fire to prove her chastity; the latter is that about an innkeeper who is nicknamed Buddha in praise of his integrity. Though Bashō gives not a word of explanation, we involuntarily make a "leap" from one passage to the other as we read them. Likewise, the passages about Hiraizumi which present the poet standing among the desolate ruins and recalling the town's past prosperity are preceded by a section that describes him plodding through a lonely woodland and arriving at a thriving harbor town called Ishinomaki. A passage on Kanazawa tells of Kosugi Isshō (1653–88), a young man devoted to the art of poetry who had died the previous winter; it is followed by the paragraph on Sanemori, the aged warrior who courageously followed the medieval samurai codes and was killed in a manner befitting a young soldier.

Some Japanese scholars have argued that *The Narrow Road to the Deep North* has the structure of a renku. Judging by these samples, we must say the argument has a measure of validity. Just as two consecutive verses in a renku are related in a uniquely poetic way, two consecutive passages in this journal work on each other and establish a theme or mood of their own—a theme or mood that is somewhat modified when a third passage is added. The fifty-odd haibun that constitute *The Narrow Road to the Deep North* are built on such an apparently casual but unobtrusively coherent structure. Of course this does not mean they lack variety. As members of a renku team consciously attempt to include a wide range of subjects such as nature, town life, love, religion, travel and so on, so Bashō in his journal now describes a beautiful scene on the northern seacoast, now writes of an interesting man he met, and now turns to express reverence for a deity enshrined at a place he visited. He even sees to it at times that women and children add a bit of color to the largely somber beauty of the north. The most effective of these passages occurs toward the end of the journal when he, after a hard day of trekking along the northern coast, meets two young courtesans at his inn:

Hitotsuya ni	Under the same roof
Yūjo mo netari	Courtesans, too, are asleep—
Hagi' to tsuki	Bush clover and the moon.

Whether Bashō was deliberately using the renku technique is, of course, irrelevant. *The Narrow, Road to the Deep North* does have unity in variety, and variety in unity, qualities that have contributed to its lasting reputation as one of the finest literary journals Japan has ever produced.

from Narrow Road to the Interior

Matsuo Bashō

Translator's Introduction

During the spring and summer of 1689, the poet Bashō, accompanied by his friend Sora, walked the roads of Japan's Northern Interior, recording with almost complete detachment the essential and transient nature of the people and places encountered along the way. Between 1690 and 1694, he polished the little travel diary of that journey, and the result, *Oku-no-hosomichi*, translated here as *Narrow Road to the Interior*, is one of the most revered books in all of Japanese literature.

Oku means "within" and "farthest" or "dead-end" place: it also means "interior" both in the sense of interior country and spiritual interior. *No* is a possessive and is prepositional. *Hosomichi* means "path" or "trail" or "narrow road." *Oku-no-hosomichi* can then be taken to mean both a narrow road through the country's mountainous interior lying between Miyagino and Matsushima, and the metaphoric narrow trail leading into one's spiritual center.

Bashō's little book is not a true travel journal. The heart and soul of his masterpiece—its *kokoro*—arises out of strenuous studies in poetry and history, Buddhism, Taoism, Confucianism, Shinto traditions, and some intense personal Zen discipline. The publication of Sora's travel notes fifty years ago reveals that Bashō's claim to have visited some places and done some things may have been fictitious. Along most of the journey, for instance, Bashō and Sora were welcomed by wealthy merchant-class patrons. But Bashō describes a much more Spartan existence. These inventions serve a useful purpose within the context of the whole book, indicating Bashō's deep faith in his art as a poet and spiritual seeker. The fact that he worked on his book over the four years following the journey indicates that he wanted the work to stand apart from any literal reading of his adventure, emphasizing spiritual over autobiographical qualities in the book. He did not, however, exaggerate his poor health and the very real physical dangers of the journey. Even though his journey took place during the Genroku period, a time of relative peace under the Tokugawa shogunate, travel was always dangerous. Bashō and Sora, like many others, dressed as Buddhist monks in part to ensure their safety.

In his mid-forties and in chronic poor health, Bashō was hardly an ideal candidate to walk the trails of the Northern Interior, even though he had already walked the roads of most of southern Honshu (the main island of Japan). One of the most renowned poets in a society that revered poetry, he found himself surrounded by followers at his little home along the banks of the Sumida River in present-day Tokyo, then called Edo. An admirer had planted a *bashō*, or plantain tree, near the house, and soon both the house and poet gained a new name.

Born Matsuo Munefusa in 1644 in the Iga Province village of Ueno, thirty miles southeast of Kyoto, Bashō served in his childhood as a companion to Yoshitada, the son of a local feudal lord, until his death in 1666. Both the death of his master and his own complicated love life—he may have been involved with ladies of the court, he had a common-law wife, and he also claimed to have become "fascinated with the ways of homosexual love"—left him ill-prepared for life as a samurai. He settled in Edo and for the next fifteen years wrote *renga* (linked verse) and haiku, living on patronage and building his reputation as a poet and teacher. In the winter of 1680, when several of his disciples built the hut that lent the poet his final nom de plume, he wrote:

Near the brushwood gate	*Shiba no to ni*
furious tea leaves scribble	*cha o konoha kaku*
nothings on the storm	*arashi kana*

The poem suggests a sense of elemental loneliness, as though the poet lived in some far wilderness rather than at the edge of a bustling, burgeoning city, and it leaves an aftertaste of *sabi*, a word that comes from *sabishisa*, loneliness. But *sabi* means far more than mere "loneliness" as we think of it: it means essential aloneness. In Zen, *sabi* is a condition of utter individuation achieved through solitary, egoless meditation. There is no ego in the poem. No one's there. The reader must project him- or herself into the flow of language and image in order to *experience* the poetry firsthand.

Modern Japanese poets often remark, "Haiku began and ended with Bashō." He had taken an essentially playful form and brought to it his profound Zen training and enormous literary scholarship, an ear for sound that was nonpareil, and a sweeping sense of the Way of Elegance (*fuga-no-michi*). In this poem even the non-Japanese reader can hear the *ah*, *o*, and *k* sounds, the *shi*, *ni*, *shi* sounds, the whole possessed of remarkable wind-in-tea-plant noises.

He had rejected bourgeois society and immersed himself in early Japanese and Chinese literature, especially the poetry of the Tang-dynasty poet Tu Fu, the twelfth-century Japanese Buddhist priest Saigyō, and the Taoist sage Chuang Tzu. Even greater than his elevation of haiku from mere literary play to the expression of profound Zen, his *haibun* (brief prose combined with haiku) established Bashō as one of the preeminent figures in all of Japanese literature. His *haibun*, especially *Oku-no-hosomichi*, relies very heavily on a literary tradition called *honkadori*, allusive poems, even revisions of poems, "answers" to poems from the classics. There is hardly a phrase in *Oku-no-hosomichi* that is not loaded with allusion, resonance, quotation, or paraphrase from Chuang Tzu, Tu Fu, Li Po, Saigyō, Kamo-no-Chōmei, the epic *Tale of Genji*, and other sources. He wrote for a highly literate, highly sophisticated audience.

By 1689, success weighed heavily on the poet. Students and sycophants alike visited constantly. He was deeply interested in the "return to original mind" (*honshin*) encouraged in Zen training; that is, he longed to find his own deepest personal connection to the very real world that lay only far beyond adoring crowds and poetry-writing contests. The fundamental teaching of Buddhism is codependent origination—that nothing is entirely self-originating. Bashō's journey would be a return to the elemental world, a return to natural, spiritual, and literary origins.

He clearly felt that social obligations interfered with his spiritual growth, and that spiritual growth was, after all, the wellspring of his verse and his life as an artist. Perhaps he was merely undergoing what our culture terms "midlife crisis." He felt nonetheless a desperate need to experience a rebirth both as an artist and as a Zennist, and it is no small testimony to his devotion to Zen practice and to his modesty as an artist that he would seek a major personal transformation at the very pinnacle of popular success.

Bashō knew well the *Samantabhadra-bodhisattva-sutra* and its primary teaching: "Of one thing it is said, 'This is good,' and of another it is said, 'This is bad,' but there is nothing inherent in either to make them 'good' or 'bad.' The 'self' is empty of independent existence." Dreaming of the full moon rising over fishing boats and tiny pine islands at Matsushima, Bashō is not looking outside himself, but rather locating "meaning" within the context of juxtaposed images that are interpenetrating and interdependent. The images themselves, true to Chinese literary Zen pedagogy, arise naturally our of the *hsin* (Japanese: *kokoro*), the heart-soul-mind of the poet. The self is empty of independent existence.

But the self, especially in the case of Bashō, is not empty of personality. The poet is not the least embarrassed by moments of sentimentality, apprehension, or outright fear, and his sense of profound irony is in good working order. For example, upon seeing the magisterial "jeweled Buddha-land" of Zuigan Temple, he suddenly longs to visit the tiny, simple temple hermitage of the mendicant priest Kembutsu; and again when he remarks about remote Eihei Temple that its location "a thousand miles from the capital" is no accident. In the midst of a terrible storm high in a mountain pass, he notes with humor and frustration the horse that spatters his pillow with piss. Unable to lead the way for a couple of young prostitutes on a pilgrimage, he later feels some regret.

Having learned from Saigyō, Kamo-no-Chōmei, and other Zen poets that seer and seen are not two things but one, Bashō remains a not-entirely-detached, compassionate participant as well as an observer. In his practice, he follows the teaching of the ninth-century Chinese Zen master Te-shan, "No mind in work, no work in mind," which directs the Zennist to be free of all self-consciousness, to be *buji*, completely free of anxiety. While working, work; while resting, rest. Bashō had often told his own students, "Learn the rules well, and then forget them," his instruction echoing that of Zen master Yun-men (864–949), "When a great act presents itself, it does so without rules."

In the spring of 1689, the famous cherry trees of Ueno and Yanaka in splendid bloom, Bashō prepared to follow the *oku-no-hosomichi* across the Shirakawa Barrier into the heart of northern Honshu, visiting famous literary sites along the way, often ignoring other, equally or even more breathtaking views, writing brief prose passages and some haiku that would connect him forever to the world's literature of travel and to the Zen tradition. He had prepared himself to meet the great act. He patched his cotton trousers, repaired his straw hat, shouldered his pack, and began a long journey into the soul's interior.

Narrow Road to the Interior

Matsuo Bashō

The moon and sun are eternal travelers. Even the years wander on. A lifetime adrift in a boat, or in old age leading a tired horse into the years, every day is a journey, and the journey itself is home. From the earliest times there have always been some who perished along the road. Still I have always been drawn by windblown clouds into dreams of a lifetime of wandering. Coming home from a year's walking tour of the coast last autumn, I swept the cobwebs from my hut on the banks of the Sumida just in time for New Year, but by the time spring mists began to rise from the fields, I longed to cross the Shirakawa Barrier into the Northern Interior. Drawn by the wanderer-spirit Dosojin, I couldn't concentrate on things. Mending my cotton pants, sewing a new strap on my bamboo hat, I daydreamed. Rubbing moxa into my legs to strengthen them, I dreamed a bright moon rising over Matsushima. So I placed my house in another's hands and moved to my patron Mr. Sampū's

summer house in preparation for my journey. And I left a verse by my door:

> Even this grass hut
> may be transformed
> into a doll's house

Very early on the twenty-seventh morning of the third moon, under a predawn haze, transparent moon still visible, Mount Fuji just a shadow, I set out under the cherry blossoms of Ueno and Yanaka. When would I see them again? A few old friends had gathered in the night and followed along far enough to see me off from the boat. Getting off at Senju, I felt three thousand miles rushing through my heart, the whole world only a dream. I saw it through farewell tears.

> Spring passes
> and the birds cry out—
> tears in the eyes of fishes

With these first words from my brush, I started. Those who remain behind watch the shadow of a traveler's back disappear.

The second year of Genroku [1689], I think of the long way leading into the Northern Interior under Go stone skies. My hair may turn white as frost before I return from those fabled places— or maybe I won't return at all. By nightfall, we come to Soka, bony shoulders sore from heavy pack, grateful for warm night robe, cotton bathing gown, writing brush, ink stone, necessities. The pack made heavier by farewell gifts from friends. I couldn't leave them behind.

Mount Kurokami still clothed in snow, faint in the mist, Sora wrote:

> Head shaven
> at Black Hair Mountain
> we change into summer clothes

Sora was named Kawai Sōgorō; Sora's his nom de plume. At my old home—called Bashō (plantain tree)—he carried water and wood. Anticipating the pleasures of seeing Matsushima and Kisagata, we agreed to share the journey, pleasure and hardship alike. The morning we started, he put on Buddhist robes, shaved his head, and changed his name to

Sogo, the Enlightened. So the "changing clothes" in his poem is pregnant with meaning.

A hundred yards uphill, the waterfall plunged a hundred feet from its cavern in the ridge, falling into a basin made by a thousand stones. Crouched in the cavern behind the falls, looking out, I understood why it's called Urami-no-Taki, "View-from-behind-Falls."

> Stopped awhile
> inside a waterfall:
> the summer begins

A friend lives in Kurobane on the far side of the broad Nasu Moor. Tried a shortcut running straight through, but it began to rain in the early evening, so we stopped for the night at a village farmhouse and continued again at dawn. Out in the field, a horse, and nearby a man cutting grass. I stopped to ask directions. Courteous, he thought awhile, then said, "Too many intersecting roads. It's easy to get lost. Best to take that old horse as far as he'll go. He knows the road. When he stops, get off, and he'll come back alone."

Two small children danced along behind, one with the curious name of Kasane, same as the pink flower. Sora wrote:

> With this *kasane*
> she's doubly pink
> a fitting name

Arriving at a village, I tied a small gift to the saddle and the horse turned back.

Set out to see the Murder Stone, Sesshō-seki, on a borrowed horse, and the man leading it asked for a poem, "Something beautiful, please."

> The horse lifts his head:
> from across deep fields
> the cuckoo's cry

Sesshō-seki lies in dark mountain shadow near a hot springs emitting bad gases. Dead bees and butterflies cover the sand.

At Ashino, the willow Saigyō praised, "beside the crystal stream," still grows along a path in fields of rice. A local official had offered to lead the way, and I had often wondered whether and where it remained. And now, today, that same willow:

> Girls' rice-planting done
> they depart:
> I emerge from willow-shade

Deeply touched by the famous pine at Takekuma, twin trunks just as long ago. The poet-priest Nōin came to mind. Before he came, Lord Fujiwara-no-Takayoshi cut down the tree for lumber, building a bridge across the Natorigawa. Nōin wrote: "No sign here now of that famous pine." Reported to have been cut down and replaced several times, it stood like a relic of a thousand years, impossibly perfect. The poet Kyohaku had given me a poem at my departure:

> Remember to show my master
> the famous Takekuma pine,
> O northern blossoming cherries

To which I now reply:

> Ever since cherry blossom time
> I longed to visit two-trunked pine:
> three long months have passed

Checking Kaemon's drawings as we walked, we followed the *oku-no-hosomichi* along the mountainside where sedge grass grew tall in bunches. The Tofu area is famous for its sedge mats, sent in tribute to the governor each year.

At Taga Castle we found the most ancient monument Tsubo-no-ishibumi, in Ichikawa Village. It's about six feet high and three feet wide. We struggled to read the inscription under heavy moss:

> This Castle was Built by Shogun Ono-no-Azumabito in 724. In 762, His Majesty's Commanding General, Emi-no-Asakari, Supervised Repairs.

Dated from the time of Emperor Shōmu, Tsubo-no-ishibumi inspired many a poet. Floods and landslides buried trails and markers, trees have grown and died, making this monument very difficult to find. The past remains hidden in clouds of memory. Still it returned us to memories from a thousand years before. Such a moment is the reason for a pilgrimage: infirmities forgotten, the ancients remembered, joyous tears trembled in my eyes.

Rose at dawn to pay respects at Myōjin Shrine in Shiogama. The former governor rebuilt it with huge, stately pillars, bright-painted rafters, and a long stone walkway rising steeply under a morning sun that danced and flashed along the red lacquered fence. I thought, "As long as the road is, even if it ends in dust, the gods come with us, keeping a watchful eye. This is our culture's greatest gift." Kneeling at the shrine, I noticed a fine old lantern with this inscribed on its iron grate:

> In the Third Year of the Bunji Era [1187]
> Dedicated by Izumi Saburo

Suddenly, five long centuries passed before my eyes. A trusted, loyal man martyred by his brother; today there's not a man alive who doesn't revere his name. As he himself would say, a man must follow the Confucian model—renown will inevitably result.

On the eighth we climbed Moon Mountain, wearing the holy paper necklaces and cotton hats of Shinto priests, following behind a mountain monk whose footsteps passed through mist and clouds and snow and ice, climbing miles higher as though drawn by invisible spirits into the gateway of the sky—sun, moon, and clouds floated by and took my breath away. Long after sunset, moon high over the peak, we reached the summit, spread out in bamboo grass, and slept. Next day, after the sun burned away the clouds, we started down toward Yudono, Bath Mountain.

Approaching the valley, we passed Swordsmith Hut, named for the twelfth-century smith Gassan, who purified himself with holy water here and used it to temper his blades. On each blade he inscribed "Gassan," Moon Mountain. He admired the famous Dragon Spring swords of China. I remembered the legendary man-and-wife smiths renowned for their dedication to detail and technique.

We stretched on a rock to rest and noticed the opening buds of a three-foot cherry tree. Buried under stubborn snow, it insists upon honoring spring, however late it arrives. Like the Chinese poem,

"Plum blossoms fragrant in burning sun!" And Gyōson Sōjō wrote, "So sad, blossoming cherry, you have no one to admire you." It's all here, in these tiny blossoms!

To say more is sacrilege. Forbidden to speak, put down the brush, respect Shinto rites. Later, back with Master Egaku, we wrote poems on the Three Holy Mountains:

> Cool crescent moon
> high above
> Feather Black Mountain

> How many rising clouds
> collapse and fall
> on the Moon's Mountain

> Forbidden to speak
> alone on Yudono Mountain
> tears on my sleeve

Sora wrote:

> Bath Mountain walkway
> paved with pilgrims' coins:
> here too are tears

Sora, suffering from persistent stomach ailments, was forced to return to his relatives in Nagashima in Ise Province. His parting words:

> Sick to the bone
> if I should fall
> I'll lie in fields of clover

He carries his pain as he goes, leaving me empty. Like paired geese parting in the clouds.

> Now falling autumn dew
> obliterates my hatband's
> "We are two"

I stayed at Zenshō-ji, a temple near the castle town of Daishōji in Kaga Province. It was from this temple that Sora departed here the night before, leaving behind:

> All night long
> listening to autumn winds
> wandering in the mountains

One night like a thousand miles, as the proverb says, and I too listened to fall winds howl around the same temple. But at dawn, the chanting of sutras, gongs ringing, awakened me. An urgent need to leave for distant Echizen Province. As I prepared to leave the temple, two young monks arrived with ink stone and paper in hand. Outside, willow leaves fell in the wind.

> Sweep the garden
> all kindnesses
> falling willow leaves repay

My sandals already on, I wrote it quickly and departed.

At the Echizen Province border, at an inlet town called Yoshizaki, I hired a boat and sailed for the famous pines of Shiogoshi. Saigyō wrote:

> All the long night
> salt-winds drive
> storm-tossed waves
> and moonlight drips
> through Shiogoshi pines

This one poem says enough. To add another would be like adding a sixth finger to a hand.

Mount Shirane faded behind us and Mount Hina began to appear. We crossed Asamuzu Bridge and saw the legendary "reeds of Tamae" in bloom. We crossed Uguisu Barrier at Yuno-o Pass and passed by the ruins of Hiuchi Castle. On Returning Hill we heard the first wild geese of autumn. We arrived at Tsuruga Harbor on the evening of the fourteenth day of the eighth moon. The harbor moonlight was marvelously bright.

I asked at the inn, "Will we have this view tomorrow night?" The innkeeper said, "Can't guarantee weather in Koshiji. It may be clear, but then again it may turn overcast. It may rain." We drank sake with the innkeeper, then paid a late visit to the Kehi Myōjin Shrine honoring the second-century Emperor Chūai. A great spirituality—moonlight in pines, white sands like a touch of frost. In ancient times Yugyō, the second high priest, himself cleared away the grounds, carried stones, and built drains. To this day, people carry sands to the shrine. "*Yugyō-no-sunamochi*," the innkeeper explained, "Yugyō's sand-bringing."

> Transparent moonlight
> shines over Yugyo's sand
> perfectly white

On the fifteenth, just as the innkeeper warned, it rained:

> Harvest moon—
> true North Country weather—
> nothing to view

The sky cleared the morning of the sixteenth. I sailed to Iro Beach a dozen miles away and gathered several colorful shells with a Mr. Tenya, who provided a box lunch and sake and even invited his servants. Tail winds got us there in a hurry. A few fishermen's shacks dotted the beach, and the tiny Hokke Temple was disheveled. We drank tea and hot sake, lost in a sweeping sense of isolation as dusk came on.

> Loneliness greater
> than *Genji*'s Suma Beach:
> the shores of autumn

> Wave after wave
> mixes tiny shells
> with bush clover flowers

Tosai wrote a record of our afternoon and left it at the temple.

A disciple, Rotsu, had come to Tsuruga to travel with me to Minō Province. We rode horses into the castle town of Ōgaki. Sora returned from Ise, joined by Etsujin, also riding a horse. We gathered at the home of Jokō, a retired samurai. Lord Zensen, the Keikō family men, and other friends arrived by day and night, all to welcome me as though I'd come back from the dead. A wealth of affection!

Still exhausted and weakened from my long journey, on the sixth day of the darkest month, I felt moved to visit Ise Shrine, where a twenty-one-year Rededication Ceremony was about to get under way. At the beach, in the boat, I wrote:

> Clam ripped from its shell
> I move on to Futami Bay:
> passing autumn

• • •

At dawn we left for Shinobu, famous for dyed cloth—called *shinobu-zuri*—named after the rock we found half buried in the mountain. Village children joined us and explained, "In the old days, the rock was on top of the mountain, but visitors trampled farmers' crops, so the old men rolled it down." Their story made perfect sense.

> Girls' busy hands plant rice
> almost like
> the ancient ones making dye

Crossed on the Ferry at Tsukinowa to the post town of Se-no-ue to see the ruins that were Satō Shōji's house, beyond town to the left, near the mountains. We were told to look at Saba Moor in Iizuka, and we eventually came to Maru Hill, where the castle ruins lay. Seeing the main gate sundered, the ancient temple nearby, seeing all the family graves, tears glazed my eyes. Especially at the tombs of two widows who had dressed in the armor of fallen sons and then lay down their lives. Like Tu Yu at Weeping Gravemound, I dried my eyes with a sleeve. Inside the temple, enjoying tea, Yoshitsune's great long sword and the priest Benkei's little Buddhist wicker chests, both enshrined:

> Sword, chest, and wind-carp
> all proudly displayed
> on boys' Festival Day

It was the first of Satsuki, rice-planting month.

Ojima Beach is not—as its name implies—an island, but a strand projected into the bay. Here one finds the ruins of Ungo Zenji's hermitage and the rock where he sat *zazen*. And still a few tiny thatched huts under pines where religious hermits live in tranquillity. Smoke of burning leaves and pine cones drew me on, touching something deep inside. Then the moon rose, shining on the sea, day turned suddenly to night. We stayed at an inn on the shore, our second-story windows opening on the bay. Drifting with winds and I clouds, it was almost like a dream. Sora wrote:

> In Matsushima
> you'll need the wings of a crane
> little cuckoo

I was speechless and tried to sleep, but rose to dig from my pack a Chinese-style poem my friend Sodō had written for me, something about Pine Islands. And also a *waka* by Hara Anteki, and haiku by Sampu and Dakushi.

Here three generations of the Fujiwara clan passed as though in a dream. The great outer gates lay in ruins. Where Hidehira's manor stood, rice fields grew. Only Mount Kinkei remained. I climbed the hill where Yoshitsune died; I saw the Kitakami, a broad stream flowing down through the Nambu Plain, the Koromo River circling Izumi Castle below the hill before joining the Kitakami. The ancient ruins of Yasuhira—from the end of the Golden Era—lie out beyond the Koromo Barrier where they stood guard against the Ainu People. The faithful elite remained bound to the castle, for all their valor, reduced to ordinary grass. Tu Fu wrote:

> The whole country devastated,
> only mountains and rivers remain.
> In springtime, at the ruined castle,
> the grass is always green.

We sat awhile, our hats for a seat, seeing it all through tears.

> Summer grasses:
> all that remains of great soldiers'
> imperial dreams

Sora wrote:

> Kanefusa's
> own white hair
> seen in blossoming briar

We managed to cross all "forty-eight rapids" of the Kurobe River on our way to the bay of Ngo. Although it was no longer spring, we thought even an autumn visit to the wisteria at Tako—made famous in the *Man'yōshū*—worth the trouble, and asked the way: "Five miles down the coast, then up and over a mountain. A few fishermen's shacks but no lodging, no place even to camp." It sounded so difficult, we pushed on instead into the province of Kaga.

> Fragrance of ripening rice
> as we pass by
> the angry Ariso Sea

We crossed Mount Unohana and Kurikara Valley at noon on the fifteenth day of the seventh moon and entered Kanazawa, where we took rooms at an inn with a merchant from Osaka, a Mr. Kasho, who was in town to attend memorial services for the haiku poet Isshō, locally renowned for his verse and devotion to craft. The poet's elder brother served as host, the poet having died last winter.

> Tremble if you can,
> Gravemound:
> this autumn wind's my cry.

At a village called Komatsu:

> Aptly named Komatsu,
> Little Pine, a breeze blows
> Over pampas grass and clover

Here we visited Tada Shrine to see Sanemori's helmet and a piece of his brocade armorcloth presented to him by lord Yoshitomo when he served the Genji clan. His helmet was no common soldier's gear: engraved with chrysanthemums and ivy from eyehole to earflap, crowned with a dragon's head between two horns. After Sanemori died on the battlefield, Kiso Yoshinaka sent it with a prayer, hand-carried to the shrine by Higuchi Jirō, Sanemori's friend. The story's inscribed on the shine.

> Ungraciously, under
> a great soldier's empty helmet,
> a cricket sings

At the Echizen province border, at an inlet town called Yoshizaki, I hired a boat and sailed for the famous pines of Shiogoshi. Saigyō wrote:

> All the long night
> Salt-winds drive
> Storm-tossed waves
> And moonlight drips
> through Shiogoshi pines

This one poem says enough. To add another would be like adding a sixth finger to a hand.

In the town of Matsuoka, I visited Tenryū Temple, renewing an old friendship with the elder. The poet Hokushi from Kanazawa, intending only to see me off a way, had come this far with me, but turned back here. His poems on views along the way were sensitive, and I wrote for him:

> Written on my summer fan
> torn in half
> in autumn

Additional Haiku of Bashõ

> Clouds will separate
> the two friends, after the migrating
> Wild goose's departure

> Against the brushwood gate
> Dead tea leaves swirl
> In the stormy wind.

> The sound of hail—
> I am the same as before
> Like that aging oak

> Should I hold it in my hand
> It would melt in my burning tears—
> Autumnal frost.

> Another year is gone—
> A travel hat on my head
> Straw sandals on my feet.

> Will you start a fire?
> I'll show you something nice—
> A huge snowball.

> Myriads of things past
> Are brought to my mind—
> These cherry blossoms!

> The rough sea
> Extending toward Sado Isle,
> The Milky Way.

> The cuckoo—
> Through the dense bamboo grove,
> Moonlight seeping.

> Year after year
> On the monkey's face,
> A monkey's mask.

> The morning-glory—
> In the daytime, a bolt is fastened
> On the front yard gate.

> This autumn
> Why am I aging so?
> Flying towards the clouds,
> a bird.

> On a journey, ailing—
> My dreams roam about
> Over a withered moor.

Rembrandt's Biblical Roles

H. Perry Chapman

What I have described in the preceding chapters as Rembrandt's emerging individuality, his development from inner anarchy to inner authority and greater autonomy, can also be traced in the biblical personas he assumed. This chapter deals with three images that span the greater part of his career: his self-portrait as one of the henchmen helping to hoist the cross in the early *Raising of the Cross* from the Passion series owned by Frederik Hendrik; the large painting in Dresden of about 1636 in which Rembrandt appears, with his wife Saskia, as the Prodigal Son in the tavern; and the late *Self-Portrait as the Apostle Paul* of 1661.

Rembrandt's knowledge of the Bible was vast and his understanding of it profound. Old and New Testament subjects formed the bulk of his production in all media at most times in his life. It is no exaggeration to say that his involvement with the Bible is unique in seventeenth-century Dutch art both in the sheer quantity of works and in the depth of religious sentiment conveyed therein. Critics increasingly recognize that his biblical works not only are deeply moving but also reflect fundamental values of Dutch Protestantism. These three biblical self-portraits, when examined in the context of his life and work and the religious climate in Holland, confirm that he was deeply affected by the dominant religious mood of his time. That the roles in which he cast himself were formulated in the framework of seventeenth-century Protestant thought, especially the encouragement of self-scrutiny, suggests that his approach to the Bible was perhaps not as idiosyncratic as was once believed. Nevertheless, the image of the artist expressed in these works is profoundly personal and increasingly independent.

Unfortunately we know little of Rembrandt's religious affiliation. Baldinucci, the only one of his early biographers to discuss his religion, wrote in 1686:

The artist professed in those days the religion of the Menisti which, though false too, is yet opposed to that of Calvin, in as much as they do not practice the rite of baptism before the age of thirty. They do not elect educated preachers, but employ for such posts men of humble condition as long as they are esteemed by them as honorable and just people, and for the rest they live following their caprice.

No documentary evidence supports Baldinucci's claim that Rembrandt belonged to the radical, fundamentalist Mennonite sect, though his information presumably came from Bernhardt Keil, who had been Rembrandt's pupil in the mid 1640s. Baldinucci's assertion is suspect because it is so conveniently consistent with the generally disapproving picture he paints of Rembrandt as an artist who flouted the rules of painting, was "different in his mental make-up from other people as regards self-control," and "was a most temperamental man and despised everyone." However, Baldinucci should not be discounted entirely. Rembrandt did have connections with a number of Mennonites, the most important being Hendrick Uylenburgh, whose business he joined upon arriving in Amsterdam. Probably, then, it was because of Uylenburgh that two of Rembrandt's first portrait commissions came from members of this sect, Nicolaes Ruts and Martin Looten. He continued to portray Mennonites, including the minister Cornelis Claesz. Anslo in 1641. Moreover, Govert Flinck, who worked as Rembrandt's assistant in the mid 1630s and took over his position as teacher in Uylenburgh's "academy," was also a Mennonite.

However, the range of faiths represented by Rembrandt's colleagues, patrons, and sitters suggests it would be a mistake to consider their beliefs as evidence of his attachment to any particular sect. If anything, it indicates that the climate of relative tolerance in the Netherlands may have fostered in him an open-minded attitude toward religion. His teachers Jacob van Swanenburgh and Pieter Lastman were both Catholic. His hometown Leiden was a center of activity for the Remonstrants, a dissenting offshoot of the Calvinist church whose members had been banned from public office and persecuted in the 1620s. One of his most important early patrons, Petrus Scriverius, who probably commissioned the *Stoning of St. Stephen* and the Leiden *Historical Scene*, was a Remonstrant leader. But during his Leiden years Rembrandt was also patronized by the Stadholder Frederik Hendrik, a staunch upholder of the Calvinist Reformed Church.

In Amsterdam, though his first clients were Mennonites, Rembrandt soon drew others, a number of them distinguished clergymen, from various faiths. In 1633 he painted, and in 1655 etched, portraits of Johannes Uytenbogaert, the leader of the Remonstrants and preacher at their church in The Hague. His Catholic patrons, all from the 1630s, included Jan Rijksen and Griet Jans, who sat for *The Shipbuilder and His Wife,* as well as the poet Jan Hermansz. Krul. In 1633 and again in 1646 he etched portraits of Jan Cornelisz. Sylvius, preacher at the Reformed Oude Kerk in Amsterdam, who was Saskia's guardian and cousin by marriage, and who had baptized their children. Other Calvinists included Johannes Elison, minister in the Dutch Reformed Church in Norwich, England, and his wife, and the prominent Amsterdammers Maerten Soolmans and his wife, Oopjen Coppit. In 1636 Rembrandt etched the portrait of Menasseh ben Israel, his neighbor and the rabbi at the synagogue near his house on the Breestraat. These portraits were made, for the most part, when Rembrandt was at the height of his popularity as a portraitist. Given the fairly high degree of religious freedom in seventeenth-century Amsterdam, it is not surprising to find that the person who commissioned a portrait cared less about the artist's religious affiliation than about his talent and fame.

Perhaps more telling are extant documents indicating that Rembrandt had a continuing, though somewhat tenuous and not particularly active, affiliation with the Dutch Reformed Church. His parents had been married in the Reformed Pieterskerk in Leiden. In 1634, Rembrandt and Saskia were married in the Reformed church in Sint Annaparochie, in the northern province of Friesland. Their first three children were baptized in Reformed

churches. When Saskia died in 1642 she was buried in the Reformed Oude Kerk in a grave purchased by Rembrandt. His companion in his later years, Hendrickje Stoffels, also belonged to the Reformed Church, as indicated by her reprimand from the local church council in 1654. Hendrickje was probably summoned because she was pregnant: that Rembrandt himself was not included in the reprimand reveals little about his relation to the church. Their daughter, Cornelia, was baptized in the Oude Kerk. In 1669 Rembrandt was the godfather—such witnesses had to profess the truth of the church's teaching—at the baptism of his granddaughter. That same year he, like Hendrickje, was buried in the Reformed Westerkerk.

That Rembrandt's strongest connections to the Reformed Church were through his family, rather than direct, suggests he may have switched his religious affiliation over the course of his life or may have been a "libertine," as the freethinking non-church-goers of his day were called. Indeed, it was not at all uncommon to choose or change one's religion in seventeenth-century Holland. Many Dutchmen, including Vermeer and Vondel, converted from one denomination to another. Rembrandt's parents reflect in microcosm the period's extraordinarily fluid approach to church affiliation. Rembrandt's father was the only Calvinist member of a Catholic family, and his mother, though originally Catholic herself, may have converted to Calvinism with her marriage and appears to have turned to the Remonstrant faith upon the death of her husband in 1630. These religious vicissitudes in Rembrandt's own family may have reinforced in him the prevailing attitude of tolerance. Religious freedom of choice may also have strengthened his already reflective nature. Just as the social and economic disruption of his move to Amsterdam forced him to redefine his place in society and aspirations as an artist, so his religious mobility may have fostered examination of his self, the state of his soul, and his relation to God.

Critics have attempted with little success to deduce Rembrandt's religious beliefs from an investigation of his biblical narratives. Rotermund unconvincingly argued that his choice of themes was specifically Mennonite. Visser 't Hooft, who saw Rembrandt's subject matter as universally Protestant and reflective of no particular sect, worked from the assumption that Rembrandt was an independent interpreter of the Bible who relied exclusively and directly on his own reading of the gospel when composing religious works. Recently a more fruitful line of investigation has revised our understanding of Rembrandt's subject matter, showing it to be consistent with the beliefs of mainstream Dutch Protestantism. Tümpel, arguing that "an age's spiritual and religious climate . . . is a more powerful formative influence than a particular person's denomination," has demonstrated that Rembrandt relied heavily on pictorial tradition and that many of the themes he treated had been handled by earlier artists. In particular, he drew on sixteenth-century biblical illustrations and series of religious prints by such artists as Lucas van Leyden and Maerten van Heemskerck. Some subjects that had appeared exclusively in prints, as parts of series, he treated in paint as independent themes for the first time.

Rembrandt's elevation of obscure biblical motifs from the graphic media to panel painting was part of the general change in biblical interpretation after the Reformation. The Protestant concern with the literal historical meaning of the Bible had a profound and far-reaching effect on religious art, as did the elimination of devotional painting from the Calvinist Church. Old and New Testament narratives, such as the Sacrifice of Isaac, the Raising of Lazarus and the parable of the Prodigal Son, were depicted not typologically but literally as historical exemplars of Christian faith. Certain types of subjects were favored, in particular moments of recognition or realization. It is possible to identify a Protestant iconography, in a rather general sense, in this new literal and moral approach to the Bible.

Rembrandt's approach to the Bible evolved from that of his predecessors, especially Pieter Lastman; like them, he isolates part of the story and drives at its literal meaning. His particular contribution is his emphasis on the human element of the narrative. In his biblical works the moralizing approach of the sixteenth century is transformed into a penetrating concern with the moral implications of a given situation and with the characters' mental and emotional responses. Rembrandt examines situations that have a direct bearing on how he and his contemporaries live their lives, and above all on how they relate to God. Specifically, a significant number of his subjects are concerned with grace, a central element of Protestant dogma, and with its corollary, man's innate sinfulness. In many

of his works, the *Supper at Emmaus* in the Louvre for example, he tries to make as comprehensible as possible how man reacts when he comes in contact with the divine. Other subjects, like *Joseph and Potiphar's Wife* or the *Denial of Peter*, seem to be attempts to grasp the nature of human failing. . . .

The Apostle Paul

Both the self-portrait in the *Raising of the Cross* and the ironic *Self-Portrait with Saskia* were, on one level, confessional statements in which Rembrandt's identification with a biblical sinner served as a metaphor for the wretchedness of man, who can be redeemed solely through the grace of God. On another level, each asserted his artistic identity. Later in his life, Rembrandt portrayed himself as St. Paul, the thinker who most clearly expressed the concept of grace and salvation that informed seventeenth-century Dutch Protestantism. The *Self-Portrait as the Apostle Paul*, painted in 1661 when Rembrandt was fifty-five years old, is one of his most moving self-images, and represents the culmination of his confessional statements of his faith. His deeply personal, heartfelt identification with Paul, an archetypal persona vastly different from that of the sinner, suggests that Rembrandt had now gained greater understanding of his religion. But Paul also provided profound inspiration for Rembrandt's artistic self, for Paul's religious genius, embodying as it did the extremes of near-godly ecstasy and earthbound humility, made him the ultimate melancholic hero of his age.

The *Self-Portrait as the Apostle Paul*, with its heavy impasto, thick brushstrokes, and rich tonalities, is a superb example of Rembrandt's late style. A directed but atmospheric light draws the figure from the enveloping darkness but is focused most strongly on his expressive face. His penetrating gaze forcefully engages the eyes of the beholder. Upon close inspection, however, this seeming immediacy gives way to an inscrutably complex facial expression. As in his finest late portraits, Rembrandt conveys the sense of a vivid presence through which the full complexities of character are only slowly revealed. Even after lengthy contemplation, the subtleties of his facial gesture are difficult but not impossible to read. His deeply furrowed forehead, arched eyebrows, and wide-open eyes reveal a thoughtful, questioning mind. His slightly pursed lips and the muscles that tighten at the corners of his mouth betray an element of uncertainty. Strong illumination supports this pensive mood and imparts specific meaning to Rembrandt's expression by isolating not only his head but also the papers he holds in his hand. This selective lighting suggests that his expression is closely related to what is written on the papers.

Rembrandt's heavy brown mantle and white turban enhance the sense of the biblical past. It has been suggested that Paul's Oriental heritage led Rembrandt to take the unusual step of portraying him in a turban. Yet this turban does not resemble the more elaborate silk headdresses in which he usually clothed his biblical figures, as for example in *King Uzziah Stricken with Leprosy*, *Belshazzar's Feast*, or the *Disgrace of Haman*. Nor is it like the dark turban in his *Portrait of a Man as the Apostle Paul*. Rather, it resembles the white painter's turban he wears in his nearly contemporary self-portraits in Kenwood House and the Louvre. In other words, Rembrandts's choice of cap in the Rijksmuseum *Self-Portrait as the Apostle Paul* visually underlines his own identification with the saint. The effect is analogous to that of the staff in the Frick self-portrait, which alludes to both a king's scepter and the painter's mahlstick.

Schmidt-Degener, in 1919, and Valentiner, in 1920, were the first to identify Rembrandt's guise as that of the Apostle Paul on the basis of his two traditional attributes, the book and the sword, the handle of which protrudes from the folds of his cloak. The discovery that the painting, long recognized as a self-portrait, also represented Paul was made in conjunction with studies of the half-length paintings of Apostles and Evangelists to which Rembrandt turned his attention in the late 1650s and early 1660s. These include, from 1661 alone, *St. Matthew and the Angel* in the Louvre, the *Apostle Bartholomew* in Malibu, and the *Apostle Simon* in Zurich. Critics have hypothesized that the self-portrait may have belonged to a series of Apostles, like earlier series by Goltzius, Rubens, and van Dyck. But, considering the differences in size, quality, and execution among the single-figure biblical "portraits" of this period, the likelihood that they arose from a single commission—and one for which there exists no documentary evidence—is remote. Furthermore, the few records of Rembrandt's pictures of saints in inventories from his lifetime indicate that they were owned separately.

Very likely, then, most if not all were produced as independent works to be sold singly.

To treat individually subjects traditionally found in series would be in keeping with Rembrandt's concerns in the late 1650s and 1660s. Then he tended to focus on the essence of a biblical story by concentrating its narrative or extracting figures from their customary settings, so that the contemplative face became his sole expressive means and the difference between portrait and history painting became increasingly difficult to discern. Thus the *Self-Portrait as the Apostle Paul* should be viewed as an independent work, produced during a period when Rembrandt was engaged almost exclusively with this one particular type of painting.

Although it has not always been recognized as such, the self-portrait fits firmly within the tradition of the historicized portrait, or *portrait historié*, that began in the late fifteenth century and was still thriving in the seventeenth, especially in the Netherlands. Whether portrayed in the form of a saint or as a participant in an Old or New Testament episode, the biblical historicized portrait served to convey the sitter's faith and devotion. One of the earliest types of historicized portrait was also the earliest type of artist-portrait: it showed the artist as St. Luke, his patron saint, drawing the Virgin. Saintly guises, which originated in donor portraits, were widespread in the sixteenth century, as evidenced by the numerous portraits of women as Mary Magdalen by such artists as Jan Gossaert and Joos van Cleve. A self-portrait in the guise of St. Paul by Antonis Mor is documented but not known. Van Mander mentions Goltzius's portrait of a man as St. Sebastian, Jan van Scorel's paintings of his wife as St. Agatha and Mary Magdalen, and a painting by Cornelis Ketel of St. Paul "naer t'leven van Rutger Jansz. gedaen." And he tells us that Ketel also painted *tronies* or heads of Christ and the twelve Apostles whose faces are portraits of painters and collectors.

By Rembrandt's time, however, portraits in religious guises had yielded in popularity to mythological and pastoral historicized portraits like Flinck's portraits of Rembrandt and Saskia. Biblical portraits of individuals were seldom done after the 1630s and had been all but abandoned by the 1650s. David Bailly's *Portrait of a Priest as St. Jerome* is a rare seventeenth-century portrait in saintly guise. The few such works from the second half of the century are almost exclusively portraits of women as Mary Magdalen or group portraits in which entire families appear in biblical scenes, such as Jan de Bray's *Christ Blessing the Children* and Barent Fabritius's *Peter in the House of Cornelius* of 1653.

In the context of seventeenth-century historicized portraiture, Rembrandt's *Self-Portrait as the Apostle Paul* is a highly individual interpretation of a pictorial convention that was already outmoded by the time it was painted in 1661. As discussed in the previous chapter, his Kenwood *Self-Portrait* and *Self-Portrait at the Easel* of about the same date revived a portrait type more prevalent in the previous century. Thus Rembrandt's portrayal of himself as the Apostle Paul is one of several instances in which he drew on the art of the previous century rather than of his own time. But pictorial tradition, while it suggests precedents for the Rijksmuseum painting, does not explain why he chose to represent himself as Paul.

The *Self-Portrait as the Apostle Paul* was the culmination of Rembrandt's lifelong attachment to this saint. Like the Prodigal Son and the Presentation in the Temple, Paul was a subject that had occupied him early in his career and to which he returned many years later. Rembrandt's interest was not in the most frequently represented episode from Paul's life, his conversion on the road to Damascus. Instead he concentrated almost exclusively on Paul the apostle, the inspired yet humble author of the epistles, an emphasis in keeping with contemporary Protestant theology.

Paul was the single most important source for the formulation and development of Reformation theology, and his teaching remained central to the beliefs of not only the Reformed Church but also other sects of Dutch Protestantism. Luther and Calvin had looked to his writing and life as their primary authority in returning to the ideals of the apostolic church. Paul's conversion, according to Calvin, was an archetypal Christian experience, for it exemplified grace received completely independently of merit:

> In this history we have a universal figure of that grace which the Lord showeth forth daily to us all. All men do not set themselves so violently against the gospel; yet, nevertheless, both pride and also rebellion against God are naturally engendered in all men. We are all wicked and cruel naturally; therefore, in that we are turned to God, that cometh to

pass by the wonderful and secret power of God contrary to nature.

Above all, Paul's message of grace and unmerited redemption became the essential truth about which Protestant theology revolved. The early reformers regarded Paul as the *stylus dei* through which God's Word had been communicated. Their theology emphasized the total helplessness of inherently sinful man, who must have faith in the mercy of the all-powerful divinity. For them Paul's epistles provided the basis for the doctrine of justification by faith, which holds that men's souls are saved by God's grace alone, and that the actions or works of men are of no consequence in achieving salvation.

Like the early reformers, theologians from the various Protestant sects in Rembrandt's Holland looked to Paul as the primary authority in interpreting the gospel. Numerous sermons—preaching was the central focus of the Protestant service, and sermons once delivered reached a wider audience in pamphlet form—reveal the current understanding of Paul. A series of nine sermons on the Epistle to the Ephesians by the Delft preacher Jan Barentsz. van Voorburch, published in 1612, presents a long defense of predestinarian Calvinism. Paul's authority was also invoked in a New Year's letter by the Remonstrant minister Edwardius Poppius, whose less rigid variety of Calvinism questioned the doctrine of predestination.' The mainstream interpretation of Paul's teaching, which very closely follows that of Calvin, is found in the extensive annotations to the *Staats Bibel*, the official Bible of the Dutch Reformed Church.

Rembrandt's earliest painting of Paul, *The apostle Paul in Prison* of 1627, concentrates on his role as *stylus dei*. Presumably this was an important painting for Rembrandt, for it was his first single-figure composition on such a large panel. It was also iconographically innovative. Departing from the usual generalized setting, Rembrandt took the unusual step of placing the elderly Paul in a bare prison cell with a grated window, leg irons, and straw on the floor. By localizing the scene in this way he gave it novel narrative immediacy. Paul had four periods of imprisonment, during which he wrote his epistles. Most likely he is shown here in his Roman captivity, writing his Epistle to the Ephesians. In that letter Paul explained his mission and reason for writing:

When ye read, ye may understand my knowledge in the mystery of Christ . . .[Of this gospel] I was made a minister, according to the gift of the grace of God . . . Unto me, who am less than the least of all saints, is this grace given, that I should preach among the Gentiles the unsearchable riches of Christ; and to make all men see what is the fellowship of the mystery, which from the beginning of the world hath been hid in God.

Paul's bearing and his face, with its deeply creased brow and wide-open eyes, suggest his overwhelming mission and what Erasmus called "the great mind of Paul hidden in the Scriptures." In a moment of divinely inspired meditation he pauses from his writing and raises his hand to his mouth. He directs his gaze not toward the manuscript on his lap, but beyond his physical surroundings to a wholly spiritual realm.

The imagery of the Epistle to the Ephesians accords with, and helps explain, certain aspects of the painting. Paul uses light as a metaphor for God's grace: "For ye were sometimes darkness, but now are ye light in the Lord." The light that streams through the prison window, striking Paul's face and forming a backdrop of illumination, connotes the divine source of his privileged rapture. It is important to note that Rembrandt made an analogous use of light in his nearly contemporary *Artist in His Studio*: there strongly directed illumination, together with a suspension of the physical activity of creation, served as a metaphor for the inspired artistic imagination.

Paul's sword, propped prominently against his pile of books and papers, signifies the Word with which he does spiritual battle: "Put on the whole armour of God, that ye may be able to stand against the wiles of the devil . . . the breastplate of righteousness . . . the shield of faith . . . the helmet of salvation, and the sword of the Spirit, which is the word of God." As in earlier images of the Apostle by Lucas van Leyden and Jacques de Gheyn III, Paul rests his foot on a large rock, which may allude to his description of the community of the faithful as "built upon the foundation of the apostles and prophets, Jesus Christ himself being the chief corner stone." Moreover, in the same epistle Paul refers to his own imprisonment, calling himself "the prisoner of the Lord," and contrasts his physical bondage with his spiritual freedom from law and sin, symbolized by his unshackled foot resting on the cornerstone of faith. Since he is a man of true

faith, armed with the sword of the Holy Spirit, the chains of the law can no longer bind his soul.

Rembrandt characterized Paul as the teacher of the true faith in another way in his *Two Old Men Disputing* of 1628, which Tümpel has identified as Peter and Paul in conversation. Among the numerous sixteenth and seventeenth-century depictions of Peter and Paul conversing, Lucas van Leyden's engraving of 1527 is the closest prototype for this painting. Typically, Rembrandt wrought an utter transformation of this traditional subject. He moved the figures from a landscape setting to a study, prompting Tümpel to suggest that the scene represents Paul's visit to Peter in Jerusalem as described in Galatians 1:18. More significantly, he gave Paul a clearly dominant position. Light strikes him as he looms over Peter, who is seen only in lost profile, left in darkness. And it is Paul, not Peter as in Lucas's print, who forcefully points to the open book as if making a particular point. Generally speaking, Paul's prominence reflects his importance to Protestant theology. More specifically, it seems incompatible with a conversation among equals in Peter's study and suggests instead that he is teaching Peter a lesson, as happens later in Galatians. In the "Antioch incident," which occurred during Peter's visit to Paul in Antioch, Peter at first ate with Gentile Christians until the criticisms of the Jewish Christians caused him to shun the Gentiles. Paul rebuked him for this hypocrisy, saying "a man is not justified by the works of the law, but by the faith of Jesus Christ." Rembrandt's Paul seems similarly to instruct the insecure and humanly wavering Peter in the true message of God.

When Rembrandt again turned to Paul in the late 1650s he revived a type, the half-length apostle, that was by then old-fashioned. In the historicized *Portrait of a Man as the Apostle Paul* of about 1659 Paul is seated at his desk, his hands clasped in an attitude of meditative faith with his sword beside him. A framed monochrome roundel on the wall to his left shows the Sacrifice of Isaac in much the same way as Rembrandt's 1655 etching of this subject. In his letter to the Hebrews Paul points to this Old Testament episode not as a typological illustration but for its human and spiritual significance. Abraham is the supreme example of faith:

By faith Abraham, when he was tried, offered up Isaac: and he that had received the promises offered up his only begotten son . . . accounting that God was able to raise him up, even from the dead.

This allusion to Abraham's test of faith provides insight into the deeply introspective historicized portrait, for Protestantism encouraged the individual to meditate on his own tests of faith, just as Paul had done. As Calvin put it,

> It remains for every one of us to apply this example to himself. The Lord, indeed, is so indulgent with our infirmity that he does not thus severely try our faith: yet he intended in the father of all the faithful [Abraham], to propose an example by which he might call us to a general trial of faith.

Abraham also features in Paul's argument that the freedom of the Gospel must be independent of the law, the idea—central to Reformation theology— that "a man is justified by faith without the deeds of the law." Thus he exemplifies grace and freedom from the law:

> For the promise, that he should be the heir of the world, was not to Abraham, or to his seed, through the law, but through the righteousness of faith . . . Therefore it is of faith, that it might be by grace.

Rembrandt's London *Paul* is evidence of a sophisticated appreciation of the Apostle that paved the way for his *Self-Portrait as the Apostle Paul*. Perhaps the legal troubles stemming from his near bankruptcy at this period strengthened Rembrandt's sympathy for Paul's attitude towards the law. And quite possibly Rembrandt, having throughout his life repeatedly depicted the events and the lessons of the scriptures, perceived his artistic mission as explicator of the Bible as akin to Paul's teaching mission. However, I am inclined to seek a fuller explanation for his identification with Paul in the broader meaning of the Apostle's message and in his introspective nature or temperament as messenger.

In his self-portrait, as in his earlier representations of Paul, Rembrandt stressed the Apostle's personal contribution as vehicle for the Word. He conveys this dearly and economically through his two attributes. The sword that he holds close to his heart is not that of his martyrdom but "the sword of the Spirit, which is the word of God." His bundle of papers is his epistles, through which he explicates the Word. Attempts to identify the particular letter have not been successful. Its text is illegible, probably intentionally, like that in some of Rembrandt's other paintings and unlike that in several earlier paintings of Paul by artists in his circle, for example the *Apostle Paul* attributed to Jan Lievens in Bremen, which shows the beginning of the Epistle to the Thessalonians. The body of the text is only summarily indicated and contains large gaps. As it exists today, the large heading across the top of the page is vague and indistinct: most likely it was never intended to be read, though many have certainly tried.

Perhaps it is unwise to expect Rembrandt to summarize Paul in one particular epistle, just as it would be unwise to seek a single reason for his identification with the Apostle. By this time in his life, Rembrandt was fully steeped in Paul's teaching. He must have had a profound understanding of his message of faith, trust in God's grace, and freedom from the law. He also must have appreciated Paul's human complexity, a complexity that derived in large part from Paul's constant self-examination.

Two moving sermons by Willem Teellinck, one of the most influential Reformed preachers, forcefully convey how the period perceived Paul's self-exploratory, self-questioning nature as essential to his message of grace. Entitled *De Clachte Pauli, over sijne natuerlijcke verdorventheyt* (The Lamentations of Paul over His Natural Depravity), Teellinck's sermons explicate Romans 7:24: "Wretched man that I am, who will deliver me from this body of death?" This verse, Teellinck explains, is Paul's cry for help in his battle with his own flesh and natural corruption, a never-ending struggle that in many ways hindered his service to God. Here Paul's lamentation that he is wretched, and that he wishes to be freed of "this body of death," or sin, is a yearning for the final severance of soul from body that is union with God. Paul similarly expressed his frustrated earthbound longing for spiritual release when he wrote elsewhere of his "desire to depart [i.e. to die], and to be with Christ."

Teellinck's *De Clachte Pauli* emphasizes Paul's confession of his own human weakness, whose contrast with the gift of divine mercy makes salvation all the more awesome. His sinfulness is likened to that of Everyman, who is equally dependent on the grace of God for forgiveness. In focusing on Paul's intensely personal expression of self-doubt, which is central to the Calvinist scheme of salvation, Teellinck captures the human aspect of his religious genius.

Paul's deeply human and self-revelatory cast of thought, which Teellinck's sermon so effectively captures, must have been at the root of the Apostle's appeal for Rembrandt. His earlier self-portraits in biblical roles accord with the Protestant view of man as inherently sinful and totally dependent on God's grace for salvation. The self-portrait in the *Raising of the Cross* and the self-portrait as the Prodigal Son are colored by a similar confessional tone. In both, the artist's identification with the biblical sinner serves to mark the enormity of Christ's sacrifice and our dependence on divine mercy. The Apostle Paul, however, embodies to an even greater degree the Calvinist insistence on reconciling one's own sinfulness with faith in God's love and grace. Faith and devotion are Paul's central message; yet they are nothing, he tells us, without humility and self-awareness.

It was precisely that self-awareness, that contrast between Paul's near-divinity and his utter humility, that must have made him so compelling to Rembrandt. As a young man Rembrandt had portrayed himself as a melancholic, an introspective, self-absorbed artistic personality prone to inspiration and enthusiasm yet painfully conscious of the limitations of human intelligence. In the sixteenth century, before the popularization of melancholy, Paul had embodied the wisest type of melancholic genius. Dürer represented him as a gloomy, fiery-eyed melancholic in his *Four Apostles*. Marsilio Ficino had classed divinely inspired poetic *furor* with Paul's ecstasy. Paul may have suggested to Rembrandt a profound analogy to his conception of his own artistic personality; moreover, Rembrandt had devoted much of his career—indeed, the majority of his works—to portraying subjects from the Bible. In identifying with Paul, he could boldly, yet respectfully, claim to be an inspired yet humble vehicle for God's Word.

But Rembrandt's identification with the saint, I propose, went beyond that to an even deeper affinity for the self-searching nature of Paul's writing. Self-examination, and the profound humility which it engenders, played a central role in Paul's thought. Though supremely gifted, he described himself as "rude in speech" and "the least of the saints;" which might have appealed to Rembrandt in the years around 1660, when he had cast off the pretensions of his earlier self-portraits to portray himself as the painter in his studio. As we have seen, Rembrandt too, in his self-portraits, was constantly reexamining his place in the world. In the *Self-portrait as the Apostle Paul* he identified not just with Paul, but with the Apostle's own conception of his calling.

Facing Up, Finally, to Bach's Dark Vision

Richard Taruskin

The Teldec Bach Cantatas

Teldec's series of Bach church cantatas, begun in 1971, when the German label was still called Telefunken, is now complete on eighty-three CDs, assembled in forty-five packages. Almost incredibly, enough Bach church cantatas are lost to fill another forty-nine CDs.

The Teldec series includes one hundred ninety of the two hundred surviving works, with one recorded in two versions. Of the other ten items, five have been found to be spurious, including the much recorded Nos. 53 and 189, and five are fragmentary works or reworkings—"parodies"—of other compositions.

Teldec's performances use a variety of European boy choirs and two period-instrument ensembles. The cellist and conductor Nikolaus Harnoncourt leads the Vienna Concentus Musicus, perhaps the oldest period-instrument ensemble still in business, and the harpsichordist and organist Gustav Leonhardt leads the Amsterdam-based Leonhardt Consort.

The series has prominently featured soloists who were or went on to become international stars, including the flutist Frans Bruggen, the countertenor Paul Esswood and the baritones Max von Egmond and, lately, Thomas Hampson. The one singer associated with the project from first release to last was the tenor Kurt Equiluz.

And now for something altogether unreviewable: eighty-three compact disks containing almost two hundred church cantatas by Johann Sebastian Bach as recorded by Teldec over an eighteen-year period (thirteen years longer than it took to write them) by a who's who of Early Music virtuosos under the joint direction of Gustav Leonhardt and Nikolaus Harnoncourt.

Eerie is the only word for the virtual silence that has greeted the end of this project, inaugurated in 1971 amid considerable fanfare and controversy. Completion was announced for 1985, the Bach tricentennial year. Had that deadline been achieved, no doubt, we would have heard more about it. Meanwhile, a competing series, inaugurated in 1975

under the leadership of the German choral specialist Helmuth Rilling, did make it to the finish line in time.

Although the Rilling traversal relied on standard instruments and a traditional (alas, rather drab if dependable) performance style, it possessed a certain musicological cachet. It was issued in the revolutionary new chronological order of cantatas that was established in the 1950s by a heroic team of German scholars, while the Teldec project followed the aimless order of the nineteenth-century Bach Gesellschaft edition. The Rilling version is also marginally more complete, since it includes the fragmentary works and parodies.

Most injurious of all to the newsworthiness of the Teldec series, perhaps, is the fact that along the way it stopped reflecting the absolute cutting edge of fashion in Bachian performance practice. In 1971, even sympathetic scholars could find the Leonhardt-Harnoncourt approach disconcerting, what with its clipped nonlegato articulations, its rhythmic alterations and dislocations, its easily satirized dynamic bulges, its brusquely punctuated recitatives, its flippant tempos, not to mention the tiny forces, the green and sickly sounding boy soprano soloists, above all the recalcitrant, sometimes ill-tuned "original instruments." Some were downright indignant at the loss of traditional scale and weight. The venerable musicologist Paul Henry Lang blasted the "frail performances with inadequate ensembles," and what he saw as the craven sacrifice of spiritual values to safe and shallow scholarly "objectivity."

Yet by the early 1980s, the ground had shifted to the point where Mr. Leonhardt and Mr. Harnoncourt had become middle-of-the-roaders. The authenticity spotlight was stolen by proponents of ever more radical theories of historical Bach performance, the most notorious being the elimination of the chorus altogether in favor of single voices. For today's authenticity mavens the Teldec performances are not nearly frail enough.

The British quarterly *Early Music* has been ignoring the series since the 1986 releases, when Mr. Harnoncourt's work in particular was primly dismissed as having "no advantages over traditional 'Romantic' interpretations," because it did not sufficiently respect what the reviewer was pleased to call "the implications of the music itself."

The music itself—what might that be? Though blandly invoked as if it were a self-evident ideal, it is really a problematical and anachronistic notion. Bach would not have understood it. Its fount was the late-eighteenth-century Enlightenment, the antimetaphysical Age of Reason. It was an Enlightened music historian named Charles Burney who in the 1770s penned the definition of music that is still paraphrased in most dictionaries: "the art of pleasing by the succession and combination of agreeable sounds." If Burney's words ring true, it is because modern musicians—composers, scholars and performers of every stripe—are essentially formalists at heart. And so are modern listeners.

We all tend to exalt what Stravinsky called the *matière sonore*—the material sound of music—over immaterial meaning (the "extramusical content," if you will). Listeners value performances to the extent that they are beautiful-sounding. Performers strive hardest for clean execution and beautiful tone. Composers and scholars define and explain musical meaning primarily in terms of an abstract ("purely musical") sound-syntax. When pressed to a logical extreme, some have even attempted to deny the reality of musical expressivity.

Because of his unparalleled technical mastery and his habit of pinning down in precise notation so much more than his contemporaries cared to do, Bach is often looked upon as music's formalist supreme. The disproportionate visibility of his highly patterned instrumental music nowadays abets this perception, as do Bach's late quasi-scholastic testaments, *The Art of Fugue,* and particularly *The Musical Offering,* which after all arose out of contact with his son's employer, Frederick the Great of Prussia, ardent Enlightener of the German lands.

The Enlightened, secularized view of Bach is the one advanced by most modern scholarship. The six columns devoted to the cantatas in the *New Grove Dictionary of Music and Musicians* contain nothing but a taxonomy, a sterile formal classification. Lip service is paid to the composer's "unfailing expressive profundity," but the whole question of expression is assimilated to innocuous notions of

beautiful form, as if to lure attention away from rhetoric and imagery and onto "the music itself."

According to such a taste, whether the genuine eighteenth-century article or its modern simulacrum, all music stands or falls as distinguished entertainment. "I don't mind so much if a performance is unhistorical," Roger Norrington told a reporter last summer, attempting an end run around the vexed notion of authenticity, "but I do mind if it isn't fun."

How utterly irrelevant this whole esthetic is to the Bach of the cantatas! How irrelevant, therefore, the cantatas are to our modern concert life. Small wonder that scarcely half a dozen out of two hundred are or ever will be known to concertgoers.

And a thoroughly unrepresentative lot it is, too, even if we exclude the fun items like the "Coffee" and "Peasant" Cantatas from the list. The favored handful includes gaudy display pieces like No. 51, *Jauchzet Gott in allen Landen,* the one church cantata Bach ever composed for a woman's voice. It includes officiously celebratory ones on familiar hymns like No. 80, *Ein' feste Burg,* usually performed—not here!—in a big band arrangement by the composer's son Wilhelm Friedemann. And it includes uncharacteristic imitations of what Bach called "the pretty little Dresden tunes" (that is, opera) like No. 140, *Wachet auf,* with its love duets between Christ and the Christian soul.

Anyone exposed to Bach's full range (as now, thanks to these records, one can be) knows that the hearty, genial, lyrical Bach of the concert hall is not the essential Bach. The essential Bach was an avatar of a pre-Enlightened—and when push came to shove, a violently anti-Enlightened—temper. His music was a medium of truth, not beauty. And the truth he served was bitter. His works persuade us—no, *reveal* to us—that the world is filth and horror, that humans are helpless, that life is pain, that reason is a snare.

The sounds Bach combined in church were often anything but agreeable, to recall Dr. Burney's prescription, for Bach's purpose there was never just to please. If he pleased, it was only to cajole. When his sounds were agreeable, it was only to point out an escape from worldly woe in heavenly submission. Just as often he aimed to torture the ear: when the world was his subject, he wrote music that for sheer deliberate ugliness has perhaps been approached—by Mahler, possibly, at times—but never equaled. (Did Mahler ever write anything as noisomely discordant as Bach's portrayal, in the opening chorus of Cantata No. 101, of strife, plague, want and care?)

Such music cannot be prettified in performance without essential loss. For with Bach—the essential Bach—there is no "music itself." His concept of music derived from and inevitably contained The Word, and the word was Luther's.

It is a predicament Bach's Enlightened rediscoverers recognized from the very first. Carl Friedrich Zelter, the conductor of the Berlin Singakademie, wrote of it to Goethe in 1827, two years before his pupil Mendelssohn revived the St. Matthew Passion. Communion with Bach's music, Zelter felt, was a means "toward apperception and awe of the Truth," but there was an obstacle: "the altogether contemptible German church texts, which suffer from the earnest polemic of the Reformation."

This was something the Enlightened mind could only resist. "The thick fog of belief stirs up nothing but disbelief," Zelter complained, with the result that Bach's sacred output "will doubtless long remain a secret, since it cannot be compared with the music we know at present."

The effort to save "the music itself" (which could be adapted to contemporary taste) from its motivating esthetic (which could not) set a vast sanitizing project in motion. It has been going on from Mendelssohn's day to our own, and has for nearly two centuries been keeping the essential Bach at bay, absent equally from the pages of *Grove* and from the latest pretty one-on-a-part renditions.

It is because they have refused to participate in the cover-up that the work of Mr. Leonhardt and (especially) Mr. Harnoncourt has been difficult of acceptance. The two divided the cantatas up, it would appear, according to temperament. Mr. Leonhardt, the Early Music movement's patrician guru, took most of the pastoral pieces, leaving the really tough sermons to the suitably fearless and contentious Mr. Harnoncourt. (Occasionally, as in Volume 40, they cast themselves whimsically against type, with the result that the phlegmatic Mr. Leonhardt unfortunately ended up playing the most neurotic piece of all—the organ solo in Cantata No. 170 that Bach himself called "an infernal bawling and drawling.")

Like any true guru, Mr. Leonhardt does not justify his ways. It is one of the stranger features of the Teldec series that the regular section in the program books devoted to "Notes on the Performance" contains only remarks by Mr. Harnoncourt on "his" cantatas. By putting his cards on the table,

Mr. Harnoncourt invites backtalk; Mr. Leonhardt's seraphic silence silences.

Yet since Mr. Harnoncourt's approach is the more challenging and the riskier, his success is all the more estimable. There is a danger of intentional fallacy in trying to account for that success, but what may well have started out as mere literalism seems to have been subverted by the essential Bach into a new, authentic musical evangelism.

Mr. Harnoncourt's style has taken on attributes that "performance practice" alone could never have vouchsafed. They can only have come from those "contemptible" Lutheran texts and their unaccommodating polemic. His increasingly hortatory and unbeautiful way of performing Bach reached a peak about halfway through the series, and the intervening decade has done nothing to lessen its power to shock—or disgust. If you seek contact with the essential Bach at full hideous strength, Mr. Harnoncourt's performances remain the only place to go.

It feels not only invidious but ridiculous to be singling out one recording from a yard-high stack. But in Volume 41, released in 1988, the essential Bach speaks through Mr. Harnoncourt with a special vehemence. Cantata No. 178, *Wo Gott der Herr nicht bei uns hält*, begins with a French overture straight from hell, a portrait of a world without God in which (as Dostoyevsky later noted) all things are possible and there is no hope. Mr. Harnoncourt applies to the dotted rhythms the awful Gnashville sound he has gradually developed for such occasions, the strings of the Concentus Musicus hurling their bows at their instruments from a great height, producing as much scratch as tone.

The "chorale-recitative" that follows illustrates the futility of human effort with a bass that is continually and arbitrarily disrupted. It is played with greatly exaggerated dynamics to underscore—needlessly, most proper authenticists would insist—the bare message of the notes. After an aria depicting a Satan-engineered shipwreck with nauseous melismas and a chorale verse evoking persecution with a crowd of claustrophobically close and syncopated imitations, we reach the heart of the cantata.

A glossed chorale verse about raging beasts finally dispenses with word-painting, which depends on mechanisms of wit and can be taken as humor. It harks back instead to the wellsprings of the Baroque in grossly exaggerated speech contours, something akin to wild gesticulation.

Now Bach the anti-Enlightener comes into his own, with a frantic tenor aria, "Shut up, stumbling Reason!" ("Schweig nur, taumelnde Vernunft!"). Past the first line the message of the text is one of comfort: "To them who trust in Jesus ever, the Door of Mercy closes never," to quote the doggerel translation in the program booklet. But Bach is fixated on that fierce and derisive opening line—indeed, on just the opening word. Out of it he builds practically the whole first section of his da capo aria, crowding all the rest into a cursory and soon superseded middle. Over and over the tenor shrieks, "Schweig nur, schweig!," leaping now a sixth, now a seventh, now an octave. Meanwhile, the accompanying orchestra, reason's surrogate, reels and lurches violently.

This one is not for you, Dr. Burney. Hands off, Maestro Norrington. There is no way this music can ever be fun. In fact, it is terrifying—perhaps more now than in Bach's own time, since we have greater reason than Bach's contemporaries ever had to wince at the sound of a high-pitched German voice stridently shouting reason down.

The cantata that follows on the same disk—No. 179, *Siehe du, dass deine Gottesfurcht nicht Heuchelei sei*—is harsh and minatory: "See to it that your fear of God is no sham!" The performance emphatically belongs to the frail, inadequate type that has given the Teldec set a bad name.

Take the aria "Liebster Gott, erbarme dich" ("Dear God, have mercy"), for soprano solo and two accompanying oboes da caccia. The solo part is quite beyond the powers of the poor boy who is called upon to sing it, and who (in the witty words of Bach scholar John Butt) has "no strong views about rhythm or tempo."

Although the aria is in the key of A minor, the middle section modulates to, and ends in, the key of C minor. Not only is the juxtaposition intensely jarring, it also puts the music in a harmonic region where the instruments simply cannot play in tune, especially as Bach takes them down to their very lowest, least tractable range. At the middle cadence the boy, too, is asked to sing lower than his tonal support permits.

The whole performance sounds loathesome and disgraceful. And these are the words: "My sins sicken me like pus in my bones; help me, Jesus, Lamb of God, for I am sinking in deepest slime." Perform this aria with a hale and hearty mezzo-soprano full of strong musical views, accompany her with a pair of brand new English horns spiffily played, and only "the music itself" will gain, not the aria, which utterly depends on its performers' failings, and on the

imperfections of their equipment to make its harrowing point.

This undermining of human agency is something Bach engineers time and again. If you want to witness a real assault by composer on performer, try the middle section of the bass aria in Cantata No. 104 (Volume 26). The text reads, "Here you taste of Jesus' goodness and look forward, as your reward for faith, to the sweet sleep of death." The vocal line extends for 18 measures in a stately 12/8 meter without a single rest, and with notes lasting as much as nine beats. It reduces the estimable Philippe Huttenlocher to a gasping, panting state in which, were the aria to continue another two minutes, he would surely receive his reward.

Nor could anyone possibly hear Frans Bruggen's incomparable enunciation of the obbligato to the great tenor aria in Cantata No. 114 (Volume 28)—*Wo wird in diesem Jammertale* ("Where, in this vale of woes, may I find refuge for my soul?")—and not realize that Bach was counting precisely on the fact, emphasized by Paul Henry Lang with asperity in 1972, that "the low region of the Baroque flute is breathy and weak."

It is for their refusal to flinch in the face of Bach's contempt for the world and all its creatures that Mr. Leonhardt and Mr. Harnoncourt deserve our admiration. Their achievement is unique and well-nigh unendurable. Unless one has experienced the full range of Bach cantatas in these sometimes all but unlistenable renditions, one simply does not know Bach. More than that, one does not know what music can do, or all that music can, be. Such performances could never work in the concert hall, it goes without saying, and who has time for church? But that is why there are records.

Postscript 1994

Many were the readers who took this piece as an attack on Bach ("God help us, on Mozart's birthday," shrieked one), accusing me of taking "a kind of sadistic delight in denigrating every aspect of the works in extremely blunt not to say offensive language" (wrote another). The idea that great music can be ugly, or ugly great, is unthinkable to most music lovers, which shows how far we have strayed from the ancient esthetic of the sublime, and nicely supports my point about "the music itself."

Others had "theological" objections to my "charges" against Bach. "Did Bach really intend or think his music ugly?" wrote a thoughtful student. "If you say that Bach's music . . . implies a world of filth and horror, you suggest he conceived a world with a cruel and tyrannical God at its helm—*not* a Christian God. Considering Bach's devotion, such a conclusion does not make sense." But as the devoted know best of all, God is not a Christian. It is for us to be Christians.

Of course, Bach is bigger than any one view of him. One exceptionally well-informed correspondent contributed some interesting—to me, most welcome—qualification, which I am happy to pass along to my readers:

> At times Bach does set texts that smack of Lutheran polemics: against the Pope and Catholicism and, yes, against reason. But "the high-pitched German voice stridently shouting reason down" is, or should be, musical—albeit declamatory—and should, perhaps, be put beside the quieter, lower German voice referring to Christ as "the light of reason" in Cantata 76, which starts with two verses of Psalm 19: "The heavens declare the glory of God." Now I should say that the Bach who set Luther's translation of the Bible is more "essential" than the Bach who set Lutheran polemics. Even when librettists present him with medical metaphors like "pus [or rottenness] in my bones" they are apt to have taken them from places like Habakkuk 3, 16.

And, she adds, "I like being harrowed by Bach—rather than Harnoncourt—and take Bach's words seriously. I doubt that he would object to some musical sublimation of the wild gestures and breathless gasps—provided the words are enunciated clearly and with conviction."

What Is Enlightenment?

Immanuel Kant

Enlightenment is man's release from his self-incurred tutelage. Tutelage is man's inability to make use of his understanding without direction from another. Self-incurred is this tutelage when its cause lies not in lack of reason but in lack of resolution and courage to use it without direction from another. *Sapere aude!*[1] "Have courage to use your own reason!"—that is the motto of enlightenment.

Laziness and cowardice are the reasons why so great a portion of mankind, after nature has long since discharged them from external direction (*naturaliter maiorennes*), nevertheless remains under lifelong tutelage, and why it is so easy for others to set themselves up as their guardians. It is so easy not to be of age. If I have a book which understands for me, a pastor who has a conscience for me, a physician who decides my diet, and so forth, I need not trouble myself. I need not think, if I can only pay—others will readily undertake the irksome work for me.

That the step to competence is held to be very dangerous by the far greater portion of mankind (and by the entire fair sex)—quite apart from its being arduous—is seen to by those guardians who have so kindly assumed superintendence over them. After the guardians have first made their domestic cattle dumb and have made sure that these placid creatures will not dare take a single step without the harness of the cart to which they are tethered, the guardians then show them the danger which threatens if they try to go alone. Actually, however, this danger is not so great, for by falling a few times they would finally learn to walk alone. But an example of this failure makes them timid and ordinarily frightens them away from all further trials.

For any single individual to work himself out of the life under tutelage which has become almost his nature is very difficult. He has come to be fond of this state, and he is for the present really incapable of making use of his reason, or no one has ever let him try it out. Statutes and formulas, those mechanical tools of the rational employment or rather misemployment of his natural gifts, are the fetters of an everlasting tutelage. Whoever throws them off makes only an uncertain leap over the narrowest ditch because he is not accustomed to that kind of free motion. Therefore, there are few who have succeeded by their own exercise of mind both in freeing themselves from incompetence and in achieving a steady pace.

But that the public should enlighten itself is more possible, indeed, if only freedom is granted, enlightenment is almost sure to follow. For there will always be some independent thinkers, even among the established guardians of the great masses, who, after throwing off the yoke of tutelage from their own shoulders, will disseminate the spirit of the rational appreciation of both their own worth and every man's vocation for thinking for himself. But be it noted that the public, which has first been brought under this yoke by their guardians, forces the guardians themselves to remain bound when it is incited to do so by some of the guardians who are themselves capable of some enlightenment—so harmful is it to implant prejudices, for they later take vengeance on their cultivators or on their descendants. Thus the public can only slowly attain enlightenment. Perhaps a fall of personal despotism or of avaricious or tyrannical oppression may be accomplished by revolution, but never a true reform in ways of thinking. Rather, new prejudices will serve as well as old ones to harness the great unthinking masses.

For this enlightenment, however, nothing is required but freedom, and indeed the most harmless among all the things to which this term can properly be applied. It is the freedom to make public use of one's reason at every point.[2] But I hear on all sides, "Do not argue!" The officer says: "Do not argue but drill!" The tax collector: "Do not argue but pay!" The cleric: "Do not argue but believe!" Only one prince in the world says, "Argue as much as you will, and about what you will, but obey!" Everywhere there is restriction on freedom.

Which restriction is an obstacle to enlightenment, and which is not an obstacle but a promoter of it? I answer: The public use of one's reason must always be free, and it alone can bring about enlightenment among men. The private use of reason, on the other hand, may often be very narrowly restricted without particularly hindering the progress on enlightenment. By the public use of one's reason I understand the use which a person makes of it as a scholar before the reading public. Private use I call that which one may make of it in a particular civil post or office which is entrusted to him. Many affairs which are conducted in the interest of the community require a certain mechanism through which some members of the community must passively conduct themselves with an artificial unanimity, so that the government may direct them to public ends, or at least prevent them from destroying those ends. Here argument is certainly not allowed—one must obey. But so far as a part of the mechanism regards himself at the same time as a member of the whole community or of a society of world citizens, and thus in the role of a scholar who addresses the public (in the proper sense of the word) through his writings, he certainly can argue without hurting the affairs for which he is in part responsible as a passive member. Thus it would be ruinous for an officer in service to debate about the suitability or utility of a command given to him by his superior; he must obey. But the right to make remarks on errors in the military service and to lay them before the public for judgment cannot equitably be refused him as a scholar. The citizen cannot refuse to pay the taxes imposed on him; indeed, an impudent complaint at those levied on him can be punished as a scandal (as it could occasion general refractoriness). But the same person nevertheless does not act contrary to his duty as a citizen when, as a scholar, he publicly expresses his thoughts on the inappropriateness or even the injustice of those levies. Similarly a clergyman is obligated to make his sermon to his pupils in catechism and his congregation conform to the symbol of the church which he serves, for he has been accepted on this condition. But as a scholar he has complete freedom, even the calling, to communicate to the public all his carefully tested and well meaning thoughts on that which is erroneous in the symbol and to make suggestions for the better organization of the religious body and church. In doing this there is nothing that could be laid as a burden on his conscience. For what he teaches a consequence of his office as a representative of the church, this he considers something about which he has no freedom to teach according to his own lights; it is something which he is appointed to propound at the dictation of and in the name of another. He will say, "Our church teaches this or that; those are the proofs which it adduces." He thus extracts all practical uses for his congregation from statutes to which he himself would not subscribe with full conviction but to the enunciation of which he can very well pledge himself because it is not impossible that truth lies hidden in them, and, in any case, there is at least nothing in them contradictory to inner religion. For if he believed he had found such in them, he could not conscientiously discharge the duties of his office; he would have to give it up. The use, therefore, which an appointed teacher makes of his reason before his congregation is merely private, because this congregation is only a domestic one (even if it be a large gathering); with respect to it, as a priest, he is not free, nor can he be free, because he carries out the orders of another. But as a scholar, whose writings speak to his public, the world, the clergyman in the public use of his reason enjoys an unlimited freedom to use his own reason and to speak in his own person. That the guardians of the people (in spiritual things) should themselves be incompetent is an absurdity which amounts to the eternalization of absurdities.

But would not a society of clergymen, perhaps a church conference or a venerable classis (as they call themselves among the Dutch), be justified in obligating itself by oath to a certain unchangeable symbol in order to enjoy an unceasing guardianship over each of its members and thereby over the people as a whole, and even to make it eternal? I answer that this is altogether impossible. Such a contract, made to shut off all further enlightenment from the human race, is absolutely null and void even if confirmed by the supreme power, by parliaments, and by the most ceremonious of peace treaties. An age cannot bind itself and ordain to put the succeeding one into such a condition that it cannot extend its (at best very occasional) knowledge, purify itself of errors, and progress in general enlightenment. That would be a crime against human nature, the proper destination of which lies precisely in this progress; and the descendants would be fully justified in rejecting those decrees as having been made in an unwarranted and malicious manner.

The touchstone of everything that can be concluded as a law for a people lies in the question whether the people could have imposed such a law on itself. Now such a religious compact might be possible for a short and definitely limited time, as it were, in expectation of a better. One might let every citizen, and especially the clergyman, in the role of scholar, make his comments freely and publicly, i.e., through writing, on the erroneous aspects of the present institution. The newly introduced order might last until insight into the nature of these things had become so general and widely approved that through uniting their voices (even if not unanimously) they could bring a proposal to the throne to take those congregations under protection which had united into a changed religious organization according to their better ideas, without, however, hindering others who wish to remain in the order. But to unite in a permanent religious institution which is not to be subject to doubt before the public even in the lifetime of one man, and thereby to make a period of time fruitless in the progress of mankind toward improvement, thus working to the disadvantage of posterity—that is absolutely forbidden. For himself (and only for a short time) a man may postpone enlightenment in what he ought to know, but to renounce it for himself and even more to renounce it for posterity is to injure and trample on the rights of mankind.

And what a people may not decree for itself can even less be decreed for them by a monarch, for his lawgiving authority rests on his uniting the general public will in his own. If he only sees to it that all true or alleged improvement stands together with civil order, he can leave it to his subjects to do what they find necessary for their spiritual welfare. This is not his concern, though it is incumbent on him to prevent one of them from violently hindering another in determining and promoting this welfare to the best of his ability. To meddle in these matters lowers his own majesty, since by the writings in which his subjects seek to present their views he may evaluate his own governance. He can do this when, with deepest understanding, he lays upon himself the reproach, *Caesar non est supra grammaticos.* Far more does he injure his own majesty when he degrades his supreme power by supporting the ecclesiastical despotism of some tyrants in his state over his other subjects.

If we are asked, "Do we now live in an enlightened age?" the answer is, "No," but we do live in an age of enlightenment.[3] As things now stand, much is lacking which prevents men from being, or easily becoming, capable of correctly using their own reason in religious matters with assurance and free from outside direction. But, on the other hand, we have clear indications that the field has now been opened wherein men may freely deal with these things and that the obstacles to general enlightenment or the release from self-imposed tutelage are gradually being reduced. In this respect, this is the age of enlightenment, or the century of Frederick.

A prince who does not find it unworthy of himself to say that he holds it to be his duty to prescribe nothing to men in religious matters but to give them complete freedom while renouncing the haughty name of tolerance, is himself enlightened and deserves to be esteemed by the grateful world and posterity as the first, at least from the side of government, who divested the human race of its tutelage and left each man free to make use of his reason in matters of conscience. Under him venerable ecclesiastics are allowed, in the role of scholars, and without infringing on their official duties, freely to submit for public testing their judgments and views which here and there diverge from the established symbol. And an even greater freedom is enjoyed by those who are restricted by no official duties. This spirit of freedom spreads beyond this land, even to those in which it must struggle with external obstacles erected by a government which misunderstands its own interest. For an example gives evidence to such a government that in freedom there is not the least cause for concern about public peace and the stability of the community. Men work themselves gradually out of barbarity if only intentional artifices are not made to hold them in it.

I have placed the main point of enlightenment—the escape of men from their self-incurred tutelage—chiefly in matters of religion because our rulers have no interest in playing the guardian with respect to the arts and sciences and also because religious incompetence is not only the most harmful but also the most degrading of all. But the manner of thinking of the head of a state who favors religious enlightenment goes further, and he sees that there is no danger to his lawgiving in allowing his subjects to make public use of their reason and to publish their thoughts on a better formulation of his legislation and even their open-minded criticisms of the laws already made. Of this we have a shining example wherein no monarch is superior to him whom we honor.

But only one who is himself enlightened, is not afraid of shadows, and has a numerous and well-disciplined army to assure public peace, can say: "Argue as much as you will, and about what you will, only obey!" A republic could not dare say such a thing. Here is shown a strange and unexpected trend in human affairs in which almost everything, looked at in the large, is paradoxical. A greater degree of civil freedom appears advantageous to the freedom of mind of the people, and yet it places inescapable limitations upon it; a lower degree of civil freedom, on the contrary, provides the mind with room for each man to extend himself to his full capacity. As nature has uncovered from under this hard shell the seed for which she most tenderly cares—the propensity and vocation to free thinking—this gradually works back upon the character of the people, who thereby gradually become capable of managing freedom; finally, it affects the principles of government, which finds it to its advantage to treat men, who are now more than machines, in accordance with their dignity.[4]

I. Kant
Konigsberg, Prussia
September 30, 1784

Notes

1   ["Dare to know!" (Horace Ars poetica). This was the motto adopted in 1736 by the Society of the Friends of Truth, an important circle in the German Enlightenment.]

2   [It is this freedom Kant claimed later in his conflict with the censor, deferring to the censor in the "private" use of reason, i.e., in his lectures.]

3   ["Our age is, in especial degree, the age of criticism, and to criticism everything must submit" (*Critique of Pure Reason*, Preface to first ed. [Smith trans.]).]

4   Today I read in the *Buschingsche Wochentliche Nachrichten* for September 13 an announcement of the Berlinische Monatsschrift for this month, which cites the answer to the same question by Herr Mendelssohn.* But this issue has not yet come to me; if it had, I would have held back the present essay, which is now put forth only in order to see how much agreement in thought can be brought about by chance.

*   [Mendelssohn's answer was that enlightenment lay in intellectual cultivation, which he distinguished from the practical. Kant, quite in line with his later essay on theory and practice, refuses to make this distinction fundamental.]

Sermon 70
The Case of Reason Impartially Considered

John Wesley

"Brethren, be not children in understanding: Howbeit in malice be ye children, but in understanding be men."

1 Cor. 14:20.

1. It is the true remark of an eminent man, who had made many observations on human nature, "If reason be against a man, a man will always be against reason." This has been confirmed by the experience of all ages. Very many have been the instances of it in the Christian as well as the heathen world; yea, and that in the earliest times. Even then there were not wanting well-meaning men who, not having much reason themselves, imagined that reason was of no use in religion; yea, rather, that it was a hinderance to it. And there has not been wanting a succession of men who have believed and asserted the same thing. But never was there a greater number of these in the Christian Church, at least in Britain, than at this day.

2. Among them that despise and vilify reason, you may always expect to find those enthusiasts who suppose the dreams of their own imagination to be revelations from God. We cannot expect that men of this turn will pay much regard to reason. Having an infallible guide, they are very little moved by the reasonings of fallible men. In the foremost of these we commonly find the whole herd of Antinomians; all that, however they may differ in other respects, agree in "making void the law through faith." If you oppose reason to these, when they are asserting propositions ever so full of absurdity and blasphemy, they will probably think it a sufficient answer to say, "O, this is your reason;" or "your carnal reason:" So that all arguments are lost upon them: They regard them no more than stubble or rotten wood.

3. How natural is it for those who observe this extreme, to run into the contrary! While they are strongly impressed with the absurdity of undervaluing reason, how apt are they to overvalue it! Accordingly, we are surrounded with those (we find them on every side) who lay it down as an undoubted principle, that reason is the highest gift of God. They paint it in the fairest colours; they extol it to the skies. They are fond of expatiating in its praise; they make it little less than divine. They are wont to describe it as very near, if not quite, infallible. They look upon it as the all-sufficient director of all the children of men; able, by its native light, to guide them into all truth, and lead them into all virtue.

4. They that are prejudiced against the Christian revelation, who do not receive the Scriptures as the oracles of God, almost universally run into this extreme: I have scarce known any exception: So do all, by whatever name they are called, who deny the Godhead of Christ. (Indeed some of these say they do not deny his Godhead; but only his supreme Godhead. Nay, this is the same thing; for in denying him to be the supreme God, they deny him to be any God at all: Unless they will assert that there are two Gods, a great one and a little one!) All these are vehement applauders of reason, as the great unerring guide. To these over-valuers of reason we may generally add men of eminently strong understanding; who, because they do know more than most other men, suppose they can know all things. But we may likewise add many who are in the other extreme; men of eminently weak understanding; men in whom pride (a very common case) supplies the void of sense; who do not suspect themselves to be blind, because they were always so.

5. Is there, then, no medium between these extremes, —undervaluing and overvaluing reason? Certainly there is. But who is there to point it out?—to mark down the middle way? That great master of reason, Mr. Locke, has done something of the kind, something applicable to it, in one chapter of his Essay concerning Human Understanding. But it is only remotely applicable to this: He does not come home to the point. The good and great Dr. Watts has wrote admirably well, both concerning reason and faith.

But neither does anything he has written point out the medium between valuing it too little and too much.

6. I would gladly endeavor in some degree to supply this grand defect; to point out, First, to the under-valuers of it, what reason can do; and then to the over-valuers of it, what reason cannot do. But before either the one or the other can be done, it is absolutely necessary to define the term, to fix the precise meaning of the word in question. Unless this is done, men may dispute to the end of the world without coming to any good conclusion. This is one great cause of the numberless altercations which have been on the subject. Very few of the disputants thought of this; of defining the word they were disputing about. The natural consequence was, they were just as far from an agreement at the end as at the beginning.

I.

1. First, then, *reason* is sometimes taken for *argument.* So, "Give me a *reason* for your assertion." So in Isaiah: "Bring forth your strong *reasons;*" that is, your strong arguments. We use the word nearly in the same sense, when we say, "He has good *reasons* for what he does." It seems here to mean, He has sufficient *motives;* such as ought to influence a wise man. But how is the word to be understood in the celebrated question concerning the "reasons of things?" particularly when it is asked, *An rationes rerum sint aeternae?* "Whether the reasons of things are eternal?" Do not the "reasons of things" here mean the *relations* of things to each other? But what are the *eternal relations* of *temporal things?* of things which did not exist till yesterday? Could the relations of these things exist before the things themselves had any existence? Is not then, the talking of such relations a flat contradiction? Yea, as palpable a one as can be put into words.

2. In another acceptation of the word, reason is much the same with *understanding.* It means a faculty of the human soul; that faculty which exerts itself in three ways;—by simple apprehension, by judgement, and by discourse. *Simple apprehension* is barely conceiving a thing in the mind; the first and most simple act of understanding. *Judgment* is the determining that the things before conceived either agree with or differ from each other. *Discourse,* strictly speaking, is the motion or progress of the mind from one judgment to another. The faculty of the soul which includes these three operations I here mean by the term *reason.*

3. Taking the word in this sense, let us now impartially consider, First, What is it that reason can do?

And who can deny that it can do much, very much, in the affairs of common life? To begin at the lowest point: It can direct servants how to perform the various works wherein they are employed; to discharge their duty, either in the meanest offices or in any of a higher nature. It can direct the husbandman at what time, and in what manner, to cultivate his ground; to plough, to sow, to reap, to bring in his corn, to breed and manage his cattle, and to act with prudence and propriety in every part of his employment. It can direct artificers how to prepare the various sorts of apparel, and a thousand necessaries and conveniences of life, not only for themselves and their households, but for their neighbours, whether nigh or afar off. It can direct those of higher abilities to plan and execute works of a more elegant kind. It can direct the painter, the statuary, the musician, to excel in the stations wherein Providence has placed them. It can direct the mariner to steer his course over the bosom of the great deep. It enables those who study the laws of their country to defend the property or life of their fellow-subjects; and those who study the art of healing to cure most of the maladies to which we are exposed in our present state.

4. To ascend higher still: It is certain reason can assist us in going through the whole circle of arts and sciences; of grammar, rhetoric, logic, natural and moral philosophy, mathematics, algebra, metaphysics. It can teach whatever the skill or industry of man has invented for some thousand years. It is absolutely necessary for the due discharge of the most important offices; such as are those of Magistrates, whether of an inferior or superior rank; and those of subordinate or supreme Governors, whether of states, provinces, or kingdoms.

5. All this few men in their senses will deny. No thinking man can doubt but reason is of considerable service in all things relating to the present world. But suppose we speak of higher things,— the things of another world; what can reason do here? Is it a help or a hinderance of religion? It may do much in the affairs of men; but what can it do in the things of God?

6. This is a point that deserves to be deeply considered. If you ask, What can reason do in religion? I answer, It can do exceeding much, both with regard to the foundation of it, and the superstructure.

The foundation of true religion stands upon the oracles of God. It is built upon the Prophets and Apostles, Jesus Christ himself being the chief corner-stone. Now, of what excellent use is reason, if we would either understand ourselves, or explain to others, those living oracles! And how is it possible without it to understand the essential truths contained therein? a beautiful summary of which we have in that which is called the Apostles' Creed. Is it not reason (assisted by the Holy Ghost) which enables us to understand what the Holy Scriptures declare concerning the being and attributes of God?—concerning his eternity and immensity; his power, wisdom, and holiness? It is by reason that God enables us in some measure to comprehend his method of dealing with the children of men; the nature of his various dispensations, of the old and new covenant, of the law and the gospel. It is by this we understand (his Spirit opening and enlightening the eyes of our understanding) what that repentance is, not to be repented of; what is that faith whereby we are saved; what is the nature and the condition of justification; what are the immediate and what the subsequent fruits of it. By reason we learn what is that new birth, without which we cannot enter into the kingdom of heaven; and what that holiness is without which no man shall see the Lord. By the due use of reason we come to know what are the tempers implied in inward holiness; and what it is to be outwardly holy—holy in all manner of conversation: In other words, what is the mind that was in Christ; and what it is to walk as Christ walked.

7. Many particular cases will occur with respect to several of the foregoing articles, in which we shall have occasion for all our understanding, if we would keep a conscience void of offence. Many cases of conscience are not to be solved without the utmost exercise of our reason. The same is requisite in order to understand and to discharge our ordinary relative duties;—the duties of parents and children, of husbands and wives, and (to name no more) of masters and servants. In all these respects, and in all the duties of common life, God has given us our reason for a guide. And it is only by acting up to the dictates of it, by using all the understanding which God hath given us, that we can have a conscience void of offense towards God and towards man.

8. Here, then, there is a large field indeed, wherein reason may expatiate and exercise all its powers. And if reason can do all this, both in civil and religious things, what is it that it cannot do?

We have hitherto endeavoured to lay aside all prejudice, and to weigh the matter calmly and impartially. The same course let us take still: Let us now coolly consider, without prepossession on any side, what it is, according to the best light we have, that reason cannot do.

II.

1. And, First, reason cannot produce faith. Although it is always consistent with reason, yet reason cannot produce faith, in the scriptural sense of the word. Faith, according to Scripture, is "an evidence," or conviction, "of things not seen." It is a divine evidence, bringing a full conviction of an invisible eternal world. It is true, there was a kind of shadowy persuasion of this, even among the wiser Heathens; probably from tradition, or from some gleams of light reflected from the Israelites. Hence many hundred years before our Lord was born, the Greek Poet uttered that great truth,—

> Millions of spiritual creatures walk the earth
> Unseen, whether we wake, or if we sleep.

But this was little more than faint conjecture: It was far from a firm conviction; which reason, in its highest state of improvement, could never produce in any child of man.

2. Many years ago I found the truth of this by sad experience. After carefully heaping up the strongest arguments which I could find, either in ancient or modern authors, for the very being of a God, and (which is nearly connected with it) the existence of an invisible world, I have wandered up and down, musing with myself: "What, if all these things which I see around me, this earth and heaven, this universal frame, has existed from eternity? What, if that melancholy supposition of the old Poet be the real case,—

> *oie per phullon genee, toiede kai andron;*

What, if 'the generation of men be exactly parallel with the generation of leaves?' if the earth drops its successive inhabitants, just as the tree drops its leaves? What, if that saying of a great man be really true,—

> *Post mortem nihil est; ipsaque mors nihil?*
> Death is nothing, and nothing is after death?

How am I sure that this is not the case; that I have not followed cunningly devised fables?"—And I have pursued the thought, till there was no spirit in me, and I was ready to choose strangling rather than life.

3. But in a point of so unspeakable importance, do not depend upon the word of another; but retire for awhile from the busy world, and make the experiment yourself. Try whether *your* reason will give you a clear satisfactory evidence of the invisible world. After the prejudices of education are laid aside, produce your strong reasons for the existence of this. Set them all in array; silence all objections; and put all your doubts to flight. alas! you cannot, with all your understanding. You may repress them for a season. But how quickly will they rally again, and attack you with redoubled violence! And what can poor reason do for your deliverance? The more

vehemently you struggle, the more deeply you are entangled in the toils; and you find no way to escape.

4. How was the case with that great admirer of reason, the author of the maxim above cited? I mean the famous Mr. Hobbes. None will deny that he had a strong understanding. But did it produce in him a full and satisfactory conviction of an invisible world? Did it open the eyes of his understanding, to see Beyond the bounds of this diurnal sphere? O no! far from it! His dying words ought never to be forgotten. "Where are you going, Sir?" said one of his friends. He answered, "I am taking a leap in the dark!" and died. Just such an evidence of the invisible world can bare reason give to the wisest of men!

5. Secondly. Reason alone cannot produce hope in any child of man: I mean scriptural hope, whereby we "rejoice in hope of the glory of God:" That hope which St. Paul in one place terms, "tasting the powers of the world to come;" in another, the "sitting in heavenly places in Christ Jesus:" That which enables us to say, "Blessed be the God and Father of our Lord Jesus Christ, who hath begotten us again unto a lively hope;—to an inheritance incorruptible, undefiled, and that fadeth not away; which is reserved in heaven for us." This hope can only spring from Christian faith: Therefore, where there is not faith, there is not hope. Consequently, reason, being unable to produce faith, must be equally unable to produce hope. Experience confirms this likewise. How often have I laboured, and that with my might, to beget this hope in myself! But it was lost labour: I could no more acquire this hope of heaven, than I could touch heaven with my hand. And whoever of you makes the same attempt will find it attended with the same success. I do not deny, that a self-deceiving enthusiast may work in himself a kind of hope: He may work himself up into a lively imagination; into a sort of pleasing dream: He may "compass himself about, "as the Prophet speaks, "with sparks of his own kindling:" But this cannot be of long continuance; in a little while the bubble will surely break. And what will follow? "This shall ye have at my hand, saith the Lord, ye shall lie down in sorrow."

6. If reason could have produced a hope full of immortality in any child of man, it might have produced it in that great man whom Justin Martyr scruples not to call "a Christian before Christ." For who that was not favoured with the written word of God, ever excelled, yea, or equalled, Socrates? In what other Heathen can we find so strong an understanding, joined with so consummate virtue? But had he really this hope? Let him answer for himself. What is the conclusion of that noble apology which he made before his unrighteous judges? "And now, O judges! ye are going hence to live; and I am going hence to die: Which of these is best, the gods know; but, I suppose, no man does." *No man knows!* How far is this from the language of the little Benjamite: "I desire to depart, and to be with Christ; which is far better!" And how many thousands are there at this day, even in our own nation, young men and maidens, old men and children, who are able to witness the same good confession!

7. But who is able to do this, by the force of his reason, be it ever so highly improved? One of the most sensible and most amiable Heathens that have lived since our Lord died, even though he governed the greatest empire in the world, was the Emperor Adrian. It is his well-known saying, "A prince ought to resemble the sun: He ought to shine on every part of his dominion, and to diffuse his salutary rays in every place where he comes." And his life was a comment upon his word: Wherever he went, he was executing justice, and showing mercy. Was not he then, at the close of a long life, full of immortal hope? We are able to answer this from unquestionable authority,—from his own dying words. How inimitably pathetic!

ADRANI MORIENTIS AD ANIMAM SUAM.

"DYING ADRIAN TO HIS SOUL."

> *Animula, vagula, blandula,*
> *Hospes, comesque corporis,*
> *Quae nunc abibis in loca,*
> *Pallidula, rigida, nudula,*
> *Nec, ut soles, dabis jocos!*

Which to the English reader may see translated into our own language, with all the spirit of the original:—

> Poor, little, pretty, fluttering thing,
> Must we no longer live together?
> And dost thou prune thy trembling wing,
> To take they flight, thou know'st not whither?
> Thy pleasing vein, they humorous folly,
> Lies all neglected, all forgot!
> And pensive, wavering, melancholy,
> Thou hop'st, and fear'st, thou know'st not what.

8. Thirdly. Reason, however cultivated and improved, cannot produce the love of God; which is plain from hence: It cannot produce either faith or hope; from which alone this love can flow. It is then only, when we "behold" by faith "what manner of love the Father hath bestowed upon us," in giving his only Son, that we might not perish, but have everlasting life, that "the love of God is shed abroad in our heart by the Holy Ghost which is given unto us." It is only then, when we "rejoice in hope of the glory of God," that "we love Him because he first loved us." But what can cold reason do in this matter? It may

present us with fair ideas; it can draw a fine picture of love: But this is only a painted fire. And farther than this reason cannot go. I made the trial for many years. I collected the finest hymns, prayers, and meditations which I could find in any language; and I said, sung, or read them over and over, with all possible seriousness and attention. But still I was like the bones in Ezekiel's vision: "The skin covered them above; but there was no breath in them."

9. And as reason cannot produce the love of God, so neither can it produce the love of our neighbour; a calm, generous, disinterested benevolence to every child of man. This earnest, steady good-will to our fellow-creatures never flowed from any fountain but gratitude to our Creator. And if this be (as a very ingenious man supposes) the very essence of virtue, it follows that virtue can have no being, unless it spring from the love of God. Therefore, as reason cannot produce this love, so neither can it produce virtue.

10. And as it cannot give either faith, hope, love, or virtue, so it cannot give happiness; since, separate from these, there can be no happiness for any intelligent creature. It is true, those who are void of all virtue may have pleasures, such as they are; but happiness they have not, cannot have. No:

> Their joy is all sadness; their mirth is all vain;
> Their laughter is madness; their pleasure is pain!

Pleasures? Shadows! dreams! fleeting as the wind! unsubstantial as the rainbow! as unsatisfying to the poor gasping soul,

> As the gay colours of an eastern cloud.

None of these will stand the test of reflection: If thought comes, the bubble breaks!

Suffer me now to add a few plain words, first to you who under-value reason. Never more declaim in that wild, loose, ranting manner, against this precious gift of God. Acknowledge "the candle of the Lord," which he hath fixed in our souls for excellent purposes. You see how many admirable ends it answers, were it only in the things of this life: Of what unspeakable use is even a moderate share of reason in all our worldly employments, from the lowest and meanest offices of life, through all the intermediate branches of business; till we ascend to those that are of the highest importance and the greatest difficulty! When therefore you despise or depreciate reason, you must not imagine you are doing God service: Least of all, are you promoting the cause of God when you are endeavouring to exclude reason out of religion. Unless you wilfully shut your eyes, you cannot but see of what service it is both in laying the foundation of true religion, under the guidance of the Spirit of God, and in raising the superstructure. You see it directs us in every point both of faith and practice: It guides us with regard to every branch both of inward and outward holiness. Do we not glory in this, that the whole of our religion is a "reasonable service?" yea, and that every part of it, when it is duly performed, is the highest exercise of our understanding?

Permit me to add a few words to you, likewise, who over-value reason. Why should you run from one extreme to the other? Is not the middle way best? Let reason do all that reason can: Employ it as far as it will go. But, at the same time, acknowledge it is utterly incapable of giving either faith, or hope, or love; and, consequently, of producing either real virtue, or substantial happiness. Expect these from a higher source, even from the Father of the spirits of all flesh. Seek and receive them, not as your own acquisition, but as the gifts of God. Lift up your hearts to Him who "giveth to all men liberally, and upbraideth not." He alone can give that faith, which is "the evidence" and conviction "of things not seen." He alone can "beget you unto a lively hope" of an inheritance eternal in the heavens; and He alone can "shed his love abroad in your heart by the Holy Ghost given unto you." Ask, therefore, and it shall be given you! Cry unto him, and you shall not cry in vain! How can you doubt? "If ye, being evil, know how to give good gifts unto your children, how much more shall your Father who is in heaven give the Holy Ghost unto them that ask him!" So shall you be living witnesses, that wisdom, holiness, and happiness are one; are inseparably united; and are, indeed, the beginning of that eternal life which God hath given us in his Son.

from A Vindication of the Rights of Women

Mary Wollstonecraft

from the Introduction

After considering the historic page, and viewing the living world with anxious solicitude, the most melancholy emotions of sorrowful indignation have depressed my spirits, and I have sighed when obliged to confess, that either nature has made a great difference between man and man, or that the civilization which has hitherto taken place in the world has been very partial. I have turned over various books written on the subject of education, and patiently observed the conduct of parents and the management of schools; but what has been the result?—a profound conviction that the neglected education of my fellow-creatures is the grand source of the misery I deplore; and that women, in particular, are rendered weak and wretched by a variety of concurring causes, originating from one hasty conclusion. The conduct and manners of women, in fact, evidently prove that their minds are not in a healthy state; for, like the flowers which are planted in too rich a soil, strength and usefulness are sacrificed to beauty; and the flaunting leaves, after having pleased a fastidious eye, fade, disregarded on the stalk, long before the season when they ought to have arrived at maturity.—One cause of this barren blooming I attribute to a false system of education, gathered from the books written on this subject by men who, considering females rather as women than human creatures, have been more anxious to make them alluring mistresses than affectionate wives and rational mothers; and the understanding of the sex has been so bubbled by this specious homage, that the civilized women of the present century, with a few exceptions, are only anxious to inspire love, when they ought to cherish a nobler ambition, and by their abilities and virtues exact respect. . . .

Yet, because I am a woman, I would not lead my readers to suppose that I mean violently to agitate the contested question respecting the equality or inferiority of the sex; but as the subject lies in my way, and I cannot pass it over without subjecting the main tendency of my reasoning to misconstruction, I shall stop a moment to deliver, in a few words, my opinion.—In the government of the physical world it is observable that the female in point of strength is, in general, inferior to the male. This is the law of nature; and it does not appear to be suspended or abrogated in favour of woman. A degree of physical superiority cannot, therefore, be denied—and it is a noble prerogative. But not content with this natural pre-eminence, men endeavour to sink us still lower, merely to render us alluring objects for a moment; and women, intoxicated by the adoration which men, under the influence of their senses, pay them, do not seek to obtain a durable interest in their hearts, or to become the friends of the fellow creatures who find amusement in their society.

I am aware of an obvious inference:—from every quarter have I heard exclamations against masculine women; but where are they to be found? If by this appellation men mean to inveigh against their ardour in hunting, shooting, and gaming, I shall most cordially join in the cry; but if it be against the imitation of manly virtues, or, more properly speaking, the attainment of those talents and virtues, the exercise of which ennobles the human character, and which raise females in the scale of animal being, when they are comprehensively termed mankind;—all those who view them with a philosophic eye must, I should think, wish with me, that they may every day grow more and more masculine. . . .

My own sex, I hope, will excuse me, if I treat them like rational creatures, instead of flattering their *fascinating* graces, and viewing them as if they were in a state of perpetual childhood, unable to stand alone. I earnestly wish to point out in what true dignity and human happiness consists—I wish to persuade women to endeavour to acquire strength, both of mind and body, and to convince them that the soft phrases, susceptibility of heart, delicacy of sentiment, and refinement of taste, are almost synonymous with epithets of weakness, and that those beings who are only the objects of pity and that kind of love, which has been termed its sister, will soon become objects of contempt. . . .

The education of women has, of late, been more attended to than formerly; yet they are still reckoned a frivolous sex, and ridiculed or pitied by the writers who endeavour by satire or instruction to improve them. It is acknowledged that they spend many of the first years of their lives in acquiring a smattering of accomplishments; meanwhile strength of body and mind are sacrificed to libertine notions of beauty, to the desire of establishing themselves,—the only way women can rise in the world,—by marriage. And this desire making mere animals of them, when they marry they act as such children may be expected to act:—they dress; they paint, and nickname God's creatures.—Surely these weak beings are only fit for a seraglio!—Can they be expected to govern a family with judgment, or take care of the poor babes whom they bring into the world?

If then it can be fairly deduced from the present conduct of the sex, from the prevalent fondness for pleasure which takes place of ambition and those nobler passions that open and enlarge the soul; that the instruction which women have hitherto received has only tended, with the constitution of civil society, to render them insignificant objects of desire— mere propagators of fools!—if it can be proved that in aiming to accomplish them, without cultivating their understandings, they are taken out of their sphere of duties, and made ridiculous and useless when the short-lived bloom of beauty is over,[1] I presume that *rational* men will excuse me for endeavouring to persuade them to become more masculine and respectable.

Indeed the word masculine is only a bugbear: there is little reason to fear that women will acquire too much courage or fortitude; for their apparent inferiority with respect to bodily strength, must render them, in some degree, dependent on men in the various relations of life; but why should it be increased by prejudices that give a sex to virtue, and confound simple truths with sensual reveries?

Women are, in fact, so much degraded by mistaken notions of female excellence, that I do not mean to add a paradox when I assert, that this artificial weakness produces a propensity to tyrannize, and gives birth to cunning, the natural opponent of strength, which leads them to play off those contemptible infantine airs that undermine esteem even whilst they excite desire. Let men become more chaste and modest, and if women do not grow wiser in the same ratio, it will be clear that they have weaker understandings. It seems scarcely necessary to say,

that I now speak of the sex in general. Many individuals have more sense than their male relatives; and, as nothing preponderates where there is a constant struggle for an equilibrium, without it has naturally more gravity, some women govern their husbands without degrading themselves, because intellect will always govern.

from Chapter II

The Prevailing Opinion of a Sexual Character Discussed

To account for, and excuse the tyranny of man, many ingenious arguments have been brought forward to prove, that the two sexes, in the acquirement of virtue, ought to aim at attaining a very different character: or, to speak explicitly, women are not allowed to have sufficient strength of mind to acquire what really deserves the name of virtue. Yet it should seem, allowing them to have souls, that there is but one way appointed by Providence to lead *mankind* to either virtue or happiness.

If then women are not a swarm of ephemeron triflers, why should they be kept in ignorance under the specious name of innocence? Men complain, and with reason, of the follies and caprices of our sex, when they do not keenly satirize our headstrong passions and groveling vices.—Behold, I should answer, the natural effect of ignorance! The mind will ever be unstable that has only prejudices to rest on, and the current will run with destructive fury when there are no barriers to break its force. Women are told from their infancy, and taught by the example of their mothers, that a little knowledge of human weakness, justly termed cunning, softness of temper, *outward* obedience, and a scrupulous attention to a puerile kind of propriety, will obtain for them the protection of man; and should they be beautiful, every thing else is needless, for, at least, twenty years of their lives. . . .

. . . the most perfect education, in my opinion, is such an exercise of the understanding as is best calculated to strengthen the body and form the heart. Or, in other words, to enable the individual to attain such habits of virtue as will render it independent. In fact, it is a farce to call any being virtuous whose virtues do not result from the exercise of its own reason. This was Rousseau's opinion respecting men: I extend it to women, and confidently assert that they have been drawn out of their sphere by false refinement, and not by an endeavour to acquire masculine qualities. Still the regal homage which they receive is so intoxicating, that till the manners of the times are changed, and formed on more reasonable principles, it may be impossible to convince them that the illegitimate power, which they obtain, by degrading themselves, is a curse, and that they must return to nature and equality, if they wish to secure the placid satisfaction that unsophisticated affections impart. But for this epoch we must wait—wait, perhaps, till kings and nobles, enlightened by reason, and, preferring the real dignity of man to childish state, throw off their gaudy hereditary trappings: and if then women do not resign the arbitrary power of beauty—they will prove that they have *less* mind than man. . . .

Many are the causes that, in the present corrupt state of society, contribute to enslave women by cramping their understandings and sharpening their senses. One, perhaps, that silently does more mischief than all the rest, is their disregard of order.

To do every thing in an orderly manner, is a most important precept, which women, who, generally speaking, receive only a disorderly kind of education, seldom attend to with that degree of exactness that men, who from their infancy are broken into method, observe. This negligent kind of guess-work, for what other epithet can be used to point out the random exertions of a sort of instinctive common sense, never brought to the test of reason? prevents their generalizing matters of fact—so they do today, what they did yesterday, merely because they did it yesterday.

This contempt of the understanding in early life has more baneful consequences than is commonly supposed; for the little knowledge which women of strong minds attain, is, from various circumstances, of a more desultory kind than the knowledge of men, and it is acquired more by sheer observations on real life, than from comparing what has been individually observed with the results of experience generalized by speculation. Led by their dependent situation and domestic employments more into society, what they learn is rather by snatches; and as learning is with them, in general, only a secondary thing, they do not pursue any one branch with that persevering ardour necessary to give vigour to the faculties, and clearness to the judgment. In the present state of society, a little learning is required to support the character of a gentleman; and boys are obliged to submit to a few years of discipline. But in the education of women, the cultivation of the understanding is always subordinate to the acquirement of some corporeal accomplishment; even while enervated by confinement and false notions of modesty, the body is prevented from attaining

that grace and beauty which relaxed half-formed limbs never exhibit. Besides, in youth their faculties are not brought forward by emulation; and having no serious scientific study, if they have natural sagacity it is turned too soon on life and manners. They dwell on effects, and modifications, without tracing them back to causes; and complicated rules to adjust behaviour are a weak substitute for simple principles.

As a proof that education gives this appearance of weakness to females, we may instance the example of military men, who are, like them, sent into the world before their minds have been stored with knowledge or fortified by principles. The consequences are similar; soldiers acquire a little superficial knowledge, snatched from the muddy current of conversation, and, from continually mixing with society, they gain, what is termed a knowledge of the world; and this acquaintance with manners and customs has frequently been confounded with a knowledge of the human heart. But can the crude fruit of casual observation, never brought to the test of judgment, formed by comparing speculation and experience, deserve such a distinction? Soldiers, as well as women, practice the minor virtues with punctilious politeness. Where is then the sexual difference, when the education has been the same? All the difference that I can discern, arises from the superior advantage of liberty, which enables the former to see more of life. . . .

Let it not be concluded that I wish to invert the order of things; I have already granted, that, from the constitution of their bodies, men seem to be designed by Providence to attain a greater degree of virtue. I speak collectively of the whole sex; but I see not the shadow of a reason to conclude that their virtues should differ in respect to their nature. In fact, how can they, if virtue has only one eternal standard? I must therefore, if I reason consequentially, as strenuously maintain that they have the same simple direction, as that there is a God.

It follows then that cunning should not be opposed to wisdom, little cares to great exertions, or insipid softness, varnished over with the name of gentleness, to that fortitude which grand views alone can inspire.

I shall be told that woman would then lose many of her peculiar graces, and the opinion of a well known poet might be quoted to refute my unqualified assertion. For Pope has said, in the name of the whole male sex,

'Yet ne'er so sure our passion to create,
'As when she touch'd the brink of all we hate.'
[Moral Essays, II]

In what light this sally places men and women, I shall leave to the judicious to determine; meanwhile I shall content myself with observing, that I cannot discover why, unless they are mortal, females should always be degraded by being made subservient to love or lust.

To speak disrespectfully of love is, I know, high treason against sentiment and fine feelings; but I wish to speak the simple language of truth, and rather to address the head than the heart. To endeavour to reason love out of the world, would be to out Quixote Cervantes, and equally offend against common sense; but an endeavour to restrain this tumultuous passion, and to prove that it should not be allowed to dethrone superior powers, or to usurp the sceptre which the understanding should ever coolly wield, appears less wild.

Youth is the season for love in both sexes; but in those days of thoughtless enjoyment provision should be made for the more important years of life, when reflection takes place of sensation. But Rousseau, and most of the male writers who have followed his steps, have warmly inculcated that the whole tendency of female education ought to be directed to one point:—to render them pleasing.

Let me reason with the supporters of this opinion who have any knowledge of human nature, do they imagine that marriage can eradicate the habitude of life? The woman who has only been taught to please will soon find that her charms are oblique sunbeams, and that they cannot have much effect on her husband's heart when they are seen every day, when the summer is passed and gone. Will she then have sufficient native energy to look into herself for comfort, and cultivate her dormant faculties? or, is it not more rational to expect that she will try to please other men; and, in the emotions raised by the expectation of new conquests, endeavour to forget the mortification her love or pride has received? When the husband ceases to be a lover—and the time will inevitably come, her desire of pleasing will then grow languid, or become a spring of bitterness; and love, perhaps, the most evanescent of all passions, gives place to jealousy or vanity.

I now speak of women who are restrained by principle or prejudice; such women, though they would shrink from an intrigue with real abhorrence, yet, nevertheless, wish to be convinced by the homage of gallantry that they are cruelly neglected by their husbands; or, days and weeks are spent in dreaming of the happiness enjoyed by congenial souls till their health is undermined and their spirits broken by discontent. How then can the great art of pleasing be such a necessary study? it is only useful to a mistress; the chaste wife, and serious mother, should only consider her power to please as the polish of her virtues, and the affection of her husband as one of the comforts that render her task less difficult and her life happier.—But, whether she be loved or neglected, her first wish should be to make herself respectable, and not to rely for all her happiness on a being subject to like infirmities with herself. . . .

. . . avoiding, as I have hitherto done, any direct comparison of the two sexes collectively, or frankly acknowledging the inferiority of woman, according to the present appearance of things, I shall only insist that men have increased that inferiority till women are almost sunk below the standard of rational creatures. Let their faculties have room to unfold, and their virtues to gain strength, and then determine where the whole sex must stand in the intellectual scale. Yet let it be remembered, that for a small number of distinguished women I do not ask a place.

It is difficult for us purblind mortals to say to what height human discoveries and improvements may arrive when the gloom of despotism subsides, which makes us stumble at every step; but, when morality shall be settled on a more solid basis, then, without being gifted with a prophetic spirit, I will venture to predict that woman will be either the friend or slave of man. We shall not, as at present, doubt whether she is a moral agent, or the link which unites man with brutes. But, should it then appear, that like the brutes they were principally created for the use of man, he will let them patiently bite the bridle, and not mock them with empty praise; or, should their rationality be proved, he will not impede their improvement merely to gratify his sensual appetites. He will not, with all the graces of rhetoric, advise them to submit implicitly their understanding to the guidance of man. He will not, when he treats of the education of women, assert that they ought never to have the free use of reason, nor would he recommend cunning and dissimulation to beings who are acquiring, in like manner as himself, the virtues of humanity.

Note

1   A lively writer, I cannot recollect his name, asks what business women turned of forty have to do in the world?—Wollstonecraft.

"Review" of Beethoven's 5th Symphony

E. T. A. Hoffmann
(translated by Robin Wallace)

The reviewer[1] has before him one of the most important works of that master who no one will now deny belongs among the first rank of instrumental composers. He is permeated by the topic that he is to discuss, and no one may take it amiss if, stepping beyond the boundaries of the customary critique, he strives to put into words what this composition made him feel deep within his soul. When music is being discussed as a self-sufficient art, this should always be understood to refer only to instrumental music, which, disdaining all help, all admixture of any other art, purely expresses the peculiar essence of this art, which can be recognized in it alone. It is the most romantic of all the arts—one almost wishes to say the only one that is *purely* romantic. Orpheus's lyre opened the gates of the underworld. Music reveals an unknown kingdom to mankind: a world that has nothing in common with the outward, material world that surrounds it, and in which we leave behind all predetermined, conceptual feelings in order to give ourselves up to the inexpressible. How little did *those* instrumental composers who tried to represent these predetermined feelings, or even to represent events, recognize this peculiar essence of music, trying instead to treat that art that is diametrically opposed to the plastic arts in a plastic way! Dittersdorf's[2] symphonies of this kind, as well as all more recent *Batailles de trois Empereurs*, etc. are ludicrous mistakes that should be punished with complete oblivion. In song, where the poetry that is added indicates specific affects by means of words, the magical power of music works like the wondrous elixir of the wise, by means of which various simpletons make every drink delicious and magnificent. Every passion—love—hate—anger—despair etc., such as we encounter in opera, is clothed by music in the purple shimmer of romanticism, and even that which we experience in life leads us out beyond life into the kingdom of the infinite. The magic of music is this strong, and, as its effect becomes more and more powerful, it must tear to pieces any impediment from another

art. The height to which composers of genius have presently raised instrumental music has been reached not only through simplification of the expressive means (perfection of the instruments, greater virtuosity of the performers) but through their deep, heartfelt recognition of the peculiar essence of music. Haydn and Mozart, the creators of recent instrumental music, first showed us this art in its full glory; he who grasped it with full devotion and penetrated its innermost essence is—Beethoven. The instrumental compositions of all three masters breathe a similar Romantic spirit, due to their all having taken possession of the peculiar essence of the art; the character of their compositions, however, is markedly different. The expression of a childlike, happy soul dominates in Haydn's compositions. His symphonies lead us into a vast, green meadow, into a joyous, colorful crowd of fortunate people. Youths and maidens glide by in round dances; laughing children, listening beneath trees, beneath rose bushes, teasingly throw flowers at each other. A life full of love, full of blessedness, as though before sin, in eternal youth; no suffering, no pain; only sweet, wistful yearning for the beloved form that hovers far away in the glow of the sunset, comes no nearer, and does not disappear; and as long as it is there, it will not become night, for it is itself the sunset, which illuminates the mountains and the woods. Into the depths of the spirit kingdom we are led by Mozart. Fear surrounds us: but, in the absence of torment, it is more a foreboding of the infinite. Love and melancholy sound forth in charming voices, the power[3] of the spirit world ascends in the bright purple shimmer, and we follow along in inexpressible longing behind the beloved forms that beckon to us in their rows, flying through the clouds in the eternal dance of the spheres. (For example, Mozart's Symphony in E♭ Major, known under the name of *Schwanengesang*.)[4] In this way, Beethoven's instrumental music also opens up to us the kingdom of the gigantic and the immeasurable. Glowing beams shoot through this kingdom's deep night, and we become aware of gigantic shadows that surge up and down, enclosing us more and more narrowly and annihilating everything within us, leaving only the pain of that interminable longing, in which every pleasure that had quickly arisen with sounds of rejoicing sinks away and founders, and we live on, rapturously beholding the spirits themselves, only in this pain, which, consuming love, hope, and joy within itself, seeks to burst our breast asunder with a full-voiced consonance of all the passions. Romantic taste is rare, Romantic talent even rarer: this is probably why there are so few who can strike that lyre that opens up the wonderful kingdom of the infinite. Haydn treats that which is human in human life romantically; he is more in accordance with the majority. Mozart lays claim to that which is more than human, that which is wondrous, and dwells within the innermost spirit. Beethoven's music moves the lever controlling horror, fear, dread, pain and awakens that interminable longing that is the essence of romanticism. Beethoven is a purely romantic (and precisely for that reason truly musical) composer, and this may be the reason that he has been less successful with vocal music,[5] which does not allow for unspecified yearning, but only represents those affects that are indicated by the words as they are experienced in the kingdom of the infinite—and that his instrumental music does not appeal to the masses. Even those masses who do not follow Beethoven into the depths do not deny that he has a high degree of imagination; on the contrary, it is customary to see in his works simply the products of a genius that, unconcerned with the form and selection of its ideas, gives itself over to its own fire and to the momentary promptings of its imagination. Nevertheless, in regard to presence of mind, he deserves to be placed on the very same level as Haydn and Mozart. Separating what is merely himself from the innermost kingdom of notes, he is thus able to rule over it as an absolute lord. The artists of aesthetic measurement have often complained about the total lack of true unity and inner coherence in Shakespeare, while it requires a deeper look to reveal a lovely tree, whose buds and leaves, flowers and fruits all grow from the same seed. Likewise, it is only by entering very

deeply into the inner structure of Beethoven's music that *the* great presence of mind of this master reveals itself, which is inseparable from true genius and is nourished by unceasing study of the art.

Beethoven bears musical romanticism deep within his soul and expresses it in his works with great genius and presence of mind. The reviewer has never felt this in a more lively way than with the present symphony, which, in a climax that builds steadily until the end, reveals this romanticism of Beethoven more than any other work of his, and sweeps the listener irresistibly into the wonderful spirit kingdom of the infinite. The first Allegro, 2/4 time in C minor, begins with a principal idea that consists of only two measures, and that, in the course of what follows, continually reappears in many different forms. In the second measure a fermata; then a repetition of this idea a tone lower, and again a fermata; both times only string instruments and clarinets. Even the key cannot yet be determined; the listener surmises E♭ major. The second violin begins the principal idea once again, and in the second measure the fundamental note of C, struck by the violoncello and bassoon, delineates the key of C minor, in which viola and violin enter in imitation, until these finally juxtapose two measures with the principal idea, which, thrice repeated (the final time with the entry of the full orchestra), and dying out in a fermata on the dominant, give to the listener's soul a presentiment of the unknown and the mysterious. The beginning of the Allegro, up until this point of rest, determines the character of the entire piece, and for this reason the reviewer inserts it here for his readers to examine:

OP. 67
Allegro con brio, mm. 1–21

After this fermata, the violins and violas imitate the principal idea, remaining in the tonic, while the bass now and then strikes a figure that resembles that idea. A constantly mounting transitional passage, which once again arouses that presentiment, even stronger and more urgently than before, then leads to a tutti whose theme once again has the rhythmic content of the principal idea and is intimately related to it:

OP. 67
Allegro con brio, mm. 44–48

The sixth chord based on D⁶ prepares the related major key of E♭, in which the horn once again recalls the principal idea. The first violin takes up a second theme, which is certainly melodious, but still remains true to the character of anxious, restless longing that the whole movement expresses. The violin carries this theme forward in alternation with the clarinet, and each time in the third measure the bass strikes that first mentioned recollection of the principal idea, by means of which this theme is again completely interlaced into the artistic web of the whole [mm. 58ff.]. In the further extension of this theme, the first violin and the violoncello repeat five times, in the key of E♭ minor, a figure that consists of only two measures, while the basses climb chromatically upward, until at last a new transitional passage leads to the conclusion, in which the wind instruments repeat the first tutti in E♭ major, and finally the full orchestra closes in E♭ major with the oft-mentioned recollection of the principal theme [mm. 83ff.]. The principal theme once again begins the second part in its initial form, only transposed a third higher and played by the clarinets and horns. The phrases of the first part follow in F minor, C minor, G minor, only differently arranged and orchestrated, until at last, after a transition once again made up of only two measures, which the violins and the wind instruments take up in alternation, while the violoncellos play a figure in contrary motion and the bases climb upwards, the following chords enter in the full orchestra:

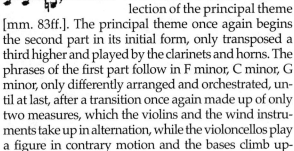

OP. 67
Allegro con brio, harmonic reduction of mm. 169–180

They are sounds by means of which the breast, oppressed and alarmed by presentiments of the gigantic, vents itself powerfully; and like a friendly form, which radiantly illuminating the deep night moves through the clouds, a theme now enters that was only touched upon by the horn in E♭ major at m. 58 of the first part.[7] First in G major, then in C major, the violins play this theme *alla 8va*, while the basses play an upward-climbing figure that somewhat recalls the tutti passage that began at m. 44 of the first part [mm. 179ff.].

the reviewer would have expected G♭ major in the chord progression that followed, which then, in the manner in which things are done here, would lead back to G major, having been enharmonically transformed into F♯ minor. The wind instruments, however, which strike the chord that follows that sixth chord, are written:

OP. 67
Allegro con brio, harmonic reduction of m. 215

Immediately thereafter, the string instruments strike this F♯-minor chord

OP. 67
Allegro con brio, harmonic reduction of m. 216

The wind instruments begin this theme *fortissimo* in F minor, but after the third measure, the string instruments take up the two final measures, and, imitating these measures, string and wind instruments alternate yet another five times and then strike individual chords, always dimenuendo and once again in alternation.

After the sixth chord

OP. 67
Allegro con brio, harmonic reduction of m. 214

which is then repeated for four measures alternately by strings and wind instruments. The chords of the wind instruments are always written as was indicated above, for no reason that the reviewer can discern.

The sixth chord

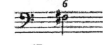

OP. 67
Allegro con brio, harmonic reduction of m. 221

now likewise follows, ever weaker and weaker. This has an unsettling and terrifying effect!—The full orchestra now strikes up a theme that is almost identical to that which was heard forty-one measures earlier,[8] while only the flutes and trumpets hold the dominant, D. This theme, however, comes to rest after only four measures, and the string instruments and horns, and then the remaining wind instruments, strike the diminished chord

OP. 67
Allegro con brio, harmonic reduction of m. 234

pianissimo seven times in alternation. In the next measure [m. 240], the basses then take up the first principal idea for two measures, with the remaining instruments *unisono*. Bass and upper voices imitate each other in this manner through five measures, followed by three measures in unison, and in the fourth measure, the full orchestra, with trumpets and drums, sounds the principal theme in its original form. The first part is now repeated with minor variations; the theme that first began in E♭ major appears now in C major and leads to a triumphant close in C major with trumpets and drums. This very conclusion, however, turns the music into F minor

OP. 67
Allegro con brio, harmonic reduction of m. 387

Through five measures of full orchestra on the sixth chord: clarinets, bassoons, and horns strike *piano* an imitation of the principal idea. One measure of general pause, then for six measures

OP. 67
Allegro con brio, harmonic reduction of mm. 390–395

all the wind instruments resume as before: and now the violas, violoncellos, and bassoons take up a theme that was heard previously in the second part in G major, while the violins, entering *unisono* in the third measure, perform a new countersubject. The music now remains in C minor, and, with small variations, the theme that began in m. 71 of the first part is repeated by the violins first alone, and then in alternation with the wind instruments. The alternations become ever closer and closer, first one measure, then a half measure; it is a driving urgency—a surging storm, whose waves strike higher and higher—until finally, twenty-four measures before the end, the beginning of the Allegro is repeated once again. There follows an organ point over which the theme is imitated until at last the final conclusion follows strongly and powerfully.

There is no simpler idea than that which the master laid as the foundation of this entire Allegro

OP. 67
Allegro con brio, mm. 1–2

and one realizes with wonder how he was able to align all the secondary ideas, all the transitional passages with the rhythmic content of this simple theme in such a way that they served continually to unfold the character of the whole, which that theme could only suggest. All phrases are short, consisting of only two or three measures, and are divided up even further in the ongoing exchanges between the string and the wind instruments. One might believe that from such elements only something disjointed and difficult to comprehend could arise; nevertheless, it is precisely this arrangement of the whole, as well as the repetitions of the short phrases and individual chords that follow continually upon one another, which hold the spirit firmly in an unnameable longing.

Completely apart from the fact that the contrapuntal treatment shows deep study of the art, it is also the transitional passages and the continual references to the principal theme that show how the master did not simply conceive the whole with all its characteristic features, within his spirit, but thought it through as well.

Like a charming spirit voice, which fills our breast with comfort and hope, sounds next the lovely (and yet meaningful) theme of the Andante in A♭ major, 3/8 time, which is performed by the viola and violoncello. The further development of the Adante recalls numerous middle movements from Haydn's symphonies, inasmuch as, just as frequently happens there, the principal theme is varied in many different ways after interjected transitional phrases. It cannot be equated with the first Allegro in terms of originality, even though the idea of continually interrupting the transitions back to A♭ major by allowing an imposing phrase in C major with trumpets and drums to intervene produces an striking effect.[9] The transition to C major occurs twice in the midst of enharmonic exchanges:

OP. 67
Adante con moto, mm. 28–30, 77–79

whereupon the grandiose theme enters and then the modulation to the dominant chord of A♭ major is completed in the following manner:

OP. 67
Adante con moto, harmonic reduction of mm. 90–97

In a simpler but very effective way, the flutes, oboes, and clarinets prepare for the third transition to this C major theme:

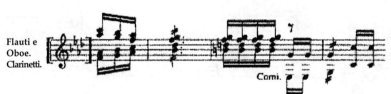

OP. 67
Adante con moto, mm. 144–147

All the phrases of the Adante are very melodious, and the principal theme is even beguiling, but the very progress of this theme, which goes through A♭ major, B♭ minor, F minor, and B♭ minor before first returning to the continual juxtaposition of the major tonalities A♭ and C, the chromatic modulations, express once again the character of the whole, and by virtue of this the Andante is a part of that whole. It is as if the frightful spirit, which in the Allegro gripped and unsettled the soul, were to step forth and threaten every moment from the storm clouds into which it had disappeared, and the friendly forms that had surrounded us comfortingly were to flee quickly from its sight.

The Minuet[10] that follows the Andante is once again as original, as gripping to the listener's soul, as one might expect from this master in the composition of that part of the symphony that, according to the example of Haydn, which he was following, should be the most piquant and ingenious of all. It is primarily the distinctive modulations, closes on the dominant-major chord, whose bass note is taken up by the bass as the tonic of the following theme in minor—the theme itself, which always extends itself by only a few measures, that strongly express the character of Beethoven's music, as the reviewer has described it above, and arouse anew that restlessness, that presentiment of the wonderful spirit kingdom with which the phrases of the Allegro assailed the listener's soul. The theme in C minor, played by the basses alone, turns in the third measure toward G minor, the horns sustain the G, and the violins and violas, joined in the second measure by the bassoons, and then by the clarinets, perform a four-measure phrase that cadences in G. The basses now repeat the theme, but after the G minor of the third measure, it turns to D minor and then to C minor, where the violin phrase is repeated. The horns now perform a phrase that leads into E♭ major, while the string instruments strike chords in quarter notes at the beginning of each measure. The orchestra, however, leads the music farther, into E♭ minor, and closes on the dominant, B♭ major. In the same measure, however, the bass begins the principal theme and performs it just as at the beginning in C minor, only now it is in B♭ minor [m. 53]. The violins, etc., too, repeat their own phrases, and there follows a point of rest in F major. The bass repeats the same theme, extending it, however, going through F minor, C minor, G minor, and then returning to C minor, whereupon the tutti, which first appeared in E♭ minor, leads through F minor to a C-major chord. However, just as it went before from B♭ major to B♭ minor, the bass now takes up the bass note C as tonic of the theme in C minor [m. 96]. Flutes and oboes, imitated by the clarinets in the second measure, now take up the phrase that was first performed by the string instruments, while these repeatedly strike a single measure from the previously mentioned tutti; the horns sustain G, the violoncellos begin a new theme, which is connected first to a further development of the violins' opening phrase, then to a new phrase in eighth notes (which had not yet been heard). Even the new theme of the violoncellos contains allusions to the principal phrase and is thereby intimately related to it, as it is also through the similar rhythm. After a brief repetition of the tutti, this section of the minuet concludes *fortissimo* in C minor with trumpets and drums. The second part (the trio) is begun by the basses with a theme in C minor, which is imitated fugally by the violas in the dominant, then by the second violin in a shortened form, and then similarly shortened by the first violins. The first half of this part closes in G major. In the second part, the basses begin the theme twice and stop again, continuing forward the third time. To many this may seem humorous, but in the reviewer it awakened an uncanny feeling.—After much imitation of the principal theme, it is taken up by the flutes, supported by oboes, clarinets, and bassoons, over the bass note G, which is sustained by the horns, and it dies out in individual notes, which are struck first by the clarinets and bassoons and then by the basses. Now follows the repetition of the theme of the first part by the basses; in place of the violins the wind instruments have the phrase now in short notes, concluding it with a point of rest. Hereupon follows, as in the first part, the extended principal phrase, but in place of the half notes there are now quarter notes and quarter-note rests. In this form, and for the most part abbreviated, the other phrases of the first part also return. The restless longing, which the theme carried within itself, is now raised to the point of anxiety, which presses powerfully upon the breast so that only individual, broken sounds can escape from it. The G-major chord seems to point to the conclusion, but the bass now sustains the bass note A♭ *pianissimo* through fifteen measures [mm. 324ff.], and violins and violas likewise sustain the third, C, while the kettledrum strikes the C, first in the rhythm of that oft-mentioned tutti, then for four measures once in each measure, then for four measures twice, and then in quarter notes. The first violin finally takes up the first theme and leads through twenty-eight measures in which this theme is continually heard, up to the seventh of the dominant of the fundamental note. The second violins and the violas have sustained the C continually with the kettledrum playing the C in quarter notes; the bass, however, after having run through the scale

from A♭ to F♯ and back to A♭, has struck the fundamental note G. Now enter first the bassoons, then one measure later the oboes, then three measures later the flutes, horns, and trumpets, while the kettledrum continually strikes the C in eighth notes, whereupon the music goes directly into the C-major chord, whereupon the final Allegro begins. The reason why the master continued the dissonant C of the kettledrum up to the conclusion is clarified by the character that he was striving to give to the whole. The heavy strokes of this dissonance, sounding like a strange, frightening voice, excite terror of the extraordinary—the fear of spirits. The reviewer has already mentioned somewhat earlier the mounting effect produced by the theme being extended for several measures, and in order to make this effect even more vivid, he will here place these extensions together:

OP. 67
Allegro (III), mm. 1–4, 8–16, 44–48, 53–64

At the repetition of the first part, this phrase appears in the following manner:

OP. 67
Allegro (III), mm. 244–252

Just as simple, and yet, when it reappears in later passages, just as gripping in its effect as the theme of the first Allegro, is the idea with which the tutti of the minuet begins.

OP. 67
Allegro (III), m. 27–28

The full orchestra, to which piccolos, trombones, and contrabassoons are now added, enters with the splendid, triumphant theme of the concluding movement, in C major—like radiant, blinding sunshine that suddenly illuminates the deep night. The phrases of this Allegro are treated more broadly than those that came before. They are not so much melodious as they are powerful, and suited to contrapuntal imitation. The modulations are unaffected and understandable; the first part has, for the most part, almost the feeling of an overture. Throughout thirty-four measures this part remains a tutti of the full orchestra in C major; then, to the accompaniment of a powerful, rising figure in the bass, a new theme in the upper voices modulates to G major and leads to the dominant chord of this key. Now begins yet another theme, consisting of quarter notes separated by triplets, which, in regard to its rhythm and its character, departs completely from what has gone before, and once again urges and impels like the phrases of the first Allegro or of the minuet:

is thoroughly worked out, to which no small contribution is made by the secondary phrases that are mixed in, the sustained notes of the trombones, and the triplet strokes in the kettledrums, trumpets, and horns. The music at last comes to rest on an organ point G [mm. 132ff.], which is struck first by the basses, and then the bass trombones, trumpets, horns, and kettledrums, while the basses are performing a concluding figure *unisono* with the violins [mm. 132ff.]. Now, for the length of fifty-four measures, this simple theme from the minuet returns,

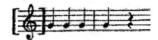

OP. 67
Allegro (IV), mm. 160–161

and there follows, in the two concluding measures, the transition from the minuet to the Allegro, only in a shorter form than before. With minor variations, and remaining in the principal key, the phrases of the first part now return, and a rushing tutti seems to lead to the conclusion. After the dominant chord, however, the bassoons, horns, flutes, oboes, and clarinets take up this theme, which was at first only touched upon, one after another [mm. 317ff.].

OP. 67
Allegro (IV), mm. 44–49

OP. 67
Allegro (IV), clarinet
mm. 322–324

Through this theme and through its further working-out through A minor toward C major, the soul is once again placed into a mood of foreboding, which had momentarily departed from it during the jubilation and rejoicing. With a short, rushing tutti the music turns once again to G major, and violas, bassoons, and clarinets begin a theme in sixths [mm. 64ff.], which is later taken up by the entire orchestra, and, after a short modulation to F minor, the first part concludes in C major with a powerful bass figure, which is then taken up by the violins in C major and then again by the basses *al rovescio*. The figure just mentioned is continued at the beginning of the second part in A minor, and that characteristic theme consisting of quarter notes and triplets enters once again. In shortened and restricted forms, this theme is now extended through thirty-four measures,[11] and in the course of this working-out the character that was already expressed in its original form

There follows yet another concluding phrase; the strings take up this phrase anew, after which it is played by the oboes, clarinets, and horns, and then again by the violins. The end seems near once again, but with the concluding chord in the tonic the violins take up, Presto (a *più stretto* begun several measures earlier), the phrase that was first heard at m. 64 of the Allegro, while the bass figure is the same one that they struck up in m. 28 of the first Allegro, and that, as has often been remarked above, is closely related to the principal theme through its rhythm, and strongly recalls it. The full orchestra (the basses enter a measure later, imitating the upper voice canonically) leads with the first theme of the last Allegro to the conclusion, which, shored up by many splendid, jubilant figures, follows after forty-one measures. The concluding chords themselves are written in a unique way; namely, after the chord that the listener takes for the last comes a measure rest, the same chord, a measure rest, once again the chord, a measure rest, then the same chord in quarter notes once every measure for three measures, a measure rest, the chord, a measure rest, and then C *unisono* struck by the entire orchestra. The perfect calm of the soul, brought about by various cadential figures following one after another, is abolished by these individual chords, struck between pauses, which recall the individual strokes in the Allegro of the symphony, and the listener is made eager anew by the final chords. They are like a fire, which was believed to have been put out, and which continually strikes out into the heights again in brightly blazing flames.

Beethoven has retained the customary succession of movements in the symphony. They appear to be put together in a fantastic way, and the whole rushes past many people like an inspired rhapsody: but the soul of every sensitive listener will certainly be deeply and closely gripped by a lingering feeling, which is precisely that unnameable, foreboding longing, and sustained in it until the final chord. Indeed, for many more moments after it, he will not be able to depart from the wonderful spirit kingdom, where pain and joy surrounded him in musical form.

Apart from the inner construction, the instrumentation, etc., it is primarily the intimate relationship that the individual themes have to one another that produces that unity that holds the listener's soul firmly in *a single* mood. In Haydn's and in Mozart's music, this unity dominates everywhere. It becomes clearer to the musician when he then discovers a fundamental bass that is common to two different passages, or when the connection between two passages reveals it; but a deeper relationship, which cannot be demonstrated in this manner, is often only expressed from the spirit to the spirit, and it is this relationship that prevails among the passages of both Allegros and of the minuet, and magnificently announces the master's presence of mind and genius. The reviewer believes that he can bring together his judgment about this magnificent work of art in a few words when he says that, ingeniously conceived and worked out with deep presence of mind, it expresses musical romanticism to a very high degree.

No instrument has difficult passagework to perform, but only an orchestra that is extraordinarily confident, practiced, and inspired by a *single* spirit, can venture to perform this symphony; for each moment that is in the least bit inadequate will spoil the whole irreparably. The continuous alternations, the exchanges between the string and wind instruments, the chords that are to be struck individually after rests, and so forth, demand the highest precision, on account of which the conductor should also be advised not, as often does occur, to play along more loudly than is

appropriate with the first violins, but much rather to hold the whole orchestra constantly in his eye and hand.[12] The first violin part is useful to this purpose, as it contains the entries of the obbligato instruments within itself.—The engraving is correct and clear. The same publisher has released this same symphony in an arrangement for pianoforte four-hands under the title: *Cinquième Sinfonie de Louis van Beethoven, arrangée pour le pianoforte à quatre mains.* Chez Breitkopf et Härtel à Leipsic (Pr. 2 Rthlr. 12 Gr.)[13] The reviewer is not otherwise much in favor of arrangements; nevertheless, it cannot be denied that the enjoyment of a masterwork, which one hears with the full orchestra, often excites the imagination as much as before in a lonely room, and sets the soul in the same mood. The pianoforte produces the great work like a sketch does a great painting, which the imagination enlivens with the colors of the original. What is more, the symphony has been arranged for the pianoforte with understanding and insight, so that the necessities of the instrument are taken appropriately into account without obscuring the peculiarities of the original.

Notes

[1] This was the first of Hoffmann's five Beethoven reviews for the AMZ. In it, he introduced many of his essential ideas about Beethoven, and, together with the review of the piano trios, op. 70, it later became the basis of his well known essay "Beethoven's Instrumental Music." First printed in the ZEW, this essay appeared in Hoffmann's *Fantasiestücke in Callots Manier*, which itself became one of the central documents of Romanticism.

Much of this review is incorporated verbatim into the essay, which has long been available in English translation. Since all of the later, more technical passages are omitted, however, the essay gives a rather distorted view of Hoffmann's critical aims. What is interesting about the original review is not simply that it contains a lengthy "analysis" of the symphony, but that Hoffmann structures this analysis so as to support his view that the symphony opens "the gates of the underworld," unleashing powerful emotions that are barely held in check by the more prosaic building blocks of the musical structure. See Wallace, *Beethoven's Critics*, 22–24, 126–143.

[2] Karl Ditters von Dittersdorf [1739–1799] was a talented composer who is still frequently cited as the epitome of everything that was staid and unimaginative about the Classical style in the hands of minor composers. It is an undeserved stigma, but, as this reference makes plain, it can be traced all the way back to Hoffmann, who was also one of the first to identify the famous triumvirate of Haydn, Mozart, and Beethoven as a stylistic unity.

3   Translator's note: many previous translators have taken the word "Macht" (might or power) as a misprint for "Nacht" (night). Both nouns form distinct metaphors (albeit with different relationships of intensity between vehicle and the metaphorical referent) when used with the verb "aufgehen," which was a common stylistic practice in early-nineteenth-century German prose. We have chosen to stay with the text as printed.

4   K. 543. The name "swan-song" was apparently a contemporary designation that has not survived. In any case, it is no more appropriate to this work than it is to Schubert's final song cycle, since a swan is supposed to sing *only* before it dies. Mozart's Symphony in E♭ Major, K. 543, was composed in 1788, three years before his death. The name may be related to the exalted style of the introduction to the first movement and the subsequent lyrical first theme.

5   Hoffmann was perhaps thinking here of the failure of Beethoven's only opera *Fidelio*, premiered in 1805 and revised in 1806. Aside from the Choral Fantasy, op. 80, and the Mass in C, op. 86 (both works also poorly received at their premieres in 1808 and 1809 respectively), almost all of Beethoven's other vocal works published or publicly performed before 1810 were *Lieder*.

6   That is, a B♭-major triad in first inversion.

7   The horn actually plays this theme at m. 59. The published score, however, contains an extra measure—the current fourth—which was not in Beethoven's manuscript. The first 100 copies of the first edition, too, were printed without this measure; the half-note D with a fermata appeared in m. 4 instead. Since Rochlitz reports that a copy of the score of the symphony was sent to Hoffmann while it was "still in the hands of the engraver," it is likely that Hoffmann wrote his review on the basis of this earlier version, even though the musical examples printed with it give the passage as it appears in modern editions. See Paul Hirsch, "A Discrepancy in Beethoven," *Music & Letters* 19 (July 1938), 265–267; and Kinsky-Halm, 159.

8   Measure 228, which Hoffmann compares to the earlier thematic statement at m. 187.

9   On the double variation form of this movement and its compositional genesis, see William Meredith, "Forming the New from the Old: Beethoven's Use of Variation in the Fifth Symphony," *Beethoven's Compositional Process*, ed. William Kinderman (Lincoln: University of Nebraska Press, 1991), 102–121.

10   Actually Allegro; Beethoven did not call this movement a minuet. In fact, in one of his early sketches, it is the second movement that is labeled "Andante quasi Menuetto."

11   Actually thirty-two measures; Hoffmann does seem to have miscounted here.

12   Hoffmann, in other words, is advising the principal first violinist, who still traditionally "led" the orchestra from his own seat, to exercise a function similar to that of the modern conductor. Like so much else in this review, this highlights the extent to which Hoffmann thought of the Fifth Symphony in terms of a unifying concept that requires intellectual depth and application to understand. It would not simply "emerge" from a technically adequate performance, but must be imposed by an interpreter who is acutely aware of everything the music contains.

13   This arrangement, by Friedrich Schneider, was published in July 1809.

Oppressed by Evolution

Matt Cartmill

As far as we can tell, all of earth's living things are descended from a distant common ancestor that lived more than 3 billion years ago. This is an important discovery, but it's not exactly news. Biologists started putting forward the idea of evolution back in the 1700s, and thanks to Darwin's unifying theory of natural selection, it's been the accepted wisdom in biology for more than a hundred years. So you might think that by now everyone would have gotten used to the idea that we are blood kin to all other organisms, and closer kin to great apes than to spiders. On the face of it, the idea makes a certain amount of plain common sense. We all know that we share more features with apes than we do with spiders or snails or cypress trees. The theory of evolution simply reads those shared features as family resemblances. It doesn't deny that people are unique in important ways. Our kinship with apes doesn't mean we're only apes under the skin, any more than the kinship of cats with dogs means that your cat is repressing a secret urge to bark and bury bones.

Yet many people don't accept the idea of evolution, and even feel downright threatened by it. Conservative Christians, in particular, have opposed it; to them, science ran off track in 1859 when Darwin's *Origin of Species* first hit the bookstores. Over the decades, we biologists have become accustomed to this opposition, but in recent years there has been a change in the antievolution camp. Now we find ourselves defending Darwin against attacks not only from the religious right but from the academic left as well.

In the United States the religious opposition to Darwin is chiefly made up of evangelical Protestants. Some of them are smart, savvy, angry, and well organized, and they have been working here for almost a hundred years to stop biologists from telling people about the history of life. In the early part of this century they persuaded the legislatures of several states to pass laws against teaching evolution. When the courts threw out those laws, the antievolutionists tried a different strategy: fighting for laws giving equal classroom time to "creation science"—that is, Bible-based biology. That didn't work, either. Now they're trying to compel teachers to present evolution as a mere theory rather than a fact. So far they haven't succeeded, but they're still working at it.

It seems clear that these religious antievolutionists aren't going to go away in the foreseeable future; biologists will have to fight them for another century or two to keep them from outlawing Darwin. But if we are to succeed, I think we'll need to give serious thought to our opponents' motives. I suspect they are deeper and subtler than most scientists like to think—or than most crusaders against evolution themselves believe.

One reason I believe this is that the motives publicly claimed by Christian antievolutionists don't make sense. Many will tell you that the evolution issue is a religious struggle between a godless scientific establishment and so-called creationists—that is, themselves. But a lot of evolutionary biologists are creationists, too—devout Christians, Jews, and Muslims, who believe in an eternal God who created the world. They just don't see any reason to think that he created it as recently as 4000 B.C.

Many opponents of the idea of evolution say they reject it because it contradicts the Bible. They claim to believe that every word in the Bible is literally true. But no one really believes that. We all know that when, in John 7:38, Jesus said, "He that believeth on me . . . out of his belly shall flow rivers of living water," he didn't mean it literally. It's a figure of speech. Practically every book of the Bible contains some such passages, which have to be read as either figures of speech or errors of fact. Consider Biblical astronomy. The Old Testament depicts the "firmament" as a strong dome or tent spread out above the Earth. It has the sun, moon, and stars set in it—and water up above it, and windows in it to let the water out when it rains (see Gen. 1:6–8, 1:14–17, 7:11, 8:2; Job 37:18; Ps. 104:2; Isa. 24:18; and Mal. 3:10). This is a lovely picture. If you read it as poetry, it's gorgeous. But taken literally, it's just plain wrong. There isn't any firmament or any water above the firmament, and the sun, moon, and stars aren't attached to anything. And if we can all agree that there isn't any firmament, then we can all agree that the literal truth of the Bible can't be the real issue here.

Some religious people say they reject the idea of evolution because it lowers human beings to the level of the beasts and blinds us to the nobility of man. In his closing speech for the prosecution in the 1925 Scopes monkey trial, William Jennings Bryan pointed angrily to a high-school textbook that classed *Homo sapiens* as a mammal. "No circle is reserved for man alone," Bryan protested. "He is, according to the diagram, shut up in the little circle entitled 'Mammals,' with thirty-four hundred and ninety-nine other species of mammals. . . . What shall we say of the intelligence, not to say religion, of those who are so particular to distinguish between fishes and reptiles and birds, but put a man with an immortal soul in the same circle with the wolf, the hyena, and the skunk? What must be the impression made upon children by such a degradation of man?"

What, indeed? But if you are going to classify living things at all, you have to group people and wolves together in some category, since they are both living things. Actually, the classification that Bryan railed against was in place a century before Darwin published his ideas on evolution. It was the pious creationist Carl von Linné, not some atheistic evolutionist, who named the Mammalia and classed *Homo sapiens* among them, back in 1758. And even then, in the mid-eighteenth century, classifying people as animals was an ancient idea. The Old Testament itself says bluntly that human beings are beasts, and no nobler than any of the others (Eccles. 3:18–21). Yes, of course we are mammals: hairy, warm-blooded vertebrates with milk glands and big forebrains, like wolves and hyenas and skunks. What's so awful about that? What else could we possibly be? Insects? Plants? Seraphim?

Most religious antievolutionists recognize that people resemble animals, but they refuse to believe it's a literal family resemblance. They think it insults human dignity to describe people as modified apes. But the Bible says that God made man from the dust of the ground (Gen. 2:7). Why is being a made-over ape more humiliating than being made-over dirt?

Given such patent contradictions, it seems apparent that there must be something else about Darwinian evolution that bothers antievolutionists. And

I think we can get some idea of what it is by studying the strange alliance against Darwin that's emerged in recent years between the forces of the religious right and the academic left.

The academic left is a diverse group. It includes all shades of opinion from the palest pink liberals to old-fashioned bright red Marxists. Probably no two of them have the same opinions about everything. But a lot of them have bought into some notions that are deeply hostile to the scientific enterprise in general and the study of evolution in particular. Although these notions are often expressed in a mindnumbing "postmodern" jargon, at bottom they're pretty simple. We can sum them up in one sentence: Anybody who claims to have objective knowledge about anything is trying to control and dominate the rest of us.

The postmodern critique of science runs something like this: There are no objective facts. All supposed "facts" are contaminated with theories, and all theories are infested with moral and political doctrines. Because different theories express different perceptions of the world, there's no neutral yardstick for measuring one against another. The choice between competing theories is always a political choice. Therefore, when some guy in a lab coat tells you that such and such is an objective fact—say, that there isn't any firmament, or that people are related to wolves and hyenas—he must have a political agenda up his starched white sleeve.

"Science is politics," writes Robert Young, editor of the journal *Science as Culture*. "Recent work has made it clear to those with eyes to see that there is no place in science, technology, medicine, or other forms of expertise where you cannot find ideology acting as a constitutive determinant."

To those who see it through a postmodernist lens, science as currently practiced is pretty bad stuff. Science is oppressive: by demanding that everyone talk and argue in certain approved ways, it tries to control our minds and limit our freedom to question authority. Science is sexist: designed by males and driven by domineering male egos, it prefers facts to values, control to nurturance, and logic to feelings—all typical patriarchal male hang-ups. Science is imperialist: it brushes aside the truths and insights of other times and cultures. ("Claims about the universality of science," insists historian Mario Biagioli, "should be understood as a form of cognitive colonialism.") And of course, science is capitalist (and therefore wicked): it serves the interests of big corporations and the military-industrial complex.

The scholar Ania Grobicki summed it up this way: "Western science is only one way of describing reality, nature, and the way things work—a very effective way, certainly, for the production of goods and profits, but unsatisfactory in most other respects. It is an imperialist arrogance which ignores the sciences and insights of most other cultures and times. . . . It is important for the people most oppressed by Western science to make use of what resources there are, to acquire skills and confidence, and to keep challenging the orthodox pretensions of 'scientific' hierarchies of power."

In this view, science is really aiming at a totalitarian control over our lives and thoughts. And though all fields of science are suspect, what most left-wing anxiety centers on is biology. You can get an idea of the fear that pervades this literature—and a taste of the convoluted prose some of these people write—by reading what the philosopher Jean Baudrillard has to say about biochemistry. "That which is hypostatized in biochemistry," he writes, "is the ideal of a social order ruled by a sort of genetic code of macromolecular calculation . . . irradiating the social body with its operational circuits. . . . Schemes of control have become fantastically perfected . . . to a neocapitalist cybernetic order that aims now at total control. This is the mutation for which the biological theorization of the code prepares the ground. . . . It remains to be seen if this operationality is not itself a myth, if DNA is not also a myth."

I don't know exactly what it means to have a genetic code irradiating things with its operational circuits, but it sounds pretty nasty. And Baudrillard isn't the only one who has it in for nucleic acids. Last year in the *Nation*, author Barbara Ehrenreich and anthropologist Janet McIntosh recounted the story of a psychologist who spoke at an interdisciplinary conference on the emotions. When several audience members rose to criticize her use of the oppressive, sexist, imperialist, and capitalist scientific method, the psychologist tried to defend science by pointing to its great discoveries—for example, DNA. The retort came back: "You believe in DNA?"

Why this suspicion of genetics? One reason is its political history. Defenders of privilege have always argued that the people below them on the social ladder deserve their lowly status because they're innately inferior; and scientists who believe this sort of thing haven't been shy about invoking biology to prove it. From the social Darwinists of the nineteenth century, the eugenics movement of the 1920s, and the race-hygiene savants of the Third Reich, down to the psychologists who today insist that social status is determined by our genes, there has

always been an abundant supply of rich white male professors gathering data to demonstrate that rich people, white people, and men are biologically superior to everyone else, No wonder genetics is greeted with raised eyebrows and snickers on the left.

But more fundamentally, many people see the biological worldview as a threat to the ideal of human freedom. If people are animals, and animals are machines driven by instinct and conditioning controlled by genes, then the way things are is pretty much the way they have to be. Consequently, trying to transform the world by human action is likely to be a futile undertaking. Those who don't much like the world the way it is—a group that includes most leftwing academics——naturally find this view abhorrent.

As a result, in academic circles outside the natural sciences today, any mention of human genetics is likely to arouse protests and angry accusations of "biological determinism," especially if you mention genes in the same breath as human psychology or behavior. In its extreme form, this left-wing hostility to biology amounts to what Ehrenreich and McIntosh call "secular creationism"—a creed that denies our biological heritage has anything to do with what people want or how they act. "Like their fundamentalist Christian counterparts," they write, "the most extreme antibiologists suggest that humans occupy a status utterly different from and clearly 'above' that of all other living beings."

In North Carolina, where I live, we recently saw how this attitude can cause the academic left to line up with the religious right. Last spring the lower house of the state legislature passed a bill requiring that "evolution shall be taught as a scientific theory, not as a proven fact" in the state's public schools. The bill eventually died in the senate. But while it was still on the table, conservative evangelicals lobbied hard for it, local evolutionists lobbied hard against it, and the newspapers were flooded with outraged letters from both sides. At the height of this dustup, Warren Nord, head of the program in Humanities and Human Values at the state university in Chapel Hill, suddenly jumped into the fight on the creationists' side—in the name of multiculturalism.

Darwin's theory, Nord complained, "undermines religious conceptions of design or purpose in nature. As we teach it, modern science is not religiously neutral. . . . [It] conflicts not just with Protestant fundamentalism . . . but with many traditional Native American, African, and Eastern religions." Nord's conclusion: "If we teach neo-Darwinian evolution and secular accounts of nature in science classes, we must also teach religious accounts of nature. . . . The only constitutional way to teach students about origins—that is, the only way to be truly neutral—is to let the contending parties (all of them) have their say."

In one sense, there's nothing wrong with Nord's argument. Of course evolution is a theory. We can imagine findings that would cause us to reject the whole idea. But that's just as true for every other big idea in science—and nobody is demanding an equal-time approach to any of the others. There are no bills cooking in America's state legislatures that will order the schools to teach the germ theory of disease and the antomic theory of matter as open questions. That might be an interesting and stimulating approach, but given that, for decades, the evidence that has come in consistently supports these two theories, the schools don't have time for it.

And nobody really wants to see science taught that way. Trying to present all ideas impartially without judging them would mean the end of science education. Like it or not, science is judgmental. It undertakes to weigh all the conflicting stories and find tests that will tell us which one is the least unlikely. If no such tests can be found, then science has nothing to say on the issue.

The idea that people evolved from apes millions of years ago is a testable scientific hypothesis. The idea that humankind was specially created in 4000 B.C. is also a testable hypothesis, and it happens to be wrong. But the idea that Nord and his evangelical allies want to introduce into biology classes—that nature expresses God's purposes—isn't a scientific issue at all, because there's no way to test it. People have been arguing about it for millennia and getting nowhere. The creationists point to all the things in nature that look beautiful, orderly, and efficient. The skeptics respond by pointing to other things that look ugly, messy, cruel, and wasteful. The creationists retort that they only seem that way to the finite human mind. Maybe so. But since no tests are possible, all that science can do is shrug.

That shrug is really what distresses the crusaders against science, on both the left and the right. Both camps believe passionately that the big truths about the world are moral truths. They view the universe in terms of good and evil, not truth and falsehood. The first question they ask about any supposed fact is whether it serves the cause of righteousness. Their notions of good and evil are different, but both see the commonplace surface of the world as a veil of illusion, obscuring the deeper moral truths behind everything that give life its meaning. "Commonsense

reality," insists the leftwing anthropologist Nancy Sheper-Hughes, "may be false, illusory, and oppressive. . . . [We must] work at the essential task of stripping away the surface forms of reality in order to expose concealed and buried truths."

For many people on the academic left, the facts reported by science are just the surface layer that has to be scraped off to expose the underlying moral and political reality. This postmodern approach to facts is a lot like that of the premodern St. Augustine, who wrote in the fifth century A.D. that we should concern ourselves with what Bible stories signify "and not worry about whether they are true."

Science, however, worries only about whether things are true and has no opinion about what they signify. In so doing, it offends both the religious right and the academic left. Both camps reject its claim to being objective and morally neutral. Because they don't think such a thing is possible, they see the pretended objectivity of science as a cover for ulterior motives. The idea of evolution is especially offensive in this regard because it implies that the universe has been value-free through 99.9 percent of its history, and that people and their values were brought into being by the mechanical operations of an inhuman reality. Both the religious and the secular creationists see human life as defined by the moral choices we make. Naturally, they shrink from the biologists' vision of people as animals (since animals don't make moral choices). The right-wingers think Darwinism promotes atheism, while the leftwingers think it promotes capitalism; but both agree it's just another competing ideology, which deserves to be cast down from its high seat of intellectual privilege.

Well, is it? Having offended both the fundamentalists and the postmodernists, I am going to annoy my scientific colleagues by admitting that the anti-evolutionists of left and right have a point nestled deep in their rhetoric.

Science has nothing to tell us about moral values or the purpose of existence or the realm of the supernatural. That doesn't mean there is nothing to be said about these things. It just means that scientists don't have any expert opinions. Science looks exclusively at the finite facts of nature, and unfortunately, logical reasoning can't carry you from facts to values, or from the finite to the infinite. As the philosopher David Hume pointed out 250 years ago, you can't infer an infinite cause from a finite effect. But science's necessary silence on these questions doesn't prove that there isn't any infinite cause—or that right and wrong are arbitrary conventions, or that there is no plan or purpose behind the world.

And I'm afraid that a lot of scientists go around saying that science proves these things. Many scientists are atheists or agnostics who want to believe that the natural world they study is all there is, and being only human, they try to persuade themselves that science gives them grounds for that belief. It's an honorable belief, but it isn't a research finding.

Evolutionists seem to be especially prone to this mistake. The claim that evolution is purposeless and undirected has become almost an article of faith among evolutionary biologists. For example, the official "Statement on Teaching Evolution" from the National Association of Biology Teachers describes evolution as "an unsupervised, impersonal, unpredictable, and natural process." That pretty much rules God out of the picture. One popular book on evolution, Richard Dawkins's *Blind Watchmaker*, is subtitled *Why the Evidence of Evolution Reveals a Universe Without Design*. In his book *Wonderful Life*, Stephen Jay Gould argues that the evolution of human beings was fantastically improbable and that a host of unlikely events had to fall out in just the right way for intelligent life to emerge on this planet. One might well take this as a sign of God's hand at work in the evolutionary process. Gould, however, bends his argument to the opposite conclusion—that the universe is indifferent to our existence and that humans would never evolve a second time if we rewound time's videotape and started over.

But to reach this conclusion, you have to assume the very thing that you are trying to prove: namely, that history isn't directed by God. If there is a God,

whatever he wills happens by necessity. Because we can't really replay the same stretch of time to see if it always comes out the same way, science has no tests for the presence of God's will in history. Gould's conclusion is a profession of his religious beliefs, not a finding of science.

The broad outlines of the story of human evolution are known beyond a reasonable doubt. However, science hasn't yet found satisfying, law-based natural explanations for most of the details of that story. All that we scientists can do is admit to our ignorance and keep looking. Our ignorance doesn't prove anything one way or the other about divine plans or purposes behind the flow of history. Anybody who says it does is pushing a religious doctrine. Both the religious creationists of the right and the secular creationists of the left object and say that a lot of evolutionists are doing just that in the name of science—and to this extent they are unfortunately right.

Fortunately, evolutionary biologists are starting to realize this. Last October, after considering several such objections, the National Association of Biology Teachers deleted the words *unsupervised* and *impersonal* from its description of the evolutionary process. To me, this seems like a step in the right direction. If biologists don't want to see the theory of evolution evicted from public schools because of its religious content, they need to accept the limitations of science and stop trying to draw vast, cosmic conclusions from the plain facts of evolution. Humility isn't just a cardinal virtue in Christian doctrine; it's also a virtue in the practice of science.

A Tale of Two Worksites

Stephen Jay Gould

Christopher Wren, the leading architect of London's reconstruction after the great fire of 1666, lies buried beneath the floor of his most famous building, Saint Paul's Cathedral. No elaborate sarcophagus adorns the site. Instead, we find only the famous epitaph written by his son and now inscribed in the floor: *si monumentum requiris, circumspice*—"if you are searching for his monument, look around." A tad grandiose perhaps, but I have never read a finer testimony to the central importance—one might even say sacredness—of actual places, rather than replicas, symbols, or other forms of vicarious resemblance.

An odd coincidence of professional life recently turned my thoughts to this most celebrated epitaph when, for the second time, I received an office in a spot loaded with history, a place still redolent with ghosts of past events both central to our common culture and especially meaningful for my own life and choices.

In 1971, I spent an academic term as a visiting researcher at Oxford University. I received a cranny of office space on the upper floor of the University Museum. As I set up my books, fossil snails, and microscope, I noticed a metal plaque affixed to the wall, informing me that this reconfigured space of shelves and cubicles had been, originally, the site of the most famous public confrontation in the early history of Darwinism. On this very spot in 1860, just a few months after Darwin published the *Origin of Species*, T. H. Huxley had drawn his rhetorical sword and soundly skewered the slick but superficial champion of creationism Bishop "Soapy Sam" Wilberforce.

As with most legends, the official version ranks as mere cardboard before a much more complicated and multifaceted truth. Wilberforce and Huxley did put on a splendid and largely spontaneous show, but no clear victor emerged from the scuffle, and Joseph Hooker, Darwin's other champion, made an even more effective reply to the bishop, since forgotten by history. (See my May 1986 essay, "Knight Takes Bishop?")

I can't claim that the lingering presence of these Victorian giants increased my resolve or improved my work, but I loved the sense of continuity vouchsafed to me by this happy circumstance. I even treasured the etymology—for "circumstance" means "standing around," and there I stood, perhaps in the very spot where Huxley had said, at least according to legend, that he preferred an honest ape to a bishop who would use his privileged position to inject scorn and ridicule into a serious scientific debate.

Last year, I received a part-time appointment as visiting research professor of biology at New York University. I was given an office on the tenth floor of the Brown Building on Washington Place, a nondescript, early-twentieth-century structure now filled with laboratories and other academic spaces. As the dean took me on a casual tour of my new digs, he made a passing remark, intended as little more than tour-guide patter, but producing an electric effect upon his new tenant. Did I know, he asked, that this building had been the site of the infamous Triangle Shirtwaist Fire of 1911? My office occupied a corner location on one of the affected floors—in fact, as I later discovered, right near the escape route used by many workers to reach safety on the roof above. The dean also told me that each year on the March 25 anniversary of the fire, the International Ladies Garment Workers Union still holds a ceremony at the site and lays wreaths to memorialize the 146 workers killed in the blaze.

If the debate between Huxley and Wilberforce defines a primary legend of my chosen profession, the Triangle Shirtwaist Fire occupies an even more central place in my larger view of life. I grew up in a family of Jewish immigrant garment workers, and this holocaust (in the literal meaning of a thorough sacrifice by burning) had set their views and helped to define their futures.

The shirtwaist—a collared blouse designed after the model of a man's shirt and worn above a separate skirt—had become the fashionable symbol of more independent women. The Triangle company, New York City's largest manufacturer of shirtwaists, occupied three floors (eighth through tenth) of the Asch Building (later bought by New York University and rechristened as Brown, partly to blot out the infamy of association with the fire). The company employed some 500 workers, nearly all young women who had recently arrived either as Jewish immigrants from eastern Europe or Catholics from Italy. The building, in addition to elevators, had only two small stairways and one absurdly inadequate fire escape. But the owners had violated no codes both because general standards of regulation were then so weak and because the structure was supposedly fireproof—as the framework proved to be (for the building, with my office, still stands), although nonflammable walls and ceilings could not prevent an internal blaze on floors crammed full of garments and cuttings. The Triangle factory was, in fact, a deathtrap—for fire hoses of the day could not pump above the sixth floor, while nets and blankets could not sustain the force of a human body falling from greater heights.

The fire broke out at quitting time. Most workers managed to escape by the elevators, down one staircase (we shall come to the other staircase later), or by running up to the roof. But 146 employees, nearly all young women, were trapped by the flames. About 50 workers met a hideous, if dramatic, end by jumping in terror from the ninth-floor windows as a wall of flame advanced from behind. Firemen and bystanders begged them not to jump, and then tried to hold improvised nets of sheets and blankets. But the men could not hold the nets against the force of fall, and many bodies plunged right through the flimsy fabrics onto the pavement below, or even right through the "hollow sidewalks" made of opaque glass circles designed to transmit daylight to basements below, still a major (and attractive) feature of my SoHo neighborhood. (These sidewalks carry prominent signs warning heavy delivery trucks not to back in.) Not a single jumper survived, and the memory of these forced leaps to death remains the most searing image of America's prototypical sweatshop tragedy.

All defining events of history develop simplified legends as official versions—primarily, I suppose, because we commandeer such events for shorthand moral instruction, and the complex messiness of actual truth always blurs the clarity of a pithy epigram. Thus, Huxley, representing the righteousness of scientific objectivity, must slay the dragon of ancient and unthinking dogma. The legend of the Triangle fire holds that workers became trapped because management had locked all the exit doors to prevent pilfering, unscheduled breaks, or access to union organizers—leaving only the fire escape as a mode of exit. All five of my guidebooks to New York architecture tell this "official" version. My favorite book, for example, states: "Although the building was equipped with fire exits, the terrified workers discovered to their horror that the ninth-floor doors had been locked by supervisors. A single fire escape was wholly inadequate for the crush of panic-stricken employees."

These official legends may exaggerate for moral punch, but they emerge from a factual basis of greater ambiguity—and this reality, as we shall see in the Triangle case, often provides a deeper and more important lesson. Huxley did argue with Wilberforce after all, even if he secured no decisive victory, and Huxley did represent the side of the angels—the true angels of light and justice. And although many Triangle workers escaped by elevators and one staircase, another staircase (that might have saved nearly everyone else) was almost surely locked.

If Wilberforce and his minions had won, I might be a laborer or a linguist or, God forbid, a lawyer today. But the Triangle fire might have blotted me out entirely. My grandmother arrived in America in 1910. On that fatal March day in 1911, she was a sixteen-year-old seamstress working in a sweatshop—but, thank God, not for the Triangle Shirtwaist Company. My grandfather, at the same moment, was cutting cloth in yet another nearby factory.

These two utterly disparate stories—half a century and an ocean apart, and maximally contrasting an industrial tragedy with an academic confrontation—might seem to stand as the most unrelatable of items: the apples and oranges, or chalk and cheese (the British version), of our mottoes. Yet I feel that the two stories share an intimate bond in illustrating the opposite poles of a central issue in the history of evolutionary theory: the application of Darwinian thought to the life and times of our own troubled species. I claim nothing beyond personal meaning—and certainly no rationale for boring anyone else—in the accidental location of my two offices in such sacred spots of history. But the emotion of a personal prod often dislodges a general theme worth sharing.

The application of evolutionary theory to *Homo sapiens* has always troubled Western culture deeply, not for any reason that might be called scientific (for humans are biological objects and must therefore take their place with all other living creatures on the genealogical tree of life) but only as a consequence of ancient prejudices about human distinctiveness and unbridgeable superiority. Even Darwin tiptoed lightly across this subject when he wrote the *Origin of Species* in 1859 (although he plunged in later, in 1871, with a book entitled *The Descent of Man*). The first edition of the *Origin* says little about *Homo sapiens* beyond the cryptic promise that "light will be thrown on the origin of man and his history." (Darwin became a bit bolder in later editions and ventured the emendation, "Much light will be thrown. . . .")

Troubling issues of this sort often find their unsurprising resolution in a bit of wisdom that has permeated our traditions from such sublime sources as Aristotle's *aurea mediocritas* (golden mean) to the vernacular sensibility of Goldilocks's decisions to split the difference between two extremes and find a solution "just right" in the middle. Similarly, one can ask either too little or too much of Darwinism in trying to understand "the origin of man and his history." As usual, a proper solution lies in the intermediary position of "a great deal, but not everything." Soapy Sam Wilberforce and the Triangle Shirtwaist Fire gain their odd but sensible conjunction as illustrations of the two extremes that must be avoided—for Wilberforce denied evolution altogether and absolutely, while the major social theory that hindered industrial reform (and permitted conditions that led to such disasters as the Triangle Shirtwaist Fire) followed the most overextended application of biological evolution to patterns of human history—the so-called theory of social Darwinism. By understanding the fallacies of Wilberforce's denial and social Darwinism's uncritical and total embrace, we may find the proper course between.

They didn't call him Soapy Sam for nothing. The orotund Bishop of Oxford saved his finest invective for Darwin's attempt to apply his heresies to human origins. In his review of the *Origin of Species* (published in the *Quarterly Review*, England's leading literary journal, in 1860), Wilberforce complained above all: "First, then, he not obscurely declares that he applies his scheme of the action of the principle of natural selection to Man himself, as well as to the animals around him." Wilberforce then uncorked a passionate argument for a human uniqueness that could only have been divinely ordained:

> Man's derived supremacy over the earth; man's power of articulate speech; man's gift of reason; man's free-will and responsibility; man's fall and man's redemption; the incarnation of the Eternal Son; the indwelling of the Eternal Spirit,—all are equally and utterly irreconcilable with the degrading notion of the brute origin of him who was created in the image of God, and redeemed by the Eternal Son.

But the tide of history rolled over the good bishop. When Wilberforce died in 1873 from a head injury after a fall from his horse, Huxley acerbically remarked that, for once, the bishop's brains had come into contact with reality—and the result had been fatal. Darwinism became the reigning intellectual novelty of the late nineteenth century. The potential domain of natural selection, Darwin's chief explanatory principle, seemed nearly endless to his devotees (although not, interestingly, to the master himself, as Darwin remained cautious about extensions beyond the realm of biological evolution). If a "struggle for existence" regulated the evolution of organisms, wouldn't a similar principle also explain the history of just about anything—from the cosmology of the universe to the languages, economics, technologies, and cultural histories of human groups?

Even the greatest of truths can be overextended by zealous and uncritical acolytes. Natural selection may be one of the most powerful ideas ever developed in science, but only certain kinds of systems can be regulated by such a process, and Darwin's principle cannot therefore explain all natural sequences that develop historically. For example, we may talk about the "evolution" of a star through a predictable series of phases over many billion years from birth to explosion, but natural selection—a process driven by differential survival and reproductive success of some individuals in a variable population—cannot be the cause of stellar development. We must look, instead, to the inherent physics and chemistry of light elements in such large masses.

Similarly, although Darwinism surely explains many universal features of human form and behavior, we cannot invoke natural selection as the controlling cause of our cultural changes since the dawn of agriculture—if only because such a limited time of some ten thousand years provides so little potential for any general biological evolution at all. Moreover, and most importantly, human cultural change operates in a manner that precludes a controlling role for natural selection. To mention the two most obvious differences: first, biological evolution proceeds by continuous division of species into independent lineages that must remain forever separated on the branching tree of life. Human cultural change works by the opposite process of borrowing and amalgamation. One good look at another culture's wheel or alphabet may alter the course of a civilization forever. If we seek any biological analogue for cultural change, I suspect that infection will work much better than evolution.

Secondly, human cultural change runs by the powerful mechanism of Lamarckian inheritance of acquired characters. Anything useful (or, alas, destructive) that our generation invents can be passed directly to our offspring by direct education. Change in this rapid Lamarckian mode easily overwhelms the much slower process of Darwinian natural selection, which requires a Mendelian form of inheritance based on small-scale, undirected variation that can then be sifted and sorted through a struggle for existence. Genetic variation is Mendelian, so Darwinism rules biological evolution. But cultural variation is largely Lamarckian, and natural selection cannot determine the recent history of our technological societies.

Nonetheless, the first blush of high Victorian enthusiasm for Darwinism inspired a rush of attempted extensions to other fields, at least by analogy. Some proved fruitful, including the decision of James Murray, editor of the *Oxford English Dictionary* (first volume published in 1884, but under way for twenty years before then), to work strictly by historical principles and treat the changing definitions of words not by current preferences in use (as in a truly normative dictionary) but by the chronology and branching evolution of recorded meanings (making the text more an encyclopedia about the history of words than a true dictionary).

But other extensions were both invalid in theory and (or so most of us would judge by modern moral sensibilities) harmful, if not tragic, in application. As the chief offender in this category, we must cite a highly influential theory that acquired the inappropriate name of social Darwinism. (As many historians have noted, this theory should really be called social Spencerism since Herbert Spencer, chief Victorian pundit of nearly everything, laid out all the basic postulates nearly a decade before the *Origin of Species* in his *Social Statics* of 1851. Darwinism did add the mechanism of natural selection as a harsher version of the struggle for existence that Spencer had long recognized. Moreover, Darwin himself maintained a most ambivalent relationship to this movement that came to bear his name. He took the pride of any creator in useful extensions of his theory—and he did hope for an evolutionary account of human origins and historical patterns. But he also understood only too well why the mechanism of natural selection applied poorly to the causes of social change in humans.)

Social Darwinism often serves as a blanket term for any genetic or biological claim made about the inevitability (or at least the "naturalness") of social inequalities among classes and sexes or military conquests of one group by another. But this usage is far too broad—although pseudo-Darwinian arguments were prominently advanced to cover all these sins. Social Darwinism, rather, usually operated as a more specific theory about the nature and origin of social classes in the modern industrial world. The short *Encyclopaedia Britannica* article on the subject correctly emphasizes this restriction by first citing the broadest range of potential meaning and then properly narrowing the scope of actual usage:

> Social Darwinism: the theory that persons, groups, and races are subject to the same laws of natural selection as Charles Darwin had perceived in plants and animals in nature. . . . The theory was used to support laissez-faire capitalism and political conservatism. Class stratification was justified on the basis of "natural" inequalities among individuals, for the control of property was said to be a correlate of superior and inherent moral attributes such as industriousness, temperance, and frugality. Attempts to reform society through state intervention or other means would, therefore, interfere with natural processes; unrestricted competition and defense of the status quo were in accord with biological selection. The poor were the "unfit" and should not be aided; in the struggle for existence, wealth was a sign of success.

Spencer believed that such harshness must be advocated in order to allow the progressive development that all "evolutionary" systems undergo if permitted to follow their natural course in an unimpeded manner. As a central principle of his system, Spencer believed that progress—defined by him as movement from a simple undifferentiated homogeneity, as in a bacterium or a "primitive" human society without social classes, to complex and structured heterogeneity, as in "advanced" organisms or industrial societies—did not arise as an inevitable property of matter in motion, but only through interaction between evolving systems and their environments. These interactions must therefore not be obstructed.

The relationship of Spencer's general vision to Darwin's particular theory has often been misconstrued or overemphasized. As stated earlier, Spencer had published the outline (and most of the details) of his system nearly ten years before Darwin presented his evolutionary theory. Spencer certainly did welcome the principle of natural selection as an even more ruthless and efficient mechanism for driving evolution forward. (Ironically, the word "evolution," as a description for the genealogical history of life, entered our language through Spencer's urgings, not from Darwin. Spencer favored the term for its vernacular English meaning of "progress," in the original Latin sense of *evolutio*, or "unfolding." At first, Darwin resisted the term—he originally called his process "descent with modification"—because his theory included no mechanism or rationale for general progress in the history of life. But Spencer prevailed, largely because no society has ever been more committed to progress as a central notion or goal than Victorian Britain at the height of its colonial and industrial expansion.)

Spencer certainly used Darwin's mechanism of natural selection to buttress his system. In fact, it was Spencer, not Darwin, who coined the term "survival of the fittest," now our conventional catch phrase for Darwin's mechanism. Darwin himself paid tribute in a sentence added to later editions of the *Origin of Species*: "I have called this principle, by which each slight variation, if useful, is preserved, by the term Natural Selection. . . . But the expression often used by Mr. Herbert Spencer of the Survival of the Fittest is more accurate, and is sometimes equally convenient."

As a mechanism for driving his universal "evolution" (of stars, species, languages, economics, technologies, and nearly anything else) toward progress, Spencer preferred the direct and mechanistic "root, hog, or die" of natural selection (as William Graham Sumner, the leading American social Darwinian, epitomized the process) to the vaguer and largely Lamarckian drive toward organic self-improvement that Spencer had originally favored as a primary cause. (In this porcine image, Sumner cited a quintessential American metaphor of self-sufficiency that my dictionary of catch phrases traces to a speech by Davey Crockett in 1843.) In a post-Darwinian edition of his *Social Statics*, Spencer wrote:

> The lapse of a third of a century since these passages were published, has brought me no reason for retreating from the position taken up in them. Contrariwise, it has brought a vast amount of evidence strengthening that position. The beneficial results of the survival of the fittest, prove to be immeasurably greater than [I formerly recognized]. The process of "natural selection," as Mr. Darwin called it . . . has shown to be a chief cause . . . of that evolution through which all living things, beginning with the lower and diverging and re-diverging as they evolved, have reached their present degrees of organization and adaptation to their modes of life.

But putting aside the question of Darwin's particular influence, the more important, underlying point remains firm: the theory of social Darwinism rests upon a set of analogies between the causes of change and stability in biological and social systems—and on a supposedly direct applicability of the biological principles to the social realm. In the *Social Statics*, Spencer rests his case upon two elaborate analogies to biological systems.

1. The struggle for existence as purification in biology and society. Darwin recognized the "struggle for existence" as metaphorical shorthand for any strategy that provides increased reproductive success, whether by outright battle, cooperation, or just simple prowess in copulation under the old principle of "early and often." But many contemporaries, including Spencer, read "survival of the fittest" only as overt struggle to the death—what Huxley dismissed as the "gladiatorial" school, or the incarnation of Hobbes's *bellum omnium contra omnes* (the war of all against all). Spencer presented this stark, limited view of nature in *Social Statics*:

> Pervading all Nature we may see at work a stern discipline which is a little cruel that it may be very kind. That state of universal warfare maintained throughout the lower creation, to the great perplexity of many worthy people, is at bottom the most merciful provision which the circumstances admit of. . . . Note that carnivorous enemies, not only remove from herbivorous herds individuals past their prime, but also weed out the sickly, the malformed, and the least fleet or powerful. By the aid of which purifying process . . . all vitiation of the race through the multiplication of its inferior samples is prevented; and the maintenance of a constitution completely adapted to surrounding conditions, and therefore most productive of happiness, is ensured.

Spencer then compounds this error by applying the same argument to human social history without ever questioning the validity of such analogical transfer. Railing against all governmental programs for social amelioration—Spencer opposed state-supported education, postal services, regulation of housing conditions, and even public construction of sanitary systems—Spencer castigated such efforts as born of good intentions but doomed to dire consequences by enhancing the survival of social dregs who should be allowed to perish for the good of all. (Spencer insisted, however, that he did not oppose private charity, although largely for the good effect of such giving upon the moral development of donors. Does any of this remind you of arguments now advanced as reformatory and spanking-new by our "modern" ultraconservatives? Shall we not profit by Santayana's famous dictum that those ignorant of history must be condemned to repeat it?) In his chapter on poor laws (which he, of course, opposed) in the *Social Statics*, Spencer wrote:

> We must call those spurious philanthropists who, to prevent present misery, would entail greater misery on future generations. That rigorous necessity which, when allowed to operate, becomes so sharp a spur to the lazy and so strong a bridle to the random, these paupers' friends would repeal, because of the wailings it here and there produces. Blind to the fact that under the natural order of things society is constantly excreting its unhealthy, imbecile, slow, vacillating,

faithless members, these unthinking, though well-meaning, men advocate an interference which not only stops the purifying process, but even increases the vitiation—absolutely encouraging the multiplication of the reckless and incompetent by offering them an unfailing provision. . . . Thus, in their eagerness to prevent the salutary sufferings that surround us, these sigh-wise and groan-foolish people bequeath to posterity a continually increasing curse.

2. The stable body and the stable society. In the universal "evolution" of all systems to progress, organization becomes ever more complex by division of labor among the increasing number of differentiating parts. All parts must "know their place" and play their appointed role lest the entire system collapse. A primitive hydra can regrow any lost part, but nature gives a man only one head and one chance. Spencer recognized the basic inconsistency in validating social stability by analogy to the integrated needs of a single organic body, for he recognized the contrary rationales of the two systems: the parts of a body serve the totality, but the social totality (the state) supposedly exists only to serve the parts (individual people). But Spencer could never be fazed by logical or empirical difficulties when pursuing such a lovely generality. (Huxley was speaking of Spencer's penchant for building grandiose systems when he made his famous remark that Spencer's idea of tragedy was "a beautiful theory, killed by a nasty, ugly little fact.") So Spencer pushed right through the numerous absurdities of such a comparison and even professed that he could find a virtue in the differences. In his famous 1860 article *The Social Organism*, Spencer described the comparison between a human body and a human society: "Such, then, are the points of analogy and the points of difference. May we not say that the points of difference serve but to bring into clearer light the points of analogy."

Spencer's article then lists the supposed points of valid comparison, including such far-fetched analogies as the historical origin of a middle class to the development in complex animals of the mesoderm, or third body layer, between the original ectoderm and endoderm; the likening of the ectoderm itself to the upper classes, for sensory organs that direct an animal arise in the ectoderm, while organs of production for such activities as digesting food emerge from the endoderm, or lower layer; the comparison of blood and money; the parallel courses of nerve and blood vessels in higher animals with the side-by-side construction of railways and telegraph wires; and, finally, in a comparison that even Spencer regarded as forced, the likening of a primitive, all-powerful monarchy with a simple brain, and an advanced parliamentary system with a complex brain composed of several lobes. Spencer

wrote: "Strange as this assertion will be thought, our Houses of Parliament discharge in the social economy, functions that are in sundry respects comparable to those discharged by the cerebral masses in a vertebrate animal."

The analogies were surely forced, but the social intent could not have been clearer: a stable society requires that all roles be filled and well executed—and government must not interfere with a natural process of sorting out and allocation of appropriate rewards. A humble worker must toil and may remain forever poor, but the industrious poor, as an organ of the social body, must always be with us:

> Let the factory hands be put on short time, and immediately the colonial produce markets of London and Liverpool are depressed. The shopkeeper is busy or otherwise, according to the amount of the wheat crop. And a potato-blight may ruin dealers in consols. . . . This union of many men into one community—this increasing mutual dependence of units which were originally independent—this gradual segregation of citizens into separate bodies with reciprocally-subservient functions—this formation of a whole consisting of unlike parts—this growth of an organism, of which one portion cannot be injured without the rest feeling it—may all be generalized under the law of individuation.

Social Darwinism grew into a major movement, with political, academic, and journalistic advocates for a wide array of particular causes. But as historian Richard Hofstadter stated in the most famous book ever written on this subject—*Social Darwinism in American Thought*, first published in 1944, in press ever since, and still full of insight despite some inevitable archaicisms—the primary impact of this doctrine lay in its buttressing of conservative political philosophies, particularly through the central, and highly effective, argument against state support of social services and governmental regulation of industry and housing:

> One might, like William Graham Sumner, take a pessimistic view of the import of Darwinism, and conclude that Darwinism could serve only to cause men to face up to the inherent hardship of the battle of life; or one might, like Herbert Spencer, promise that, whatever the immediate hardships for a large portion of mankind, evolution meant progress and thus assured that the whole process of life was tending toward some very remote but altogether glorious consummation. But in either case the conclusions to which Darwinism was at first put were conservative conclusions. They suggested that all attempts to reform social processes were efforts to remedy the irremediable, that they interfered with the wisdom of nature, that they could lead only to degeneration.

The industrial magnates of America's Gilded Age ("robber barons" in a terminology favored by many people) loved the argument against regulation, evidently for self-serving reasons, however much they mixed their lines about nature's cruel inevitability with expressions of standard Christian piety. John D. Rockefeller stated in a Sunday school address:

> The growth of a large business is merely a survival of the fittest. . . . The American Beauty rose can be produced in the splendor and fragrance which bring cheer to its beholder only by sacrificing the early buds which grow up around it. This is not an evil tendency in business. It is merely the working-out of a law of nature and a law of God.

And Andrew Carnegie, who had been sorely distressed by the apparent failure of Christian values, found his solution in Herbert Spencer, then sought out the English philosopher for friendship and substantial favors. Carnegie wrote about his discovery of Spencer's work: "I remember that light came as in a flood and all was clear. Not only had I got rid of theology and the supernatural, but I had found the truth of evolution. 'All is well since all grows better' became my motto, and true source of comfort." Carnegie's philanthropy, primarily to libraries and universities, ranks as one of the great charitable acts of American history, but we should not forget his ruthlessness and resistance to reforms for his own workers (particularly his violent breakup of the Homestead strike of 1892) in building his empire of steel—a harshness that he defended with the usual Spencerian line that any state regulation would derail an inexorable natural process eventually leading to progress for all. In his most famous essay (entitled "Wealth," published in the *North American Review* of 1889), Carnegie stated:

> While the law may be sometimes hard for the individual, it is best for the race, because it insures the survival of the fittest in every department. We accept and welcome, therefore, as conditions to which we must accommodate ourselves, great inequality of environment, the concentration of wealth, business, industrial and commercial, in the hands of a few, and the law of competition between these, as being not only beneficial, but essential for the future progress of the race.

I don't want to advocate a foolishly grandiose view about the social and political influence of academic arguments—and I also wish to avoid the common fallacy of inferring a causal connection from a correlation. Of course I do not believe that the claims of social Darwinism directly caused the ills of unrestrained industrial capitalism and suppression of workers' rights. I know that most of these Spencerian lines acted as mere window dressing for social

forces well in place and largely unmovable by any merely academic argument.

On the other hand, academic arguments are not entirely impotent either—for why else would those in charge invoke such claims so forcefully? The general thrust of social change unfolded in its own complex manner without much impact from purely intellectual rationales, but many particular issues—especially the actual rates and styles for changes that would have eventually occurred in any case—could be substantially affected by academic discourse. It really did matter to millions of people when a given reform suffered years of legislative delay, and then became vitiated in legal battles and compromises. The social Darwinian argument of the superrich and the highly conservative did stem, weaken, and slow the tides of amelioration, particularly for workers' rights.

Most historians would agree that the single most effective argument of social Darwinism lay in Spencer's own centerpiece—the argument against state-enforced standards for industry, education, medicine, housing, public sanitation, and so on. Few Americans, even the robber barons, would go so far, but Spencerian dogma did become a powerful bludgeon against regulation of industry to insure better working conditions for laborers. On this particular point—the central recommendation of Spencer's system from the beginning—we may argue for a substantial effect of academic doctrine upon the actual path of history.

Armed with this perspective, we may return to the Triangle Shirtwaist Fire, the deaths of 146 young workers, and the palpable influence of a doctrine that applied too much of the wrong version of evolution to human history. The battle for increased safety of workplaces and healthier environments for workers had been waged with intensity for several decades. The trade union movement put substantial priority upon these issues, but management had often reacted with intransigence or even violence, citing their Spencerian rationale for the perpetuation of apparent cruelty. Government regulation of industry had become a major struggle of American political life—and the cause of benevolent state oversight had advanced from the Sherman Antitrust Act of 1890 to the numerous and crusading reforms of Theodore Roosevelt's recent presidency (1901–09). When the Triangle fire broke out in 1911, regulations for health and safety of workers were so weak, and so unenforceable by tiny and underpaid staffs, that the company's managers—cynically and technically "up to code" in their firetrap building—could pretty much impose whatever the weak and nascent labor union movement couldn't prevent.

If the standard legend were true—and the Triangle workers died because all the doors had been locked by cruel owners—then the story might convey no moral beyond the personal guilt of management. But the loss of 146 lives occurred for much more complicated reasons, all united by the pathetic weakness of legal regulations for health and safety of workers. And I do not doubt that the central thrust of social Darwinism—the argument against regulation as forestalling a necessary and natural process—had major impact in slowing the passage of basic regulations that almost everyone today, even our archconservatives, regard as beneficial and humane. I accept that these regulations would eventually have been instituted even if Spencer had never been born—but it made a world of difference to the Triangle workers that forces of pure laissez-faire, buttressed by their Spencerian centerpiece, managed to delay some implementations until the 1920s, rather than acceding to the just demands of unions and social reformers in 1910.

One of the two Triangle stairways was apparently locked on that fateful day—although lawyers of company owners won acquittal for their clients on this issue, largely by using legal legerdemain to confuse, intimidate, and draw inconsistencies from young witnesses with a poor command of English. Two years earlier, an important strike had begun at the Triangle company and had spread to shirtwaist manufacturers throughout the city. The union won in most factories but not, ironically, at Triangle—where management held out and compelled the return of workers without anything gained. Tensions remained high at Triangle in 1911, and management had become particularly suspicious, even paranoid, about thefts. Therefore, when the fire erupted at quitting time (and against weakly enforced laws for maintaining multiple active exits), managers had locked one of the doors to force all the women to exit by the Greene Street stairwell, where a supervisor could inspect every handbag to guard against thefts of shirtwaists.

But the bosses were breaking a weak and unenforceable law in this instance. All other causes of death can be traced to managerial compliance with absurdly inadequate standards, largely kept so weak by active political resistance to legal regulation of worksites, buttressed by the argument of social Darwinism. Fire hoses could not pump above the sixth floor, but no law prevented the massing of workers into crowded floors above. No statute required fire drills or other forms of training for fire safety. In other cases, weak regulations were risibly inadequate, easy to flout, and basically unenforced in any case. For example, by law, each worker required 250 cubic feet of air space—a good rule to prevent crowding. But companies had managed to circumvent the intent of this law, and maintain their traditional (and dangerous) density of workers, by moving into large loft buildings with high ceilings and substantial irrelevant space that could be included in the 250 cubic foot minimum.

When the Asch Building was completed in 1900, an inspector for the Building Department informed the architect that a third staircase should be provided. But the architect sought and received a variance, arguing that the single fire escape effectively served as the missing staircase required by law for structures with more than 10,000 square feet per floor. Moreover, the single fire escape—which buckled and fell during the fire, as a result of poor maintenance and too great a weight of workers trying to escape—led only to a glass skylight in a closed courtyard. The building inspector had also complained about this arrangement, and the architect had promised to make the necessary alterations. But no changes were ever made, and the falling fire escape plunged right through the skylight, greatly increasing the death toll.

Two final quotations highlight the case for inadequate legal protection as a primary cause of the unconscionable death toll in the Triangle Shirtwaist Fire (Leon Stein's excellent book, *The Triangle Fire*, [J. B. Lippincott Company, 1962] served as my chief source for information about this event).

Rose Safran, a survivor of the fire and supporter of the 1909 strike, said, "If the union had won we would have been safe. Two of our demands were for adequate fire escapes and for open doors from the factories to the street. But the bosses defeated us and we didn't get the open doors or the better fire escapes. So our friends are dead."

A building inspector who had actually written to the Triangle management just a few months before, asking for an appointment to discuss the initiation of fire drills, commented after the blaze: "There are only two or three factories in the city where fire drills are in use. In some of them where I have installed the system myself, the owners have discontinued it. The neglect of factory owners in the matter of safety of their employees is absolutely criminal. One man whom I advised to install a fire drill replied to me: 'Let 'em burn. They're a lot of cattle, anyway.'"

The Triangle fire galvanized the reform movement as never before. An empowered force, now irresistible, of labor organizers, social reformers, and liberal legislators pressed for stronger regulation under the theme of "never again." Hundreds of laws were passed as a direct result of this belated agitation. But nothing could wash the blood of 146 workers from a sidewalk of New York.

This tale of two worksites—of a desk where Huxley debated Wilberforce, and an office on a floor that burned during the Triangle Shirtwaist Fire—has no end, for the story illustrates a theme of human intellectual life that must always be with us, however imbued with an obvious and uncontroversial solution. Extremes tend to be untenable, even dangerous, places on complex and subtle continua. For the application of Darwinian theory to human history, Wilberforce's "none" marks an error of equal magnitude with the "all" of an extreme social Darwinism.

In a larger sense, the evolution of a species like *Homo sapiens* should fill us with notions of glory for our odd mental uniqueness, and of deep humility for our status as a tiny and accidental twig on such a sturdy and luxuriantly branching tree of life. Glory *and* humility! Since we can't abandon either feeling for a unitary stance in the middle, we had best make sure that both attitudes always walk together, hand in hand, and secure in the wisdom of Ruth's promise to Naomi: "Where thou goest, I will go; and where thou lodgest, I will lodge."

Saint Manuel Bueno, Martyr

Miguel de Unamuno

If in this life only we have hope in Christ, we are of all men most miserable.

Saint Paul: I Cor. 15:19

Now that the bishop of the diocese of Renada, to which this my beloved village of Valverde de Lucerna belongs, is said to be urging the process of beatification of our Don Manuel, or rather, Saint Manuel Bueno, who was parish priest here, I want to put in writing, by way of confession (although to what end only God, and not I can say), all that I know and remember about that matriarchal man who pervaded the most secret life of my soul, who was my true spiritual father, the father of my spirit, the spirit of myself, Angela Carballino.

The other, my flesh-and-blood temporal father, I scarcely knew, for he died when I was still very young. I know he came to Valverde de Lucerna from elsewhere—he was a stranger to the place—and that he settled here when he married my mother. He had brought a number of books with him: *Don Quixote*, some classical plays, some novels, a few histories, the *Bertoldo*, a veritable grab bag. These books (practically the only ones in the entire village), set me daydreaming, and I was devoured by my daydreams. My dear mother told me very little about the words or the deeds of my father. For the words and deeds of Don Manuel, whom she worshiped, of whom she was enamored, in common with all the rest of the village—in an exquisitely chaste manner, of course—had obliterated all memory of the words and deeds of her husband whom she fervently commended to God, as she said her daily rosary.

I remember Don Manuel as if it were yesterday, from the time when I was a girl of ten, just before I was taken to the convent school in the cathedral city of Renada. At that time Don Manuel, our saint, must have been about thirty-seven years old. He was tall, slim; he carried himself erect, his head the way our Buitre Peak carries its crest, and his eyes had all the blue depth of our lake. As he walked he commanded all eyes, and not only the

eyes but the hearts of all; gazing round at us he seemed to look through our flesh as through glass and penetrate our hearts. We all loved him, especially the children. And the things he said to us! The villagers could scent the odor of sanctity, they were intoxicated with it.

It was at this time that my brother Lázaro, who was in America, from where he regularly sent us money with which we lived in decent comfort, had my mother send me to the convent school, so that my education might be completed outside the village; he suggested this move despite the fact that he had no special fondness for the nuns. "But, since, as far as I know," he wrote us, "there are no lay schools there yet—especially not for young ladies—we will have to make use of the ones that do exist. The important thing is for Angelita to receive some polish and not be forced to continue among village girls." And so I entered the convent school. At one point I even thought of becoming a teacher; but pedagogy soon palled.

At school I met girls from the city and I made friends with some of them. But I still kept in touch with people in our village, and I received frequent news from them and sometimes a visit. And the fame of the parish priest even reached the school, for he was beginning to be talked of in the cathedral city. And the nuns never tired of asking me about him.

Ever since I was a child I had been endowed, I don't really know why, with a large degree of curiosity and uneasiness, due in part at least to that jumble of books which my father had collected, and at school these qualities were stimulated, especially in the course of a friendship I developed with a girl who grew excessively attached to me. At times she suggested that we enter the same convent together, swearing to an everlasting "sisterhood" and even that we seal the oath in blood. At other times she talked to me, with half-closed eyes, of sweethearts and marriage adventures. Strangely enough, I have never heard anything of her since, nor of what became of her, despite the fact that whenever our Don Manuel was mentioned, or when my mother wrote me something about him in her letters—which happened in almost every letter—and I read it to her, the girl would cry out ecstatically: "What a lucky girl you are to be able to live near a saint like that, a living saint, of flesh and blood, and to be able to kiss his hand; when you go back to your village write to me a lot and tell me lots of things about him."

I spent five years at school, five years which have now evanesced in memory like a dream at dawn, and when I was fifteen I returned to my own Valverde de Lucerna. By now everything there revolved around Don Manuel: Don Manuel, the lake, and the mountain. I arrived home anxious to know him, to place myself in his care, and hopeful that he would set me on my path in life.

It was rumored that he had entered the seminary to become a priest so that he might thus look after the children of a recently widowed sister and provide for them in place of their father; that in the seminary his keen mind and his talents had distinguished him and that he had subsequently turned down opportunities of a brilliant career in the Church because he wanted to remain exclusively a part of his Valverde de Lucerna, of his remote village which lay like a brooch between the lake and the mountain reflected in it.

How he loved his people! He spent his life salvaging wrecked marriages, forcing unruly children to submit to their parents, or reconciling parents to their children, and, above all, he consoled the embittered and weary in spirit and helped everyone to die well.

I recall, among other incidents, the occasion when the unfortunate daughter of old Aunt Rabona returned to our town. She had been living in the city and lost her virtue there; now she returned unmarried and abandoned, and she brought back a little son. Don Manuel did not rest until he had persuaded an old sweetheart, Perote by name, to marry the poor girl and, moreover, to legitimize the infant with his own name. Don Manuel told Perote:

"Come now, give this poor waif a father, for he hasn't got one except in heaven."

"But, Don Manuel, it's not my fault . . . !"

"Who knows, my son, who knows . . . ! And in any case, it's not a question of guilt."

And today, poor old Perote, inspired on that occasion to saintliness by Don Manuel, and now a paralytic and invalid, has the support and consolation of his life in the son he accepted as his own when the boy was not his at all.

On Midsummer's Night, the shortest night of the year, it was, and still is, a local custom here for all the old crones, and a lot of old men, who thought they were possessed or bewitched—they were, in fact, hysterical for the most part, and in some cases epileptics—to flock to the lake. Don Manuel undertook to fulfill the same function as the lake, to serve as a pool of healing, to treat his people and even, if possible, to cure them. And such was the effect of his presence, of his gaze, and above all of his voice—his miraculous voice!—and the infinitely sweet authority of his words, that he actually did achieve some remarkable cures. Whereupon his fame increased, drawing all the sick of the environs to our lake and our priest. And yet, once, when a mother came to ask for a miracle on behalf of her son, he answered her with a sad smile:

"Ah, but I don't have my bishop's permission to perform miracles."

He was particularly interested in seeing that all the villagers kept themselves clean. If he chanced upon someone with a torn garment he would say: "Go and see the sacristan, and let him mend that tear." The sacristan was a tailor. And when, on the first day of the year, everyone went to congratulate the priest on his saint's day—his holy patron was Our Lord Jesus Himself—it was Don Manuel's wish that everyone should appear in a new shirt, and those that had none received the present of a new one from Don Manuel himself.

He treated everyone with the greatest kindness; if he favored anyone, it was the most unfortunate, and especially those who rebelled. There was a congenital idiot in the village, the fool Blasillo, and it was toward him that Don Manuel chose to show the greatest love and concern; as a consequence he succeeded in miraculously teaching him things which had appeared beyond the idiot's comprehension. The fact was that the embers of understanding feebly glowing in the idiot were kindled whenever, like a pitiable monkey, he imitated his Don Manuel.

The marvel of the man was his voice; a divine voice which brought one close to weeping. Whenever he officiated at Solemn High Mass and intoned the Preface, a tremor ran through the congregation and all who heard his voice were moved to the depths of their being. The sound of his chanting, overflowing the church, went on to float over the lake and settle at the foot of the mountain. And when on Good Friday he chanted, "My God, my God, why hast Thou forsaken me?" a profound shudder swept through the multitude, like the lash of the northeast wind across the waters of the lake. It was as if these people heard Our Lord Jesus Christ Himself, as if the voice sprang from the ancient crucifix, at the foot of which generations of mothers had offered up their sorrows. And it happened that on one occasion when his mother heard him, she was unable to contain herself, and cried out to him right in the church, "My son!" And the entire congregation was visibly affected, tears pouring down every cheek. It was as if the mother's cry had issued from the half-open lips of the Mater Dolorosa—her heart transfixed by seven swords—which stood in one of the side chapels. Afterwards, the fool Blasillo went about piteously repeating, like an echo, "My God, my God, why hast Thou forsaken me?" with such effect that everyone who heard him was moved to tears, to the great satisfaction of the fool, who prided himself on this triumph of imitation.

The priest's effect on people was such that no one ever dared to tell him a lie, and everyone confessed to him without need of a confessional. So true was this that one day, after a revolting crime had been committed in a neighboring village, the judge—a dull fellow who badly misunderstood Don Manuel—called on the priest and said:

"Let's see if *you*, Don Manuel, can get this bandit to admit the truth."

"So that *you* may punish him afterwards?" asked the saintly man. "No, Judge, no; I will not extract from any man a truth which could be the death of him. That is a matter between him and his God. . . . Human justice is none of my affair. 'Judge not that ye be not judged,' said Our Lord."

"But the fact is, Father, that I, a judge . . ."

"I understand. You, Judge, must render unto Caesar that which is Caesar's, while I shall render unto God that which is God's."

And, as Don Manuel departed, he gazed at the suspected criminal and said:

"Make sure, only, that God forgives you, for that is all that matters."

Everyone in the village went to Mass, even if it were only to hear him and see him at the altar, where he appeared to be transfigured, his countenance lit from within. He introduced one holy practice into popular worship; it consisted in assembling the whole town inside the church, men and women, old and young, about a thousand souls; there we recited the Creed, in unison, so that it sounded like a single voice. "I believe in God, the Father almighty, creator of heaven and earth . . ." and all the rest. It was not a chorus, but a single voice, all the voices blending into one forming a kind of mountain, whose peak, lost at times in the clouds, was Don Manuel. As we reached the section "I believe in the resurrection of the flesh and eternal life," Don Manuel's voice was submerged, drowned in the voice of the populace as in a lake. In truth, he was silent. And I could hear the bells of the city which is said hereabouts to be at the bottom of the lake—bells which are said also to be audible on Midsummer's Night—the bells of the city which is submerged in the spiritual lake of our people. I was hearing the voice of our dead, resurrected in us by the communion of saints. Later, when I had learned the secret of our saint, I understood that it was as if a caravan crossing the desert lost its leader as they approached the goal of their trek, whereupon his people lifted him up on their shoulders to bring his lifeless body into the promised land.

When it came to dying themselves, most of the villagers refused to die unless they were holding onto Don Manuel's hand, as if to an anchor chain.

In his sermons he never inveighed against unbelievers, Freemasons, liberals, or heretics. What for, when there were none in the village? Nor did it occur to him to speak out against the wickedness of the press. On the other hand, one of his most frequent themes was the sinfulness of gossip. As he himself forgave everything and everyone, he would not accept the existence of forked tongues.

"Envy," he liked to repeat, "is nurtured by those who prefer to think they are envied, and most persecutions are the result of a persecution complex rather than of an impulse to persecute."

"But Don Manuel, just listen to what that fellow was trying to tell me. . . ."

"We should concern ourselves less with what people are trying to tell us than with what they tell us without trying. . . ."

His life was active rather than contemplative, and he constantly fled from idleness, even from leisure. Whenever he heard it said that idleness was the mother of all vices, he added: "And also of the greatest vice of them all, which is to think idly." Once I asked him what he meant and he answered: thinking idly is thinking as a substitute for doing, or thinking too much about what is already done instead of about what must be done. What's done is done and over with, and one must go on to something else, for there is nothing worse than remorse without possible solution." Action! Action! Even in those early days I had already begun to realize that Don Manuel fled from being left to think in solitude, and I sensed that some obsession haunted him.

And so it was that he was always busy, sometimes even busy looking for things to do. He wrote very little on his own, so that he scarcely left us anything in writing, not even notes; on the other hand, he acted as scribe for everyone else, especially composing letters for mothers to their absent children.

He also worked with his hands, pitching in to help with some of the village tasks. At threshing time he reported to the threshing floor to flail and winnow, meanwhile teaching and entertaining the workers by turn. Sometimes he took the place of a worker who had fallen sick. One bitter winter's day he came upon a child half-dead with cold. The child's father had sent him into the woods to bring back a calf that had strayed.

"Listen," he said to the child, "you go home and get warm, and tell your father that I am bringing back the calf." On the way back with the animal he ran into the father, who had come out to meet him, thoroughly ashamed of himself.

In winter he chopped wood for the poor. When a certain magnificent walnut tree died—"that matriarchal walnut," he called it, a tree under whose shade he had played as a boy and whose nuts he had eaten for so many years—he asked for the trunk, carried it to his house and, after he had cut six planks from it, which he kept at the foot of his bed, he made firewood of the rest to warm the poor. He also was in the habit of making handballs for the boys and many toys for the younger children.

Often he used to accompany the doctor on his rounds, and stressed the importance of following the doctor's orders. Most of all he was interested in maternity cases and the care of children; it was his opinion that the old wives' sayings "from the cradle to heaven" and the other one about "little angels belong in heaven" were nothing short of blasphemy. The death of a child moved him deeply.

"A stillborn child, or one who dies soon after birth are, like suicides, the most terrible mystery to me," I once heard him say. "Like a child crucified!"

And once, when a man had taken his own life and the father of the suicide, an outsider, asked Don Manuel if his son could be buried in consecrated ground, the priest answered:

"Most certainly, for at the last moment, in the very last throes, he must surely have repented. There is no doubt of it whatsoever in my mind."

Often he would visit the local school too, to help the teacher, to teach alongside him—and not only the catechism. The simple truth was that he fled relentlessly from idleness and from solitude. He went so far in this desire of his to mingle with the villagers, especially the young people and the children, that he even attended the village dances. And more than once he played the drum to keep time for the boys and girls dancing; this kind of activity, which in another priest would have seemed like a grotesque mockery of his calling, in him somehow took on the appearance of a divine office. When the Angelus rang out, he would put down the drum and sticks, take off his hat (all the others doing the same) and pray: "The angel of the Lord declared unto Mary: Hail Mary . . ." And afterwards: "Now let us rest until tomorrow."

The most important thing," he would say, "is for the people to be happy; everyone must be happy just to be alive. To be satisfied with life is of first importance. No one should want to die until it is God's will."

"I want to die now," a recently widowed woman once told him, "I want to follow my husband. . . ."

"But why?" he asked. "Stay here and pray God for his soul."

Once he commented at a wedding: "Ah, if I could only change all the water in our lake into wine, into a gentle little wine which, no matter how much of it one drank, would always make one joyful without making one drunk . . . or, if it made one drunk, would make one joyfully tipsy."

One day a band of poor circus people came through the village. Their leader—who arrived with a gravely ill and pregnant wife and three children to help him—played the clown. While he was in the village square making all the children, and even some of the adults, laugh with glee, his wife suddenly fell desperately ill and had to leave; she went off accompanied by a look of anguish from the clown and a howl of laughter from the children. Don Manuel hurried after her, and a little later, in a corner of the inn's stable, he helped her give up her soul in a state of grace. When the performance was over and the villagers and the clown learned of the tragedy, they came to the inn, and there the poor, bereaved clown, in a voice overcome with tears, said to Don Manuel, as he took his hand and kissed it: "They are quite right, Father, when they say you are a saint." Don Manuel took the clown's hand in his and replied in front of everyone:

"It is you who are the saint, good clown. I watched you at your work and understood that you do it not only to provide bread for your own children, but also to give joy to the children of others. And I tell you now that your wife, the mother of your children, whom I sent to God while you worked to give joy, is at rest in the Lord, and that you will join her there, and that the angels, whom you will make laugh with happiness in heaven, will reward you with their laughter."

And everyone present wept, children and adults alike, as much from sorrow as from a mysterious joy in which all sorrow was drowned. Later, recalling that solemn hour, I came to realize that the imperturable happiness of Don Manuel was merely the temporal, earthly form of an infinite, eternal sadness which the priest concealed from the eyes and ears of the world with heroic saintliness.

His constant activity, his ceaseless intervention in the tasks and diversions of his flock, had the appearance of a flight from himself, a flight from solitude. He confirmed this suspicion: "I have a fear of solitude," he would say. And still, from time to time he would go off by himself, along the shores of the lake, to the ruins of the abbey where

the souls of pious Cistercians seem still to repose, although history has long since buried them in oblivion. There, the cell of the so-called Father-Captain can still be found, and it is said that the drops of blood spattered on the walls as he flagellated himself can still be seen. What thoughts occupied our Don Manuel as he walked there? I remember a conversation we held once when I asked him, as he was speaking of the abbey, why it had never occurred to him to enter a monastery, and he answered me:

"It is not at all because my sister is a widow and I have her children and herself to support—for God looks after the poor—but rather because I simply was not born to be a hermit, an anchorite; the solitude would crush my soul; and, as far as a monastery is concerned, my monastery is Valverde de Lucerna. I was not meant to live alone, or die alone. I was meant to live for my village, and die for it too. How should I save my soul if I were not to save the soul of my village as well?"

"But there have been saints who were hermits, solitaries . . . ," I said.

"Yes, the Lord gave them the grace of solitude which He has denied me, and I must resign myself. I must not throw away my village to win my soul. God made me that way. I would not be able, alone, to carry the cross of birth. . . ."

I trust that these recollections, which keep my faith alive, will portray our Don Manuel as he was when I, a young girl of almost sixteen, returned from the convent of Renada to our "monastery of Valverde de Lucerna," to kneel once more at the feet of our "abbot."

"Well, here is Simona's daughter," he said as soon as he saw me, "quite a young woman, and knowing French, and how to play the piano, and embroider, and heaven knows what else besides! Now you must get ready to give us a family. And your brother Lázaro, when is he coming back? Is he still in the New World?"

"Yes, Father, he is still in America."

"The New World! And we in the Old. Well, then, when you write to him, tell him from me, on behalf of the parish priest, that I should like to know when he is returning from the New World to the Old, to bring us the latest from over there. And tell him that he will find the lake and the mountain as he left them."

When I first went to him for confession, I became so confused that I could not enunciate a word. I recited the "Forgive me, Father, for I have sinned," in a stammer, almost sobbing. And he, observing this, said:

"Good heavens, my dear, what are you afraid of, or of whom are you afraid? Certainly you're not trembling under the weight of your sins, nor in fear of God. No, you're trembling because of me, isn't that so?"

At this point I burst into tears.

"What have they been telling you about me? What fairy tales? Was it your mother, perhaps? Come, come, please be calm: you must imagine you are talking to your brother. . . ."

At this I plucked up courage and began to tell him of my anxieties, doubts, and sorrows.

"Bah! Where did you read all this, Miss Bluestocking? All this is literary nonsense. Don't believe everything you read just yet, not even Saint Teresa. If you want to amuse yourself, read the *Bertoldo*, as your father before you did."

I came away from my first confession to that holy man deeply consoled. The initial fear—simple fright more than respect—with which I had approached him, turned into a profound pity. I was at that time a very young woman, almost a girl still; and yet, I was beginning to be a woman, in my innermost being I felt the maternal instinct, and when I found myself in the confessional at the side of the saintly priest, I sensed a kind of unspoken confession on his part in the soft murmur of his voice. And I remembered how when he had chanted in the church the words of Jesus Christ: "My God, my God, why hast Thou forsaken me?" his own mother had cried out in the congregation: "My son!"; and I could hear the cry that had rent the silence of the temple. And I went to him again for confession—and to comfort him.

Another time in the confessional I told him of a doubt which assailed me, and he responded:

"As to that, you know what the catechism says. Don't question me about it, for I am ignorant; in Holy Mother Church there are learned doctors of theology who will know how to answer you."

"But you are the learned doctor here."

"Me? A learned doctor? Not even in my dreams! I, my little theologian, am only a poor country priest. And those questions, . . . do you know who whispers them into your ear? Well . . . the Devil does!"

Then, making bold, I asked him point-blank:

"And suppose he were to whisper these questions to you?"

"Who? To me? The Devil? No, we don't even know each other, my child, we haven't even met."

"But if he did whisper them? . . ."

"I wouldn't pay any attention. And that's enough of that; let's get on, for there are some sick people, some really sick people, waiting for me."

I went away thinking, I don't know why, that our Don Manuel, so famous for curing the bedeviled, didn't really believe in the Devil. As I started home, I ran into the fool Blasillo, who had probably been hovering around outside; as soon as he saw me, and by way of treating me to a display of his virtuosity, he began repeating—and in what a manner!—"My God, my God, why hast Thou forsaken me?" I arrived home utterly saddened and locked myself in my room to cry, until finally my mother arrived.

"With all these confessions, Angelita, you will end up going off to a nunnery."

"Don't worry, Mother," I answered her. "I have plenty to do here; the village is my convent."

"Until you marry."

"I don't intend to," I rejoined.

The next time I saw Don Manuel I asked him, looking him straight in the eye:

"Is there really a Hell, Don Manuel?"

And he, without altering his expression, answered:

"For you, my child, no."

"For others, then?"

"Does it matter to you, if you are not to go there?"

"It matters to me for the others. Is there a Hell?"

"Believe in Heaven, the Heaven we can see. Look at it there"—and he pointed to the heavens above the mountain, and then down into the lake, to the reflection.

"But we are supposed to believe in Hell as well as in Heaven," I said.

"Yes, that's true. We must believe everything that our Holy Mother Church believes and teaches, our Holy Mother Church, Catholic, Apostolic, and Roman. And now, that's enough of that!"

I thought I read a deep sadness in his eyes, eyes as blue as the waters of the lake.

Those years went by as if in a dream. Within me, a reflected image of Don Manuel was unconsciously taking form. He was an ordinary enough man in many ways, as everyday as the daily bread we asked for in our Paternoster. I helped him whenever I could with his tasks, visiting his sick, our sick, the girls at school, and helping, too, with the church linen and the vestments; I served in the role, as he said, of his deaconess. Once I was invited to the city for a few days by an old schoolfriend, but I had to hurry back home, for the city stifled me—something was missing, I was thirsty for a sight of the waters of the lake, hungry for a sight of the peaks of the mountain; and even more, I missed my Don Manuel, as if he were calling me, as if he were endangered by my being so far away, as if he were in need of me. I began to feel a kind of maternal affection for my spiritual father; I longed to help him bear the cross of birth.

My twenty-fourth birthday was approaching when my brother Lázaro came back from America with the small fortune he had saved up. He came back to Valverde de Lucerna with the intention of taking me and my mother to live in a city, perhaps even in Madrid.

"In the country," he said, "in these villages, a person becomes dull, brutalized, and spiritually impoverished." And he added: "Civilization is the very opposite of everything countrified. The idiocy of country life! No, that's not for us; I didn't have you sent away to school so that afterwards you might go to waste here, among these ignorant peasants."

I said nothing, though I was ready to oppose any idea of moving. But our mother, already past sixty, took a firm stand from the start: "Change pastures at my age?" she demurred at once. A little

later she made it quite clear that she could not live away from her lake, her mountain, and above all, her Don Manuel.

"You are both of you like those cats that get attached to houses," my brother kept saying.

When he realized the extent of the sway exercised over the entire village—especially over my mother and myself—by the saintly priest, my brother began to resent him. He saw in this situation an example of the obscurantist theocracy which, according to him, smothered Spain. And he began to spout the old anticlerical commonplaces, to which he added antireligious and "progressive" propaganda brought back from the New World.

"In this Spain of useless, easy-going men, the priests manipulate the women, and the women manipulate the men. Not to mention the idiocy of the country, and this feudal backwater!"

"Feudal," to him, meant something frightful. "Feudal" and "medieval" were the epithets he employed to condemn something out of hand.

The absolute failure of his diatribes to move us and their lack of effect upon the village—where they were listened to with respectful indifference—disconcerted him no end. "The man does not exist who could move these clods." But he soon began to understand—for he was an intelligent man, and therefore a good one—the kind of influence exercised over the village by Don Manuel, and he came to appreciate the effect of the priest's work in the village.

"This priest is not like the rest of them," he announced. "He is, in fact, a saint."

"How do you know what the rest of them are like?" I asked him, and he replied:

"I can imagine."

Even so, he did not set foot inside the church nor did he miss an opportunity to parade his lack of belief—though he always exempted Don Manuel from his scornful accusations. In the village, an unconscious expectancy began to build up, the anticipation of a kind of duel between my brother Lázaro and Don Manuel—in short, it was expected that Don Manuel would convert my brother. No one doubted but that in the end the priest would bring him into the fold. On his side, Lázaro was eager (he told me so himself, later) to go and hear Don Manuel, to see and hear him in the church, to get to know him and to talk with him, so that he might learn the secret of his spiritual sway over our souls. And he let himself be coaxed to this end, so that finally—"out of curiosity," as he said—he went to hear the preacher.

"Now, this is something else again," he told me as soon as he came back from hearing Don Manuel for the first time. "He's not like the others; still, he doesn't fool me, he's too intelligent to believe everything he has to teach."

"You mean you think he's a hypocrite?"

"A hypocrite . . . no! But he has to live by his job."

As for me, my brother was determined I should read the books he brought me, and others which he urged me to buy.

"So your brother Lázaro wants you to read," Don Manuel declared. "Well, read, my child, read and make him happy. I know you will only read worthy books. Read, even if you only read novels; they are as good as histories which claim to be 'true.' You are better off reading than concerning yourself with village gossip and old wives' tales. Above all, though, you will do well to read some devotional books which will bring you contentment in life, a quiet, gentle contentment, and peace."

And he, did he enjoy such contentment?

It was about this time that our mother fell mortally sick and died. In her last days her one wish was that Don Manuel should convert Lázaro, whom she hoped to see again in heaven, in some little corner among the stars from where they could see the lake and the mountain of Valverde de Lucerna. She felt she was going there now, to see God.

"You are not going anywhere," Don Manuel kept telling her; "you are staying right here. Your body will remain here, in this earth, and your soul also, in this house, watching and listening to your children though they will not see or hear you."

"But, Father," she said, "I am going to see God."

"God, my daughter, is all around us, and you will see Him from here, right from here. And all of us see in Him, and He in all of us."

"God bless you," I whispered to him.

"The peace in which your mother dies will be her eternal life," he told me.

And, turning to my brother Lázaro: "Her heaven is to go on seeing you, and it is at this moment that she must be saved. Tell her you will pray for her."

"But . . ."

"But what? . . . Tell her you will pray for her, to whom you owe your life. And I know that once you promise her, you *will* pray, and I know that once you pray. . ."

My brother, with tears in his eyes, went up to our dying mother and gave her his solemn promise to pray for her.

"And I, in heaven will pray for you, for all of you," my mother replied. And then, kissing the crucifix and fixing her eyes on Don Manuel, she gave up her soul to God.

"Into Thy hands I commend my spirit," prayed the priest.

My brother and I stayed on in the house alone. What had happened at the time of my mother's death had established a bond between Lázaro and Don Manuel. The latter seemed even to neglect some of his charges, his patients, and his other needy to look after my brother. In the afternoons, they would go for a walk together, beside the lake or toward the ivy-covered ruins of the old Cistercian abbey.

"He's an extraordinary man," Lázaro told me. "You know the story they tell of how there is a city at the bottom of the lake, submerged beneath the water, and that on Midsummer's Night at midnight the sound of its church bells can be heard. . . ."

"Yes, a city 'feudal and medieval' . . ."

"And I believe," he went on, "that at the bottom of Don Manuel's soul there is a city, submerged and drowned, and that sometimes the sound of its bells can be heard. . . ."

"Yes. . . . And this city submerged in Don Manuel's soul, and perhaps—why not?—in yours as well, is certainly the cemetery of the souls of our ancestors, the ancestors of our Valverde de Lucerna . . . ' eudal and medieval'!"

Eventually my brother began going to Mass. He went regularly to hear Don Manuel. When it became known that he was prepared to comply with his annual duty of receiving Communion, that he would receive Communion when the others did, an inner joy ran through the town, which felt that by this act he was restored to his people. The rejoicing was so simple and honest, that Lázaro never did feel that he had been "vanquished" or "overcome."

The day of his Communion arrived; of Communion before and with the entire village. When my brother's turn came, I saw Don Manuel—white as the January snow on the mountain, and moving like the surface of the lake when it is stirred by the northeast wind—come up to him with the holy wafer in his hand, trembling violently as he reached out to Lázaro's mouth; at that moment the priest shook so that the wafer dropped to the ground. My brother himself recovered it and placed it in his mouth. The people saw the tears on Don Manuel's cheeks, and everyone wept, saying: "How he loves him!" And then, because it was dawn, a cock crowed.

On returning home I shut myself in with my brother; alone with him I put my arms around his neck and kissed him.

"Lázaro, Lázaro, what joy you have given us all today; the entire village, the living and the dead, especially our mother. Did you see how Don Manuel wept for joy? What joy you have given us all!"

"That's why I did it," he answered me.

"Is that why? Just to give us pleasure? Surely you did it for your own sake, because you were converted."

And then Lázaro, my brother, grew as pale and tremulous as Don Manuel when he was giving Communion, and bade me sit down, in the chair where our mother used to sit. He took a deep breath, and, in the intimate tone of a family confession, he told me:

"Angelita, it is time for me to tell you the truth, the absolute truth, and I shall tell it, because I must, because I cannot and ought not to conceal it from you, and because sooner or later, you are bound to find it out anyway, if only halfway—which would be worse."

Thereupon, serenely and tranquilly, in a subdued voice, he recounted a tale that cast me into a lake of sorrow. He told me how Don Manuel had begged him, particularly during the walks to the ruins of the old Cistercian abbey, to set a good example, to avoid scandalizing the townspeople, to take part in the religious life of the community, to feign belief even if he did not feel any, to conceal his own ideas—this without attempting in any way to catechize him, to instruct him in religion, or to effect a true conversion.

"But is it possible?" I asked in consternation.

"Very possible and absolutely true. When I said to him: 'Is it really you, the priest, who suggests that I pretend?' he replied, hesitatingly: 'Pretend? Not at all! It would not be pretending. "Dip your fingers in holy water, and you will end by believing," as someone said.' And I, gazing into his eyes, asked him: 'And you, by celebrating the Mass, have you ended up by believing?' He looked away and stared out at the lake, until his eyes filled with tears. And it was in this way that I came to understand his secret."

"Lázaro!" I moaned.

At that moment the fool Blasillo came along our street, crying out his: "My God, my God, why hast Thou forsaken me?" And Lázaro shuddered, as if he had heard the voice of Don Manuel, or even that of Christ.

"It was then," my brother at length continued, "that I really understood his motives and his saintliness; for a saint he is, Sister, a true saint. In trying to convert me to his holy cause—for it is a holy cause, a most holy cause—he was not attempting to score a triumph, but rather was doing it to protect the peace, the happiness, the illusions, perhaps, of his flock. I understood that if he thus deceives them— if it *is* deceit—it is not for his own advantage. I submitted to his logic—and that was my conversion. And I shall never forget the day on which I said to him: 'But, Don Manuel, the truth, the truth, above all!'; and he, all a-tremble, whispered in my ear—though we were all alone in the middle of the countryside—'The truth? The truth, Lázaro, is perhaps something so unbearable, so terrible, something so deadly, that simple people could not live with it!'

" 'And why do you allow me a glimpse of it now, here, as if we were in the confessional?' I asked. And he said: 'Because if I did not, I would be so tormented by it, so tormented that I would finally shout it in the middle of the Plaza, which I must never, never, never do. . . . I am put here to give life to the souls of my charges, to make them happy, to make them dream they are immortal—and not to destroy them. The important thing is that they live undisturbed, in concord with one another—and with the truth, with my truth, they could not live at all. Let them live. That is what the Church does, it lets them live. As for true religion, all religions are true insofar as they give spiritual life to the people who profess them, insofar as they console them for having been born only to die. And for each race the truest religion is their own, the religion that made them. . . . And mine? Mine consists in consoling myself by consoling others, even though the consolation I give them is not ever mine.' I shall never forget his words."

"But then this Communion of yours has been a sacrilege," I dared interrupt, regretting my words as soon as I said them.

"Sacrilege? What about the priest who gave it to me? And his Masses?"

"What martyrdom!" I exclaimed.

"And now," said my brother, "there is one more person to console the people."

"To deceive them, you mean?" I said.

"Not at all," he replied, "but rather to confirm them in their faith."

"And they, the people, do you think they really believe?"

"As to that, I know nothing! . . . They probably believe without trying, from force of habit, tradition. The important thing is not to stir them up. To let them live on the thin diet of their emotions rather than acquiring the torments of luxury. Blessed are the poor in spirit!"

"So that is what you have learned from Don Manuel. . . . And tell me, do you feel you have carried out your promise to our mother on her deathbed, when you promised to pray for her?"

"Do you think I could fail her? What do you take me for, Sister? Do you think I would go back on my word, my solemn promise made at the hour of death to a mother?"

"I don't know. . . . You might have wanted to deceive her so she could die in peace."

"The fact is, though, that if I had not lived up to my promise, I would be totally miserable."

"And . . ."

"I have carried out my promise and I have never neglected for a single day to pray for her."

"Only for her?"

"Well, for whom else?"

"For yourself! And now, for Don Manuel."

We parted and each went to his room, I to weep through the night, praying for the conversion of my brother and of Don Manuel. And Lázaro, to what purpose, I know not.

From that day on I was nervous about finding myself alone with Don Manuel, whom I continued to help in his pious works. And he seemed to sense my inner state and to guess at its cause. When at last I approached him in the confessional's penitential tribunal (who was the judge, and who the offender?) the two of us, he and I, bowed our heads in silence and began to weep. It was Don Manuel who finally broke the silence, with a voice that seemed to issue from a tomb:

"Angelita, you have the same faith you had when you were ten, don't you? You believe, don't you?"

"Yes, I believe, Father."

"Then go on believing. And if doubts come to torment you, suppress them utterly, even to yourself. The main thing is to live. . . ."

I summoned up my courage, and dared to ask, trembling:

"But, Father, do you believe?"

For a brief moment he hesitated, and then, taking hold of himself, he said:

"I believe!"

"In what, Father, in what? Do you believe in the life hereafter? Do you believe that when we die, we do not die altogether? Do you believe that we will see each other again, that we will love each other in the next world? Do you believe in the next life?"

The poor saint was sobbing.

"My child, leave off, leave off!"

Now, as I write this memoir, I ask myself: Why did he not deceive me? Why did he not deceive me as he deceived the others? Why did he torture himself? Why could he not deceive himself, or why could he not deceive me? And I prefer to think that he was tormented because he could not deceive himself into deceiving me.

"And now," he said, "pray for me, for your brother, and for yourself—for all of us. We must go on living. And giving life."

And, after a pause:

"Angelita, why don't you marry?"

"You know why."

"No, no; you must marry. Lázaro and I will find you a suitor. For it would be good for you to marry, and rid yourself of these obsessions."

"Obsessions, Don Manuel?"

"I know what I am saying. You should not torment yourself for the sake of others, for each of us has more than enough to do answering for himself."

"That it should be you, Don Manuel, saying this! That you should advise me to marry and answer for myself alone and not suffer over others! That it should be you!"

"Yes, you are right, Angelita. I am no longer sure of what I am saying since I began to confess to you. Only, one must go on living. Yes! One must live!"

And when I rose to leave the church, he asked me:

"Now, Angelita, in the name of the people, do you absolve me?"

I felt pierced by a mysterious and priestly prompting and said:

"In the name of the Father, the Son, and the Holy Ghost, I absolve you, Father."

We left the church, and as I went out I felt the quickening of maternal feelings within me.

My brother, now totally devoted to the work of Don Manuel, had become his closest and most zealous collaborator and companion. They were bound together, moreover, by their common secret. Lázaro accompanied the priest on his visits to the sick, and to schools, and he placed his fortune at the disposition of the saintly man. And he nearly learned to help celebrate Mass. All the while he was sounding deeper the unfathomable soul of the priest.

"What an incredible man!" he exclaimed to me once. "Yesterday, as we were walking along beside the lake he said: 'There lies my greatest temptation.' When I interrogated him with my eyes, he went on: 'My poor father, who was close to ninety when he died, was tormented all his life, as he himself confessed to me, by a temptation to commit suicide, by an instinct toward self-destruction, which had come to him from a time before memory—from birth, from his *nation*, as he said—and he was forced to fight against it always. And this struggle grew to be his life. So as not to succumb to this temptation he was forced to take precautions, to guard his life. He told me of terrible episodes. His urge was a form of madness—and I have inherited it. How that water beckons me with its deep quiet! . . . an apparent serenity reflecting the sky like a mirror—and beneath it the hidden current! My life, Lázaro, is a kind of continual suicide, or a struggle against suicide, which is the same thing. . . . Just so long as our people go on living!' And then he added: 'Here the river eddies to form a lake, so that later, flowing down the plateau, it may form cascades, waterfalls, and torrents, hurling itself through gorges and chasms. Thus life eddies in the village; and the temptation to commit suicide is greater beside the still waters which at night reflect the stars, than it is beside the crashing falls which drive one back in fear. Listen, Lázaro, I have helped poor villagers to die well, ignorant, illiterate villagers who had scarcely ever been out of their village, and I have learned from their own lips, or sensed it when they were silent, the real cause of their sickness unto death, and there at their deathbed I have been able to see into the black abyss of their life-weariness. A weariness a thousand times worse than hunger! For our part, Lázaro, let us go on with our kind of suicide working for the people, and let them dream their lives as the lake dreams the heavens.'

"Another time," said my brother, "as we were coming back, we caught sight of a country girl, a goatherd, standing tall, on the crest of the mountain slope overlooking the lake and she was singing in a voice fresher than the waters. Don Manuel stopped me, and pointing to her said: 'Look, it's as though time had stopped, as though this country girl had always been there just as she is, singing the way she is, and it's as though she would always be there, as she was before my consciousness began, as she will be when it is past. That girl is a part of nature—not of history—along with the rocks, the clouds, the trees, and the water.' He has such a subtle feeling for nature, he infuses it with feeling! I shall never forget the day when snow was falling and he asked me: 'Have you ever seen a greater mystery, Lázaro, than the snow falling, and dying, in the lake, while a headdress is laid upon the mountain?'"

Don Manuel had to moderate and temper my brother's zeal and his neophyte's rawness. As soon as he heard that Lázaro was going about inveighing against some of the popular superstitions he told him firmly:

"Leave them alone! It's difficult enough making them understand where orthodox belief leaves off and where superstition begins. And it's even harder for us. Leave them alone, then, as long as they get some comfort. . . . It's better for them to believe everything, even things that contradict one another, than to believe nothing. The idea that someone who believes too much ends up not believing anything is a Protestant notion. Let us not protest! Protestation destroys contentment and peace."

My brother told me, too, about one moonlit night when they were returning to the village along the lake, whose surface was being stirred by a mountain breeze, so that the moonbeams topped the white-crested waves, and Don Manuel turned to him and said:

"Look, the water is reciting the litany and saying: *ianua caeli, ora pro nobis*; gate of heaven, pray for us."

And two tears fell from his lashes to the grass, where the light of the full moon shone upon them like dew.

And time sped by, and my brother and I began to notice that Don Manuel's spirits were failing, that he could no longer control completely the deep-rooted sadness which consumed him; perhaps some treacherous illness was undermining his body and soul. In an effort to arouse his interest, Lázaro spoke to him of the good effect the organization of something like a Catholic agrarian syndicate in the Church would have.

"A syndicate?" Don Manuel replied sadly. "A syndicate? And what is that? The Church is the only syndicate I know of. And you have certainly heard 'My kingdom is not of this world.' Our kingdom, Lázaro, is not of this world. . . ."

"And of the other?"

Don Manuel bowed his head:

"The other is here. Two kingdoms exist in this world. Or rather, the other world. . . . Ah, I don't really know what I am saying. But as for the syndicate, that's a carry-over from your radical days. No, Lázaro, no; religion does not exist to resolve the economic or political conflicts of this world, which God handed over to men for their disputes. Let men think and act as they will, let them console themselves for having been born, let them live as happily as possible in the illusion that all this has a purpose. I don't propose to advise the poor to submit to the rich, nor to suggest to the rich that they submit to the poor; but rather to preach resignation in everyone, and charity toward everyone. For even the rich man must resign himself—to his riches, and to life; and the poor man must show charity—even to the rich. The Social Question? Ignore it, for it is none of our business. So, a new society is on the way, in which there will be neither rich nor poor, in which wealth will be justly divided, in which everything will belong to everyone—and so, what then? Won't this general well-being and comfort lead to even greater tedium and weariness of life? I know well enough that one of those leaders of what they call the Social Revolution said that religion is the opium of the people. Opium . . . Opium . . . Yes, opium it is. We should give them opium, and help them sleep, and dream. I, myself, with my mad activity am giving myself opium. And still I don't manage to sleep well, let alone dream well. . . . What a fearful nightmare! . . . I, too, can say, with the Divine Master: 'My soul is exceedingly sorrowful, even unto death.' No, Lázaro, no; no syndicates for us. If *they* organize them, well and good—they would be distracting themselves in that way. Let them play at syndicates, if that makes them happy."

The entire village began to realize that Don Manuel's spirit was weakening, that his strength was waning. His very voice—that miracle of a voice—acquired a kind of tremor. Tears came into his eyes at the slightest provocation—or without provocation. Whenever he spoke to people about the next world, about the next life, he was forced to pause at frequent intervals, and he would close his eyes. "It is a vision," people would say, "he has a vision of what lies ahead." At such moments the fool Blasillo was the first to burst into tears. He wept copiously these days, crying now more than he laughed, and even his laughter had the sound of tears.

The last Easter Week which Don Manuel was to celebrate among us, in this world, in this village of ours, arrived, and all the village sensed that the tragedy was coming to an end. And how those words struck home when for the last time Don Manuel cried out before us: "My God, my God, why hast Thou forsaken me?" And when he repeated the words of the Lord to the Good Thief—"all thieves are good," Don Manuel used to tell us—: "Today shalt thou be with me in paradise." And then, the last general Communion which our saint was to give! When he came to my brother to give him the Host—his hand steady this time—just after the liturgical ". . . *in vitam aeternam*," he bent down and whispered to him: "There is no other life but this, no life more eternal . . . let them dream it eternal . . . let it be eternal for a few years. . . ." And when he came to me, he said: "Pray, my child, pray for us all." And then, something so extraordinary happened that I carry it now in my heart as the greatest of mysteries: he leant over and said, in a voice which seemed to belong to the other world: ". . . and pray, too, for our Lord Jesus Christ."

I stood up weakly like a sleepwalker. Everything around me seemed dreamlike. And I thought: "Am I to pray, too, for the lake and the mountain?" And next: "Am I bedeviled, then?" Home at last, I took up the crucifix my mother had held in her hands when she had given up her soul to God, and, gazing at it through my tears and recalling the "My God, my God, why hast Thou forsaken me?" of our two Christs, the one of this earth and the other of this village, I prayed: "Thy will be done on earth as it is in heaven," and then, "And lead us not into temptation. Amen." After this I turned to the Statue of the Mater Dolorosa—her heart transfixed by seven swords—which had been my poor mother's most sorrowful comfort, and I prayed again: "Holy Mary, Mother of God, pray for us sinners, now and at the hour of our death. Amen." I had scarcely finished the prayer, when I asked myself: "Sinners? Us, sinners? And what is our sin, what is it?" And all day I brooded over the question.

The next day I went to see Don Manuel—now in the full sunset of his magnificent religiosity—and I said to him:

"Do you remember, my Father, years ago when I asked you a certain question you answered: 'That is a question you must not ask me; for I am ignorant; there are learned doctors of the Holy Mother Church who will know how to answer you'?"

"Do I remember? . . . Of course, I do. And I remember I told you those were questions put to you by the Devil."

"Well, then, Father, I have come again, bedeviled, to ask you another question put to me by my Guardian Devil."

"Ask it."

"Yesterday, when you gave me Communion, you asked me to pray for all of us, and even for . . ."

"That's enough! . . . Go on."

"I arrived home and began to pray; when I came to the part 'Pray for us sinners, now and at the hour of our death,' a voice inside me asked: 'Sinners? Us, sinners? And what is our sin?' What is our sin, Father?"

"Our sin?" he replied. "A great doctor of the Spanish Catholic Apostolic Church has already explained it; the great doctor of *Life Is a Dream* has written 'The greatest sin of man is to have been born.' That, my child, is our sin: to have been born."

"Can it be atoned, Father?"

"Go away and pray again. Pray once more for us sinners, now and at the hour of our death. . . . Yes, at length the dream is atoned . . . at length life is atoned . . . at length the cross of birth is expiated and atoned, and the dogma comes to an end. . . . And as Calderón said, to have done good, to have feigned good, even in dreams, is something which is not lost."

The hour of his death arrived at last. The entire village saw it come. And he made it his finest lesson. For he did not want to die alone or at rest. He died preaching to his people in the church. But first, before being carried to the church—his paralysis made it impossible for him to move—he summoned Lázaro and me to his bedside. Alone there, the three of us together, he said:

"Listen to me: watch over my poor flock; find some comfort for them in living, and let them believe what I could not. And Lázaro, when your hour comes, die as I die, as Angela will die, in the arms of the Holy Mother Church, Catholic, Apostolic, and Roman; that is to say, the Holy Mother Church of Valverde de Lucerna. And now farewell; until we never meet again, for this dream of life is coming to an end. . . ."

"Father, Father," I cried out.

"Do not grieve, Angela, only go on praying for all sinners, for all who have been born. Let them dream, let them dream. . . . Oh, how I long to sleep, to sleep, to sleep without end, to sleep for all eternity, and never dream! Forgetting this dream! . . . When they bury me, let it be in a box made from the six planks I cut from the old walnut tree—poor old tree!—in whose shade I played as a child, when I began the dream. . . . In those days, I really did believe in life everlasting. That is to say, it seems to me now that I believed. For a child, to believe is the same as to dream. And for a people too . . . You'll find those six planks I cut at the foot of the bed."

He was seized by a sudden fit of choking, and then, feeling better, he went on:

"You will recall that when we prayed together, animated by a common sentiment, a community of spirit, and we came to the final verse of the Creed, you will remember that I would fall silent. . . . When the Israelites were coming to the end of their wandering in the desert, the Lord told Aaron and Moses that because they had not believed in Him they would not set foot in the Promised Land with their people; and he bade them climb the heights of Mount Hor, where Moses ordered Aaron to be stripped of his garments, so that Aaron died there, and then Moses went up from the plains of Moab to Mount Nebo, to the top of Pisgah, looking into Jericho, and the Lord showed him all of the land promised to His people, but He said to him: 'Thou

shalt not go over thither.' And there Moses died, and no one knew his grave. And he left Joshua to be chief in his place. You, Lázaro, must be my Joshua, and if you can make the sun stand still, make it stop, and never mind progress. Like Moses, I have seen the face of God—our supreme dream—face to face, and as you already know, and as the Scriptures say, he who sees God's face, he who sees the eyes of the dream, the eyes with which He looks at us, will die inexorably and forever. And therefore, do not let our people, so long as they live, look into the face of God. Once dead, it will no longer matter, for then they will see nothing. . . ."

"Father, Father, Father," I cried again.

And he said:

"Angela, you must pray always, so that all sinners may go on dreaming, until they die, of the resurrection of the flesh and life everlasting. . . ."

I was expecting "and who knows it might be . . ." but instead, Don Manuel had another choking fit.

"And now," he finally went on, "and now, at the hour of my death, it is high time to have me taken, in this very chair, to the church, so that I may take leave there of my people, who are waiting for me."

He was carried to the church and taken, in his armchair, into the chancel, to the foot of the altar. In his hand he held a crucifix. My brother and I stood close to him, but the fool Blasillo wanted to stand even closer. He wanted to grasp Don Manuel by the hand, so that he could kiss it. When some of the people nearby tried to stop him, Don Manuel rebuked them and said:

"Let him come closer. . . . Come, Blasillo, give me your hand."

The fool cried for joy. And then Don Manuel spoke:

"I shall say very few words, my children; I scarcely have strength except to die. And I have nothing new to tell you either. I have already said everything I have to say. Live together in peace and happiness, in the hope that we will all see each other again some day, in that other Valverde de Lucerna up there among the stars of the night, the stars which the lake reflects over the image of the reflected mountain. And pray, pray to the Most Blessed Virgin, and to our Lord. Be good . . . that is enough. Forgive me whatever wrong I may have done you inadvertently or unknowingly. After I give you my blessing, let us pray together, let us say the Paternoster, the Ave Maria, the Salve, and the Creed."

Then he gave his blessing to the whole village, with the crucifix held in his hand, while the women and children cried and even some of the men wept softly. Almost at once the prayers were begun. Don Manuel listened to them in silence, his hand in the hand of Blasillo the fool, who was falling asleep to the sound of the praying. First the Paternoster, with its "Thy will be done on earth as it is in heaven," then the Ave Maria, with its "Pray for us sinners, now and at the hour of our death"; followed by the Salve, with its "mourning and weeping in this vale of tears"; and finally, the Creed. On reaching "The resurrection of the flesh and life everlasting" the people sensed that their saint had yielded up his soul to God. It was not necessary to close his eyes even, for he died with them closed. When we tried to wake up Blasillo, we found that he, too, had fallen asleep in the Lord forever. So that later there were two bodies to be buried.

The whole village immediately went to the saint's house to carry away holy relics, to divide up pieces of his garments among themselves, to carry off whatever they could find as a memento of the blessed martyr. My brother kept his breviary, between the pages of which he discovered a carnation, dried as in a herbarium and mounted on a piece of paper, and upon the paper a cross and a certain date.

No one in the village seemed willing to believe that Don Manuel was dead; everyone expected to see him—perhaps some of them did—taking his daily walk along the shore of the lake, his figure mirrored in the water, or silhouetted against the background of the mountain. They continued to hear his voice, and they all visited his grave, around which a veritable cult grew up; old women "possessed by devils" came to touch the walnut cross, made with his own hands from the tree which had given the six planks of his coffin. And the ones least willing to believe in his death were my brother and I.

Lázaro carried on the tradition of the saint, and he began to compile a record of the priest's work. Some of the conversations in this account of mine were made possible by his notes.

"It was he," said my brother, "Who made me into a new man. I was a true Lazarus whom he raised from the dead. He gave me faith."

"Faith? . . ." I interrupted.

"Yes, faith, faith in life itself, faith in life's consolations. It was he who cured me of my delusion of 'progress,' of my belief in its political implications. For there are, Angela, two types of dangerous and harmful men: those who, convinced of life beyond the grave, of the resurrection of the flesh, torment other people—like the inquisitors they are—so that they will despise this life as a transitory thing and work for the other life; and then, there are those who, believing only in this life . . ."

"Like you, perhaps . . ."

"Yes, and like Don Manuel. Believing only in this world, this second group looks forward to some vague future society and exerts every effort to prevent the populace from finding consolation in the belief in another world. . . ."

"And so . . ."

"The people should be allowed to live with their illusion."

The poor priest who came to replace Don Manuel found himself overwhelmed in Valverde de Lucerna by the memory of the saint, and he put himself in the hands of my brother and myself for guidance. He wanted only to follow in the footsteps of the saint. And my brother told him: "Very little theology, Father, very little theology. Religion, religion, religion." Listening to him, I smiled to myself, wondering if this were not a kind of theology, too.

And at this time I began to fear for my poor brother. From the time of Don Manuel's death it could scarcely be said that he lived. He went to the priest's tomb daily; he stood gazing into the lake for hours on end. He was filled with nostalgia for deep, abiding peace.

"Don't stare into the lake so much," I begged him.

"Don't worry. It's not this lake which draws me, nor the mountain. Only, I cannot live without his help."

"And the joy of living, Lázaro, what about the joy of living?"

"That's for others. Not for those of us who have seen God's face, those of us on whom the Dream of Life has gazed with His eyes."

"What; are you preparing to go and see Don Manuel?"

"No, Sister, no. Here at home now, between the two of us, the whole truth—bitter as it may be, bitter as the sea into which the sweet waters of our lake flow—the whole truth for you, who are so set against it. . . ."

"No, no, Lázaro. You are wrong. Your truth is not the truth."

"It's my truth."

"Yours, perhaps, but surely not . . ."

"His, too."

"No, Lázaro. Not now, it isn't. Now, he must believe otherwise; now he must believe . . ."

"Listen, Angela, once Don Manuel told me that there are truths which, though one reveals them to oneself, must be kept from others; and I told him that telling me was the same as telling himself. And then he said, he confessed to me, that he thought that more than one of the great saints, perhaps the very greatest himself, had died without believing in the other life."

"It's not possible!"

"All too possible! And now, Sister, you must be careful that here, among the people, no one even suspects our secret. . . ."

"Suspect it!" I cried out in amazement. "Why, even if I were to try, in a fit of madness, to explain it to them, they wouldn't understand it. The people do not understand your words, they have only understood your actions. To try and explain all this to them would be like reading some pages from Saint Thomas Aquinas to eight-year-old children, in Latin!"

"All the better. In any case when I am gone, pray for me and for him and for all of us."

At length, his own hour came. A sickness which had been eating away at his robust constitution seemed to flare up with the death of Don Manuel.

"I don't so much mind dying," he said to me in his last days, "as the fact that with me another piece of Don Manuel dies, too. The remainder of him must live on with you. Until, one day, even we dead will die forever."

When he lay in the throes of death, the people, as is customary in our villages, came to bid him farewell and they commended his soul to the care of Don Manuel—Saint Manuel the Good, Martyr. My brother said nothing to them; he had no more to say. He had already said everything there was to say. He had become a link between the two Valverdes de Lucerna—the one at the bottom of the lake and the one reflected on its surface. He was already one more of us who had died of life, and, in his way, one more of our saints.

I was disconsolate, more than disconsolate; but I was, at least, among my own people, in my own village. Now, having lost my Saint Manuel, the father of my soul, and my own Lázaro, my more than flesh and blood brother, my spiritual brother, it is now that I realize that I have aged. But have I really lost them then? Have I grown old? Is my death approaching?

Life must go on! And he taught me to live, he taught us to live, to feel life, to feel the meaning of life, to merge with the soul of the mountain, with the soul of the lake, with the soul of the village, to lose ourselves in them so as to remain in them forever. He taught me by his life to lose myself in the life of the people of my village, and I no longer felt the passing of the hours, and the days, and the years, any more than I felt the passage of the water in the lake. It began to seem that my life would always be like this. I no longer felt myself growing old. I no longer lived in myself, but in my people, and my people lived in me. I tried to speak as they spoke, as they spoke without trying. I went into the street—it was the one highway—and, since I knew everyone, I lived in them and forgot myself (while, on the other hand, in Madrid, where I went once with my brother, I had felt a terrible loneliness, since I knew no one, and had been tortured by the sight of so many unknown people).

Now, as I write this memoir, this confession of my experience with saintliness, with a saint, I am of the opinion that Don Manuel the Good, my Don

Manuel, and my brother, too, died, believing they did not believe, but that, without believing in their belief, they actually believed, in active, resigned desolation.

But why, I have asked myself repeatedly, did not Don Manuel attempt to convert my brother through deception, pretending to be a believer himself without being one? And I have finally come to the conclusion that Don Manuel realized he would not be able to delude him, that with him a fraud would not do, that only through the truth, with his truth, would he be able to convert him; that he knew he would accomplish nothing if he attempted to enact the comedy—the tragedy, rather—which he played out for the benefit of the people. And so, he won him over to his pious fraud; he won him over to the cause of life with the truth of death. And thus did he win me, and I never permitted anyone to see through his divine, his most saintly, game. For I believed then, and I believe now, that God—as part of I know not what sacred and inscrutable purpose—caused them to believe they were unbelievers. And that at the moment of their passing, perhaps, the blindfold was removed.

And I, do I believe?

As I write this—here in my mother's old house, and I past my fiftieth year and with my memories growing as dim and faded as my hair—outside it is snowing, snowing upon the lake, snowing upon the mountain, upon the memory of my father, the stranger, upon the memory of my mother, my brother Lázaro, my people, upon the memory of my Saint Manuel, and even on the memory of the poor fool Blasillo, my Saint Blasillo—and may he help me in heaven! The snow effaces corners and blots out shadows, for even in the night it shines and illuminates. Truly, I do not know what is true and what is false, nor what I saw and what I merely dreamt—or rather, what I dreamt and what I merely saw—nor what I really knew or what I merely believed to be true. Neither do I know whether or not I am transferring to this paper, white as the snow outside, my awareness, for it to remain in writing, leaving me without it. But why cling to it any longer?

Do I really understand any of it? Do I really believe in any of it? What I am writing about here, did it actually take place, and did it take place in just the way I am telling it? Can such things really happen? Can all this be more than a dream dreamed within another dream? Can it be that I, Angela Carballino, a woman in her fifties, am the only one in this village to be assailed by these far-fetched thoughts, thoughts unknown to everyone else? And the others, those around me, do they believe? At least they go on living. And now they believe in Saint Manuel the Good, Martyr, who, with no hope of immortality for himself, preserved that hope in them.

It appears that our most illustrious bishop, who set in motion the process of beatifying our saint from Valverde de Lucerna, is intent on writing an account of Don Manuel's life, something which would serve as a guide for the perfect parish priest, and with this end in mind he is gathering information of every sort. He has repeatedly solicited information from me; he has come to see me more than once; and I have supplied him with all sorts of facts and details. But I have never revealed the tragic secret of Don Manuel and my brother. And it is curious that he has never suspected anything. I trust that what I have set down here will never come to his knowledge. For, all temporal authorities are to be feared; I distrust all authorities on this earth even when they are Church authorities.

And here I end this memoir. Let its fate be what it will. . . .

How, you may ask, did this document, this memoir of Angela Carballino, fall into my hands? That, dear reader, is something I must keep secret. I have transcribed it for you just as it was written, with only a few, a very few editorial emendations. Does it remind you of other things I have written? This fact does not gainsay its objectivity nor its reality. Moreover, for all I know, perhaps I created real, actual beings, independent of me, beyond my control, characters with immortal souls. For all I know, Augusto Pérez in my novel *Mist* was right when he claimed to be more real, more objective than I am, I who thought I had invented him. As for the reality of this Saint Manuel the Good, Martyr—as he is revealed to me by his disciple and spiritual daughter, Angela Carballino—it has not occurred to me to doubt his reality. I believe in it more than the saint himself did. I believe in it more than I do in my own reality.

And now, before I bring this epilogue to a close, I wish to remind you, patient reader, of the ninth verse of the Epistle of the forgotten Apostle, Saint Jude—what power in a name!—where we are told how my heavenly patron, Saint Michael Archangel (Michael means "Who such as God?" and archangel means arch-messenger) disputed with the Devil (Devil means accuser, prosecutor) over the body of Moses, and would not allow him to carry it off as a prize, to damnation. Instead, he told the Devil: "May the Lord rebuke thee." And may he who wishes to understand, understand!

I should like also, since Angela Carballino introduced her own feelings into the story—I don't know how it could have been otherwise—to comment on her statement to the effect that if Don Manuel and his disciple Lázaro had confessed their convictions to the people, they, the people, would not have understood. Nor, I should like to add, would they have believed the two of them. They would have believed in their works and not in their words. And works

stand by themselves, and need no words to back them up. In a village like Valverde de Lucerna one makes one's confession by one's conduct.

And as for faith, the people scarcely know what it is, and care less.

I am well aware of the fact that no action takes place in this narrative, this *novelistic* narrative, if you will—the novel is, after all, the most intimate, the truest history, so that I scarcely understand why some people are outraged to have the Gospels called a novel, when such a designation actually sets it above some mere chronicle or other. In short, nothing happens. But I hope that this is because everything in it remains, remains forever like the lakes and the mountains and the blessed simple souls, who, beyond faith and despair, the blessed souls who, in the lakes and the mountains, outside history, took refuge in a divine novel.

Salamanca
November 1930

The Post-Enlightenment World

Sir John Polkinghorne

The practice of religion and a belief in God appear to have been almost universal phenomena, with the exception of the modern Western world. We live in a pluralist society of belief and unbelief. That exception is often attributed to the rise of science. Our enhanced understanding of the physical world is held to have undermined the belief of many in a spiritual reality. Thus baldly stated the proposition has the air of a logical *non sequitur.* Are not physical and spiritual matters concerned with different levels of meaning and thus no more in direct opposition than is the character of the page in front of you, discerned as composed of paper and ink, in conflict with the assertion that it is also the means by which its author is attempting to set his thoughts before you? The most comprehensive discussion of its chemical composition could not exclude consideration of its possible intellectual content. To see how science and theology have come to be thought of by many as being in some way in opposition requires an historical, rather than a logical, assessment.

Science first achieved a recognizably modern form in the seventeenth century. Those concerned in its early development were, almost to a man, people who took seriously the existence of a religious dimension to life. Many of the first Fellows of the Royal Society were of a puritan persuasion. Indeed it has been suggested that the Christian doctrine of creation, with its emphasis on the Creator's rationality (so that his world was intelligible) and freedom (so that its nature had a contingent character which could only be discovered by investigation, rather than by speculation) provided an essential matrix for the coming into being of the scientific enterprise. Of course, some of those early scientists had problems in their relations with the ecclesiastical authorities and with orthodox belief. We cannot feel that the Galileo affair reflects much credit on the Church, even if it was not quite the confrontation between a lonely hero, imbued with a simple desire for truth, and the forces of clerical obscurantism, that popular mythology depicts. Newton had his difficulties in accepting trinitarian belief, but neither he nor Galileo was a sceptic and Newton appears to have held the mistaken view that his writings on the book of Daniel were of equal importance to the *Principia.*

Yet in the seventeenth century we can also see the beginnings of what was to become thought of as the conflict between science and religion. Thomas Hobbes eagerly, if inexpertly, seized on the mechanical ideas then being developed to make the Democritean assertion that reality was nothing but a concourse of atoms in motion. That was a materialistic take-over bid, leaving no place for the mental, let alone the religious. Few were inclined to be so dismissive of the claims of mind to its own existence, but the manner in which those claims were defended itself contained the seeds of future difficulty.

Descartes proclaimed the duality of mind and matter. How the thinking substance of mind and the extended substance of matter were related was not so easy to say. Ultimately he had to invoke God as the guarantor of their connection. The Cartesian system, wittily characterized by Gilbert Ryle as the ghost in the machine, had grave problems. William Temple said that he considered that day on which Descartes conceived it ('shut up alone in a stove'—a heated room—as he tells us) was 'the most disastrous day in the history of Europe'. Such a judgement is the pardonable exaggeration of a philosophically inclined person, but there is no doubt that Cartesianism had a dangerous tendency. Its author's fondness for clear ideas drove him to a focal divorce between mind and matter as the only tolerable way of preserving the claims of the former to equal consideration with the latter. Yet if too sharp a separation is made, the tangible nature of matter is liable eventually to promote a feeling of the unreality of intangible mind. Moreover the Cartesian system is stiffly rationalistic. Clear ideas are excellent when we are able to conceive them but it may be that at certain times with certain problems it is better to be content with a creative confusion than to strive for an oversimplified solution. Clarity can be purchased at the expense of the complexity of the truth. Even today our ignorance of matters germane to the relationship of brain and mind is such that we can only proceed with modesty and caution.

It was in the Enlightenment of the eighteenth century that the chill of mechanistic ideas communicated itself widely in a form less crude than that of Hobbes, and so more persuasive. The remarkable success of Newton's ideas in explaining the behaviour of physical systems, both terrestrial and celestial, encouraged reliance on a discourse of reason whose paradigm was seen in the power of mathematics. That there might be aspects of reality, intuitively discerned, whose nature was fittingly expressed in the cloudier language of symbol was not taken seriously. The thinkers of the Enlightenment sought by cold clear reason to comprehend an objective world of determinate order. They saw themselves as self-sufficient and were confident of their powers and of human perfectibility. Even theology was affected. When it did not lapse into a detached deistic belief in a God who had set the world a-spinning but cared little for it thereafter, it adopted a coolly rational tone, placing great reliance on natural theology's supposed demonstrations from the intricate design of the world. In line with the spirit of the age, God had become the divine Mechanic. There was considerable suspicion of religious experience less ordered and decorous than that provided by attendance at public worship. The principal role of religion was thought to be the encouragement of morality. In England in the eighteenth century one of the great theological figures was Bishop Joseph Butler, author of *The Analogy of Religion*. He warned John Wesley about the dangers of enthusiasm, saying: 'Sir, pretending to extraordinary revelations and gifts of the Holy Ghost is a horrid thing, a very horrid thing.' Indeed it is, if it is a matter of pretence, as Wesley agreed. But it is always possible that what is involved is, in fact, a valid experience which goes beyond the staid limits of conventional expectation.

Wesley and the other great preachers of the Evangelical Revival represent religion's protest against the frigid rationalism of the Enlightenment. Their preaching of human sinfulness may have been unhealthily guilt-ridden but it took a more realistic view of the flawed condition of mankind than that provided by optimistic ideas of human perfectibility. Other protests were also made against prevailing rationalism. The poets and artists of the Romantic movement intuitively rejected the desiccated analytic method of the Enlightenment which, in Wordsworth's phrase, murdered to dissect. William Blake proclaimed with mystic intensity the pre-eminence of the symbolic over the scientific: ' "What," it will be questioned, "when the sun rises, do you not see a round disc of fire somewhat like a guinea?" O no, no, I see an innumerable company of the heavenly host crying, "Holy, Holy, Holy is the Lord God Almighty." ' Blake's vision is powerful and disturbing but too idiosyncratic to have been widely influential.

In fact, as the nineteenth century progressed, the light of reason seemed to shine with ever greater clarity on a comprehensible and determinate world. Clerk Maxwell brought an order into the phenomena of electromagnetism which was fit to stand beside Newton's achievements in mechanics. The principle of physics seemed complete. All that was left was their application to problem solving. Above all, Darwin showed how competitive selection could sift favourable mutations from random variations, creating thereby the appearance of design without need for the intervention of a Designer. The one apparently convincing demonstration of the existence of God, on which the eighteenth-century theologians had placed such great reliance, was found to be fatally flawed. Paley had compared the likelihood of the intricate structure of the world being the result of chance to the assertion that a watch had been assembled by random causes. However it now seemed that after all one could find a watch without a watchmaker's having had to put it there.

None of this logically denied the validity of religious experience or the existence of God. Yet it marginalized such claims in the minds of men. Like Laplace, whose demonstration of the inherent stability of the solar system made unnecessary Newton's belief in a divine corrective occasionally applied to stop the planets wobbling apart, people came to feel that they had no need of the hypothesis of God. The Enlightenment attitude had done its acid work and many people's faith dissolved away.

By a curious irony, as the nineteenth century came to an end, the method and view of the Enlightenment were themselves beginning to dissolve in their turn. We now live in a post-Enlightenment age. The essential character of Enlightenment thinking was to allow the clear light of reason to play upon an objective and determinant world. Scarcely a feature of that description now survives intact.

The insights of depth psychology have modified our understanding of the operation of human reason. We are more than rational egos. The exact nature of the polarities within the psyche is a matter of dispute between Freud and Jung and their successors. Yet it is clear that our conscious minds are counterbalanced by an unconscious component, at once creative, chaotic and teeming with symbol. These deep levels within ourselves need to be spoken to, and they themselves speak to and influence the ego of which we are aware. There is an element of Blake within all of us.

At the same time that the human psyche has revealed its shadowy and elusive depths, the physical world has denied determinate objectivity at its constituent roots. Heisenberg tells us concerning electrons and other elementary particles that if we know what they are doing we do not know where they are, and if we know where they are we do not know what they are doing. His uncertainty principle proclaims the unpicturability of the quantum world. Naive objectivity is a status inappropriate for its inhabitants. Moreover the fitfulness inherent in quantum theory breaks the bonds of strict determinism. In general we can only give relative probabilities for differing possible outcomes of an experimental observation and no cause is to be assigned for obtaining a particular result on a specific occasion. The world known to the twentieth century is a good deal curiouser and more shadowy than the eighteenth and nineteenth centuries could have conceived.

That in itself is no great cause for religious rejoicing. The ancient Hebrews knew well the dangers of the waters of chaos. Our century has seen a recurrent cult of the Absurd which is destructive of true understanding. To acknowledge the limits of rationality, objectivity and determinism is not to relinquish a belief in reason, a respect for reality or a search for order. It may however lead to greater openness to the variety of the world and our experience of it, an acceptance that beside the insights of science, expressible in the quantitative language of mathematics, there are the equally necessary insights of religion, expressible in the qualitative language of symbol.

Hidden History

Patrick Smith

Look closely and you will see what an enormous variety of human types are represented in the huge crowd.

—Shimei Futabatei, *Drifting Clouds*, 1889

In Kanazawa, a city on the Sea of Japan noted for its old samurai quarter, there is a family that traces its ancestors back four centuries. Their name is Meboso, and they have made sewing needles and fishhooks for nineteen generations.

The Meboso's are as proud of their uncommon name as they are of their craft, for the two cannot be separated. "Meboso" comes from *meboso-bari,* narrow-eyed needle. In the sixteenth century their skill was such that the local daimyo, the feudal lord, let them take a surname and carry swords. "An unusual honor," Tadayoshi Meboso said when he explained this to me. "Almost no one of our status could have a name or own a sword." Today the Mebosos sell fly-fishing gear, along with boxes of tailor's needles, from the same shop they have run since 1575. It is on Meboso-dori—Meboso Avenue.

It was hardly unusual for people under feudal rule to have only a given name and to be identified according to their village or some other obvious attribute. But where else among the advanced countries is this point of a family name still important, still dwelt upon in casual conversation?

The feudal past is near in Japan. Until late in the last century only daimyo and samurai, and an exceptional few like the Meboso's, had family names. Everyone else was nameless. Allowing everyone a surname was among the early reforms of the Meiji era, Japan's great period of modernization, which began in 1868. It is because names were so recently granted that many still correspond to villages or rural features. Kurokawa: Blackriver; Ishibashi: Stonebridge.

What is to be learned from the simple historical fact that the great-grandparents of many Japanese alive today had no names? Seeing Japan as a group society, we conclude that there was no notion of individuality among the Japanese until a few generations before our own. No individuality, and for the vast majority no history—just as the serfs of feudal Europe lived out lives as unrecorded as the lives of farm animals.

Such reasoning is logical enough. It is a commonplace that the Japanese are given to groups. No matter what version of Japan one subscribes to, it is likely to include the assumption that the individual's worth and power are secondary to the worth of the collective, whether it is a village, a baseball team, or a corporation. History offers abundant evidence to support this idea. The fact that the Japanese were nameless until little more than a century ago is but one of numerous examples.

But this is a misreading. For the group is a kind of fiction in Japan. It is within the group that the Japanese put on their masks. To assume a mask is to assume a role—a public, designated role in the group. The masks of the Japanese are also masks of sameness. By wearing them, the Japanese signify to themselves that there are no differences among them, and that having no differences is part of what it means to be Japanese.

One of the first Westerners to live in Japan, a Jesuit called João Rodrigues, seems to have understood the Japanese mask uncannily well. Rodrigues arrived in 1576, around the time the Mebosos got their name, and remained more than thirty years. He was fluent in the language and eventually translated for the shogun. The Japanese have three hearts, Rodrigues surmised: "a false one in their mouths for all the world to see, another within their breasts only for their friends, and the third in the depths of their hearts, reserved for themselves alone and never manifested to anyone."

To wear a mask among others: Is there a better measure of how thoroughly the individual is effaced, of how well the Japanese personality learned to peek out through the reed screen of a purposely blank expression that hides the true face from public view? These habits of mind and physiology have been so completely internalized that Japanese even today have difficulty discussing their own ways of thinking or feeling. But a nation of effaced personalities is different from one in which individual personalities—somehow, miraculously—do not exist.

Neither individuality nor a sense of history is missing from the assumptions by which ordinary Japanese live. Nor were they absent in the past. These basic aspects of human life have simply been submerged. So there is a more accurate conclusion to draw from the nameless majority that lived and died in Japan until a century ago. Then as now, it was not individuality that was missing so much as public individuality, the open manifestation of the self, the self unmasked within the group. In the same way, the Japanese did not live without their own history—no more, at least, than anyone else in a feudal society. Their history was merely hidden by the society that preferred them to remain nameless.

There is a vast chasm between the simplicity arriving foreigners often find in Japan and the furtive, unrevealed complexity that lies within. In this space the Japanese still make their hidden history—the record of their endeavor to achieve public, unmasked individuality.

The term for "group" is *nakama*. The first character, *naka*, means "inside," and the second, *ma*, refers to an enclosure in either space or time—a room, a field, an interval, a long duration. The importance not only of belonging but of being hidden within can be judged from the first lines of poetry Japan ever produced:

> Eight clouds arise.
>
> The eightfold fence of Izumo
>
> Makes an eightfold fence
>
> For the spouses to retire within.
>
> Oh! that eightfold fence.

These lines are about the whole of Japan. There were eight clouds and eight fences because in the old chronicles Japan consisted of eight islands. One still finds a suggestion of the much-treasured fence in Izumo, a coastal city in southwestern Japan where an ancient god is said to have descended from heaven. The Izumo shrine, Shinto's oldest, is still enclosed by a fence beyond which ordinary mortals may not pass. Outside of it there are several torii, the classic Shinto gates, which reveal perfectly the essential abstraction of the belonging ritual. No fence ever flanks a torii. It is freestanding but nonetheless alters the space around it. The outermost torii

at Izumo is most of a mile from the shrine along a busy commercial street. Candy stores, trinket shops, and garages stretch out on either side, yet the gate marks the difference between outer and inner space, the profane and sacred.

The duality of outside and inside, the enclosed and the exposed, is the first thing to confront the arriving visitor. The standard term for oneself is "gaijin," outside person. It is one's first notice that life in Japan will consist of a series of acceptances and rejections. Nothing is excepted. What is sumo, the popular wrestling tradition held to extend back to 23 B.C., if not a ritual celebration of the distinction made between the included and excluded? The two wrestlers purify the circle where they stand by dusting it with salt. They square off, squat, and stare. There is almost nothing to see, for the match usually lasts no more than a minute or two, and often mere seconds. What matters is the consequence. The sumo contest produces not so much a winner and a loser as a change in status: The vanquished is the man pushed out of the circle.

In feudal Japan the matter of belonging came down to one's *ie*, or household. The *ie* was more than a family in that those not related by blood could be adopted into it. Villages were groups of *ie*; commercial enterprises were organized as *ie*. The *ie* remained important until 1945, a building block of imperial Japan. In the *ie* one learned to suppress the self. And all of Japan was an *ie*, the emperor being the head of the Japanese household. The prewar ideologues claimed that Japan was unique in the world because it was a "family-state." In modern terms, Japan was corporatist—a society in which individual agency is denied and the individual is instead "incorporated" into one or another special interest. The ground for public discourse is then carved up among these various interests.

Today the Japanese live in a universe of intersecting, constantly shifting circles—"households" made of families, schools, graduating classes, universities, sports clubs, sects, social cliques, nightclub regulars, companies. The list is infinite, the question of belonging continuous. Alone, two people from different sections of the same organization are outsiders to each other; joined by a third from another organization, they become insiders, and the third is the outsider. Such variations occur over and over in the course of daily life and are signified in commonplace objects: not just fences and gates, but walls, bridges, banks of desks, paper screens.

Japanese is rich in its descriptions of this essential distinction. There are words denoting what is outside and inside, public and private, the spoken and authentic versions of the truth. One pair of these terms will be useful. *Omote* and *ura* mean the explicit and the implicit, the outer and the inner, the front and the back, or, more broadly, the revealed and the hidden. In old Japanese they meant "face" and "mind." Today one speaks of *omote-dori* and *ura-dori*, main streets and back lanes; *omote-ji* is kimono cloth, *ura-ji* is kimono lining. *Futo no omote* is the front of an envelope; *ura-niwa* is a back garden. These terms have numerous dimensions and, like others, can be revealing. *Urameshii* means to feel bitter, *urayamu* to feel envious, and *urami* is a grudge. None of these is an acceptable thing to reveal in Japan, where the group's primary purpose is to preserve harmony and the appearance of sameness. So feelings of envy and bitterness are by definition *ura*, hidden.

Common to the various terms for inside and outside are the values of belonging versus exclusion, revelation versus concealment. What is public has always been the higher social value in Japan. And what is public is associated with order and the group, while what is private is individual and therefore secretive, selfish, and corrupting. One may belong to a group, and that group to a larger group, but the price of belonging is the subjugation of the individual to the group, the private to the public, the authentic to the represented.

João Rodrigues, the Jesuit who found three hearts in the Japanese, was smarter than we are in one respect. Our images of the Japanese encourage us to assume that there simply is no individuality among them—that in some other than human way they are content to live, like penguins or lemmings, with nothing to distinguish one from another. Rodrigues understood that the individual was only obscured. But the Jesuit was wrong in another way. There is nothing "false" about the faces the Japanese present to the world, not so far as they are concerned, and nothing about unshared thoughts and feelings that make them truer or more valuable. This is a mistake only a Westerner could make, for we, like Father Rodrigues, do not share Japan's notion of the group as the superior value.

It is also true that the Japanese reserve a special place for what is concealed. They are dedicated diarists for the simple reason that so much of life must be hidden. One of Japan's aesthetic traditions, famously displayed in a temple garden in Kyoto, is called *mie gakure*, the seen and unseen. In the garden, fifteen stones protrude from a sea of combed gravel.

But from no vantage point are all of the stones visible; wherever you stand, one is always hidden. In a friend's office I once saw an ink drawing of two peasants pulling a harness. The harness trailed off at the edge of the picture; nothing else was depicted. When I mentioned the drawing my friend smiled. "Yes," he said. "Can you see the cart?"

Mie gakure, applied to people, also means "to appear and disappear," or "to hide oneself." And there is nothing the Japanese are more accustomed to hiding than themselves, their inner beings. True heart, called *kokoro*, and *ninjo*, human feelings, are rarely manifest but all the more precious for it. Emotions are unsullied and innocent, which is why, when the Japanese expose them, they appear childishly sentimental—as, for example, when they are drunk, or singing in a karaoke bar. Emotions are part of the "*ura* of the *ura*," the inside of the inside, and it is because they are withheld that each Japanese lives with a certain sense of crisis in his relations with the outer world.

"What is concealed is the flower," wrote Ze-ami, the fourteenth-century Noh master. "What is not concealed cannot be the flower." The thought survives in many contexts and is not irrelevant in this one. It is cited by the psychiatrist Takeo Doi in his explorations of the Japanese personality. Doi was a deeply traditional man. He believed that to live amid elaborate concealments was a normal, healthy thing. And he saw no tension between the security of belonging, which is undeniable among the Japanese, and the individual desire to break free of the group—which, though traditionally unacknowledged, is also undeniable. "The ideal condition of the mind, the condition from which mental health derives," Doi wrote in 1985, "is one in which we can feel comfortable having secrets."

The confinements in which the Japanese live are enveloping and complete, affording only the dimmest view of a life without them. Something as simple as asking directions in Japan can often reveal the peculiar isolation the habit of concealment produces at the core of Japanese life. It is perfectly ordinary to find a person willing to oblige. But it is also common to be completely ignored, as if you had not spoken, as if you were not standing there—as if you were a ghost. This is not so much impolite behavior as it is a recognition that there is (in the Jesuit's terms) no heart between you: With neither formal relations nor friendship there is only strangeness, a kind of nonbeing. Even if the passerby pauses to help, you may discover he knows nothing of a street or building only a hundred yards away, for it is not part of the tiny universe in which he lives.

Foreigners who reside in Japan are part of the system by virtue of their exclusion. Rarely does the "outside person" enter the intricate, burdensome web of duties and obligations that covers all interaction among the Japanese and binds each to the group. According to custom a resident gaijin, like a Japanese, will be known as Fuji Film's Wilson or Smith of the *International Herald Tribune*. One is considered to be part of a group, as every Japanese is. But the foreigner soon recognizes that just as Japan is a nation of insiders, it is equally one of "others."

There never seem to be enough groups to create new "others," new outsiders. It is as if people will resort to any ruse to obscure the matter of public individuality. Pseudoscience is popular in this regard. A European executive once sat with his Japanese manager to meet job applicants. After the routine questions, the manager ended each interview with, "And what is your blood type?" All but one candidate replied matter-of-factly and without surprise. (The exception laughed and did not know.) Later the gaijin asked about the strange inquiry. It is best, the manager explained, not to mix blood types in the same work space. The idea has many adherents; newspapers sometimes assess new governments according to whether cabinet members are A, B, O, or some other blood type.

When I arrived in Tokyo and began to staff my newspaper's bureau, I found many young Japanese intrigued by the prospect of joining a gaijin company—an act that carried a whiff of individual risk and nonconformity, even of defiance. The Japanese have made a womb of their society. But if the temptation to exit it was strong, most found their fears still stronger. The womb of life is confining, but it is also secure, and so most Japanese remain, as it were, unborn. By the time I met Kay Itoi, who worked with me at the *Herald Tribune* for the duration of my tour in Japan, I understood that I was looking for someone with a certain courage and restlessness, even impatience.

It is in restlessness and impatience and the temptation of risk that we find clues to the individual's struggle with the enveloping web. This is nothing new; it is a long thread in the history of the Japanese, and to describe the Japanese today is to note only the new prominence this thread has taken in the weave. It is a kind of eternal tension—between freedom and belonging, community and autonomy—and it is part of what I call hidden history because it, too, is concealed—submerged but never nonexistent.

• • •

After the Pacific war an interesting debate took place among the Japanese. It concerned something called *shutai-sei*. The term literally means "subjecthood," but it is translated variously as "subjectivity," "selfhood," "authenticity," or "autonomy." It refers to the perceiving, judging, deciding individual. To achieve *shutai-sei* was to leave behind all the old conventions: the enveloping mutual duties, the acceptance of inclusion and exclusion, the suppression of individuality for the sake of the displayed consensus. *Shutai-sei* meant to establish an autonomous identity. The term also had strong connotations. It implied an energetic, assertive individuality—what I have called public individuality. The autonomous person was capable not only of making moral commitments but of acting openly upon them.

It is remarkable to realize how little the Japanese of the late 1940s knew of such matters. Japan had recently deployed millions of soldiers, ships, planes, and weapons across vast parts of the Pacific. But, midway in our century, the Japanese had no socially accepted notion of something as ordinary elsewhere, as taken-for-granted, as individuality. Except in their private hearts, as the old Jesuit would have put it, or in open opposition to accepted norms, they could cultivate no sense of self. Their thoughts and values were the thoughts and values imposed by the community. We ordinarily assume that group identity is something the Japanese cling to so as to keep foreigners out. But we must consider the opposite proposition: Was the group not also made to keep the Japanese people in—and to keep them from becoming individuals?

Those who debated the meaning of *shutai-sei* believed that cultivating the autonomous self was postwar Japan's fundamental task, more essential than any other. It was the failure of the Japanese to make subjective judgments, they said, that led them to acquiesce when the wartime dictatorship draped a blanket of ideology over them and pushed the nation into tragedy. The core of the postwar project, therefore, was psychological. As the best-known exponent of autonomy put it, "An internal reform of the psychological structure of Japanese society must occur."

These words belong to a man named Masao Maruyama. Maruyama, who passed away in 1996 at the age of eighty-two, was without question the most influential thinker Japan has produced in our century. In the great debate over *shutai-sei* he led a camp called the "modernists," who posited two kinds of autonomy. One was individual: the self as a private, independent being. The other was social:

the free individual who also understood his place within the larger whole. These two ideas of autonomy were advanced in opposition to the old notion of community, in which people had no identity and no free choices. The object of all this theorizing was nothing more nor less than democracy—that is to say, corporatism's opposite. The modernists called for the creation among the Japanese of "a new, democratic human type." Their views are easily boiled down: Democracy does not work without individual liberty, and individual liberty is impossible to sustain without a democratic context.

The debate over *shutai-sei* collapsed in the late 1940s. The new democratic human type never appeared, a casualty of the reverse course. Under the restored prewar elite the Japanese were unable to escape from the old, confining notions of community. That is why Japan took on the machinery of democracy after the war but has had no authentic democracy. In the Cold War climate many of those who urged the notion of autonomy upon the Japanese, including Maruyama, were dismissed as dangerous leftists. And here we arrive at one of the fundamental ironies in the way we look upon the modern Japanese. There was indeed an active left in Japan after the war—a left of many hues. But so what? Examining the postwar situation today, the notion of a Soviet-style Japan looks a bit ridiculous. Much of what we took to be the subversive left stood not for collectivism but an escape from collectivism, not the suppression of private endeavor but the embrace of it. They had argued for the very thing Westerners profess to believe in most profoundly: the primacy of the individual.

The *shutai-sei* episode has many echoes in the past. So we must ask, Why has the group had such a tenacious hold on the Japanese? Where in history did so deep-seated a notion of community come from?

The group in Japan is as ancient as its people. Rice cultivation required communities based on mutual dependence. Geography isolated the Japanese: one community from another by the islands' mountainous landscapes, and the islands from the Asian mainland by the rough waters of the Japan Sea. There is nothing peculiar about the community ethos that resulted. Ancient Japan was a primitive society that had much in common with any other. Japan took its first unusual turn in the seventh century, under a scholarly prince regent named Shotoku. It was then the Japanese began to build the group society that would endure until our time.

Under Shotoku Japan began to borrow wholesale from China much of what we now think of as Japanese. Along with Buddhism, urban design, a central bureaucracy, and much else, Shotoku imported the Confucian classics. Through these Japan learned the revered virtues—benevolence, filial piety, sincerity, and so on—and the five relationships that define the human stations: ruler and ruled, father and son, elder brother and younger, husband and wife, friend and friend. We might consider Shotoku Japan's first great Orientalist—the first to imagine a "Japan" other than what it was. He brought order and hierarchy to people who had been notably informal in such matters. The Japanese court was typical: It, too, had been rather informal. Then it assumed elaborate ranks, all of them quintessentially Confucian—Greater Benevolence and Lesser Benevolence, Greater and Lesser Propriety, and on through the Chinese sage's catalogue of righteousness.

The feudal period began at the end of the twelfth century, when provincial warriors, the earliest samurai, forced the emperor into obscurity and built a military dictatorship that lasted seven centuries under a succession of generals—the shoguns. We are familiar with many of the samurai's features: his discipline and austerity, his rigorously simple aesthetic, his adherence to an honor code similar in outline to the chivalry of medieval Europe. The code of the samurai was elaborately Confucian, with a complex system of mutual duties: a system of give-and-take interdependence meant to keep samurai—professional killers, martial arts cultists—from destroying one another. Over time the shogun told the samurai what to wear, how to settle a dispute, how to prepare meals, what kind of pottery to have around the house, how much to spend on a gift. Rules were everything. Rank and "house," signified in the precise colors, fabrics, and patterns of one's clothing, were also everything.

For the nameless majority the samurai were the stuff of heroic legend, the doers of high deeds. But they were not really individuals. When they internalized the code they built an edifice within. Each act, no matter how perilous or against the odds, was at once a mark of distinction and an affirmation of conformity to the code. It was a display of will—which was also cultivated according to the code. There is, for instance, the matter of loyalty. The great sage was clear about the virtues. Loyalty was not first among them—benevolence was. And loyalty meant allegiance according to one's conscience. But the samurai made loyalty paramount and made no allowance for the inner voice. In the Japanese conception, loyalty and filial piety together required obedience, even at the sacrifice of reason or conscience. It is no wonder that the Buddhism of the samurai was Zen, a native-hatched sect. Zen taught emptiness of mind: the suppression of self by an exertion of will so complete as to enable action without conscious thought.

The samurai can be viewed as the first Japanese whose individuality was essentially private. How else to describe people who found purity in the utmost detachment from everything they did that was visible to others? Satori, Zen enlightenment, was a matter of private salvation. Seppuko, ritual suicide, was an honorable way out of disgrace because it was an act of private individuality. In this we can wonder about the excessive care with which seppuku was carried out: the crosswise cut through the belly, then upward toward the navel—incisions that made death certain but damaged no vital organs. Was it a ritual revelation of the intact self within, or a final, public assertion that there was no self, that the self was obliterated so that honor could be posthumously restored?

It is not difficult to see in the samurai things we try to understand today: the concealment of personality, rigorous loyalty to the group—loyalty to a fault. But how were these habits of mind prolonged so far into our own time?

In 1542 three Portuguese sailors landed on an island off the coast of Kyushu. The lost mariners were the first Europeans to reach Japan. Francis Xavier, the Jesuit from Goa, arrived seven years later to plant the cross. Notably, there was little interest in how these first Westerners lived and thought, but much in the things they brought: clocks, musical instruments, medicines, maps. Muskets prompted Japan's first try at industrial copying: They were reproduced in great numbers.

As Christianity spread, successive shoguns feared it would unite the daimyo, or feudal lords, each with an army of his own, against them. The first ban on missionaries came in 1587. By 1639, a century after foreigners first stepped ashore, isolation edicts called *sakoku*, "closed country," were in effect: Gaijin were barred with the exception of a few Dutch merchants; "Dutch learning," open to a select few, became the sole source of outside knowledge. Anyone attempting to leave Japan would be put to death; no ship could be built to carry more than a thousand *koku*—which was a ban on oceangoing vessels.* *Sakoku* was the work of a family of shoguns named Tokugawa. The first of them, Ieyasu, took power in 1603 and moved the military government from Kyoto, the decadent imperial capital, to a swampy hamlet then called Edo and now Tokyo (Eastern Capital).

The Tokugawa ruled for two and a half centuries, until 1868. Theirs was the most extreme form of feudalism Japan had ever known. The Japanese lived like figurines in a bell jar—locked in hereditary status and the ancient, cyclical time of masters and cultivators. Progress was prohibited—the enemy of changelessness. The Tokugawa were the greatest Orientalists Japan has yet produced. Their notion of Japan was grotesque, utterly static. It became more imaginary as the Edo centuries wore on, so requiring ever greater bureaucratic will to enforce it.

Edo Japan was a society of distinctions—beneath which lay a profound conformity. It stands, I believe, among the purest examples of corporatism ever devised. Everyone was ranked according to caste: samurai, peasants, artisans, merchants. Each caste had its assigned role. Each was segregated by dress, means of transport, and countless other details. Only the samurai could bear swords—long ones in the countryside, short ones in town. Samurai were permitted no contact with peasants, the peasants none with townsmen. A townsman's kimono was to be this long. Peasants must rise at this hour, consume such and such a meal, avoid tea, plant bamboo this close to their huts, dig latrines that far away.

Japan as a caste society was nothing new. The last family of shoguns—there were fifteen Tokugawa rulers before the end—merely took the feudal rigidities to their limits. They were Confucian fundamentalists. The Tokugawa were obsessed with edicts, decrees, prohibitions, gruesome punishments—everything needed to maintain a climate of terror. Edo kept an immense network of enforcers—secret police, frontier guards, censors, undercover agents. Villages were organized into five-person groups: Each member was required to spy on the other four, each group on other groups. In spite of this (or because of it) there were roughly three thousand peasant uprisings during the Tokugawa centuries—one a month, on average, though they gained in frequency as time went on. There were another three thousand "disturbances" that never went as far as the house trashings and riots scholars count as uprisings.

Feudalism in this strangely illuminated twilight is an essential piece of Japan's past—not only because it lasted so long or because we can trace back to it so much of what the Japanese are today, but because the history of Edo has been the battleground in modern Japan, or a large part of it. Edo Japan gives us a classic example of the power of leaving things out. And what is always left out is the conflict and

---

*A koku equaled slightly more than five bushels.

tension that existed just below the surface—the history that was hidden.

Today we have a peculiar idea of the Edo era—a half-true distortion of this bizarre age. Our received image is of a dull but orderly time, well expressed in the standard term "the Tokugawa peace." In *Japan: Past and Present*, Edwin Reischauer gave a neat summary of the orthodoxy, as uncomplicated as one of the period's woodblock prints: "The prolonged, complete peace of the Tokugawa period brought to Japan years of unprecedented prosperity, and industrial production and trade grew rapidly." Based upon such imagery, we are invited to think of the Edo era as "early modern Japan"—never the derogatory "late Feudalism." This is an exceptional irony, for from the Edo era onward it has been a mark of Japan's leaders that they have, in one way or another, sought to defer the true arrival of modern society in Japan.

Edo's advances cannot be denied. Rudimentary manufacturing began; restless merchants laid the groundwork for modern trade, and a lively popular culture—Kabuki, pulpy literature—took root in the pleasure quarters of Edo, Osaka, and Kyoto. But there was no peace in Edo Japan. There was a sort of federalist settlement between the shoguns and the daimyo, but otherwise the era was marked by merciless exploitation, purposeful deprivation, paranoic police controls, coercion, more or less constant official violence—and more or less constant popular resistance to all of these things. In its terror and totality, its nightmarish bureaucracy and manipulation of knowledge, Edo Japan is usefully compared with the later Soviet Union. In its violent dream of Oriental agrarianism it suggests the Cambodia of the Khmer Rouge.

The lasting gift of the Tokugawa was to deliver the Japanese to the doorstep of the industrial age with the feudal edifice crumbling all around but still intact within each of them. Today there are the corporate samurai—as obsessed with "house" and hierarchy as the old warriors. The Japanese still puzzle over the precise value of gifts to be given for precisely which favors received, precisely the proper clothing for each occasion, the precise seating in a room according to rank, inclusion, and exclusion.

Many Japanese entertain a kind of ersatz nostalgia for the Edo era—ersatz because it is cartoonish, sanitized. Among the old sayings one still hears in the countryside, for instance, is "Three houses in front, one on either side." It is a simple admonition not to act before surveying all those around you. And it is a neat description of how the complex system of duties and obligations works. Those who still dwell in the old villages often advance this phrase as a measure of community spirit and the endurance of village values. Perhaps it is that, partly. But the saying requires its full context. Properly understood, it also suggests something of the individual's wariness toward all others, a wariness the Japanese learned long ago to carry within.

There is a remarkable description of the Edo era—remarkable because it remains so oddly apt today. It was written by Yukichi Fukuzawa, an educator in the era that followed, and it appeared in one of his best-known works, *Outline of Civilization*. Fukuzawa appears today on the face of the ten-thousand-yen note, stern but wistful, wearing a somber kimono but with a Western haircut. One senses he looks forward in that pose. But in *Outline*, published in 1873, he looked back to a people atomized but unrealized, intensely private but intensely unfree. The passage is a concise description of a society in which individuality lives only in the secrets of each of its members:

> They all depended on the government and did not concern themselves with national affairs. Among a million people there were a million different minds. Each person shut himself up in his own house and ignored the outside world as if it were a foreign country. They failed to consult one another even about the best way to clean their wells, let alone ways to repair roads. If they chanced to come upon a dog's excrement, they went around it. They were so preoccupied with trying to avoid getting involved in anything that they had no time to discuss things together. This long-ingrained habit became a custom and produced the present sad state of affairs.

Respect for and dependence upon authority, unswerving loyalty, austerity, and a rigorous work ethic—all are marks late feudalism has left upon the Japanese. We are invited to conclude that Japan is by tradition and culture a vertical society and that Japanese ethics are situational—based not on principle but on the ever-shifting net of relationships in which the Japanese live. The best-known explanation of these matters is *The Chrysanthemum and the Sword*, a book published in 1946 by the anthropologist Ruth Benedict. Benedict distinguished Japan as a shame culture as opposed to a guilt culture: "True shame cultures rely on external sanctions for good behavior, not, as true guilt cultures do, on an internalized conviction of sin."

These observations cannot be dismissed. But they obscure as much as they explain. The Japanese are shamed when they transgress, for they have disgraced their household. But are there really people in the world who never feel the pangs of guilt, who have no conscience? Loyalty can be a fine thing, but Japan's notion of loyalty, loyalty that admits of no questions, led it into a world war, after all. Hard work, by the same token, has historically been a matter of desperate necessity. As to respect for authority, it is better understood as obsequiousness bred of fear.

A clear picture of the past leads to a fundamental point about the Japanese, an understanding that changes everything. Once we recognize the conflict beneath the surface, we understand that group identity had more to do with coercion and power than with tradition and culture. Then we must rethink our conclusions about the attributes of the Japanese we are encouraged to admire. Are they so enviable as to be emulated? More admirable, by any measure, is the long, buried struggle against feudal terror and tyranny—the same struggle we admire in our own history. The prevailing psychology among the Japanese may indeed startle, as Lafcadio Hearn noted nearly a century ago. But there is nothing especially "Japanese" about what we call the Japanese character or personality, we must conclude. We can talk only about people subjected to certain conditions and their response to those conditions.

It was the primitive habit of confinement and exclusion, fixed during the Edo centuries, that the Japanese tried to overcome within themselves when they considered such questions as autonomy in the late 1940s. They found nothing wrong with a strong sense of community. Among the essential ideas advanced by Masao Maruyama's modernists, so far as I understand them, was that individuality is fully realized only in the context of community. But only when community is freely entered upon. So long subject to a coerced, unmodern kind of belonging, the Japanese found themselves, then as now, only half at home in the modern world. Alone among primitive societies, Japan is "advanced"; alone among advanced societies, Japan has remained primitive.

We know Japan today as a late developer. When, in the 1860s and 1870s, it sent emissaries abroad for the first time in two and a half centuries, the objects of Western industry—threshers, railroads, air compressors, iron bridges—left them shocked. So, it must be added, did everything they attributed to Western individualism: political debate, labor strife, each person running off in his own direction. The West, especially America, seemed to live in a state of barely controlled anarchy. Capitalism struck the Japanese as "warfare in peacetime," as an early diplomatic diarist put it. These first travelers across the Pacific were like experiments with time, people who were born into the modern world but who had seen nothing of it.

We also know Japan as an addicted borrower, first from China and, beginning in the late nineteenth century, from us. In this the Japanese were discriminating, choosing from each country only what they wanted. From France they learned of oil painting, from England of warships, from America of manufacturing. But they missed something essential about all that they borrowed. They did not understand that a piece of machinery—to say nothing of a school system or a set of laws—had a long past, that it was an expression of the society that produced it. Like the feudal Japanese who encountered the first Europeans, Japan's first modernizers were concerned only with *mono*—things, hardware.

But as much as Japan was a late developer, it was also an early one—indeed, the earliest. If, among advanced countries, Japan was near to last, among Third World countries it was first. The Japanese were the first non-Western people to absorb the things of the Western world. And Japan's modern leaders did no more than what many Third World leaders have done since: They adopted the technological ways of the West while preserving the social, spiritual, and psychological identity of the past. A century ago the Japanese called this *wakon yosai*, Japanese spirit, Western things. Today they would profess to believe in "Asian values"—as distinct from universal values.

Japan quickly followed the West's belief in humanity's alienation from nature and so set about subjugating the natural world. That was a prerequisite of industrialization. But it rejected the West's notion of the sovereign individual. Instead Japan tried to remain a communal society—hence the idea of a "family state"—in which the individual was dependent upon the authority of the group. To put it another way, Japan rejected the idea that people were the makers of their own history, autonomous agents of reason and judgment. Such a proposition was blocked at the border like a contaminated vegetable or an uncensored foreign newspaper. In short, Japan did not become modern so much as a consumer of the modern.

Is this to say that, as the West had an Enlightenment, so must the Japanese and the rest of humanity? That is the error of the Chrysanthemum Club and its "modernization theory": To be modern is to be Western, and everyone must sooner or later follow our path. But neither do we want to make the opposite mistake—to assert that the liberation of the individual was something peculiar to Western societies at a certain moment in history. The Japanese never had an Enlightenment, but that is hardly the point. No one familiar with the coercion and resistance of the feudal centuries—and of the modern era, for that matter—can conclude that the Japanese failed to evolve toward greater autonomy and individuality because they did not want to or were not ready to.

In July of 1853 Matthew Perry anchored four steamships off the coast south of Edo. The shogun and his immense, creaking bureaucracy had advance word and expected him. But local fishermen on the water that day tell us more about Japan's true sentiment. They thought Perry's "black ships" were some sort of floating volcano, and they scattered like birds at the sight of a sudden intruder.

Japan was about to get its first dose of *gaiatsu*, foreign pressure. Four years after Perry arrived, the shogunate—confused, decayed, desperate—signed treaties with the United States, Britain, Holland, Russia, and France that extended their jurisdiction onto Japanese soil and limited Edo's right to tax imports. In 1867 the last shogun abdicated, and Japan began its age of modernization. It never forgot the humiliation of the unequal treaties. They shaped Japan's goal to make itself the West's industrial and military equal and lent the endeavor an urgency that left no Japanese untouched.

It is easy to misunderstand the West's part in all this. Perry's ships were merely catalysts, arguably not even constructive catalysts. At the moment of their arrival all the principal agents of the great change to come were within. Japan may even have been better off without Perry, for it might have felt less urgency in the task ahead, and it might have done things less expediently, so avoiding the tragic consequences that lay in the future.

The Meiji era, named for its emperor's reign, began with the restoration of imperial sovereignty. For seven centuries Japan had been ruled by shoguns, and before that by regents. They wielded power in the emperor's name, but by 1867 the throne was far from public view, its transcendent authority a myth. With the restoration the emperor suddenly exited the neurasthenic shadows and stepped back onto center stage. So at the core of all the advances there lay a return. The emperor was to become a modern monarch, but he was also a god-king of the sort not seen since ancient days.

The events leading up to the restoration were extremely bizarre. In 1866 the political scene was a tangle of forces backing either the shogun or the throne. The fires of antiforeign chauvinism, long fanned by the bureaucracy, were raging. Crop failures and the new foreign trade—imports of manufactured goods, exports of gold and silver—had wrecked the economy. Popular unrest was at a peak: more than a hundred rural uprisings, and urban riots at the rate of several a month. A thread of premonitory superstition ran through all of this. A comet that year was taken as a portent of some imminent but incalculable change.

Early in 1867 everything went strangely quiet. Popular unrest more or less ceased. But in the autumn Japan broke out in ecstatic revelry—a combination of rioting, religious hysteria, sake-powered partying, and spontaneous, orgiastic street dancing. Houses were hung with brightly colored rice cakes, straw, and flowers. Dancers—men and women, young and old—clogged the streets to clamoring bells, drums, gongs, chimes, and whistles. Drunken commoners tramped through the houses of the privileged without—unforgivably—removing their shoes. Popular lyrics celebrated food, sake, and sex. People gave clothing away to strangers and threw money in the streets. The frenzy swept from Edo to Hiroshima after thousands of amulets, paper charms with Shinto and Buddhist gods painted on them, begin falling from the sky.

No historian has explained the rain of amulets. But they were not the only peculiar feature of this altogether odd interlude. Cross-dressing was widespread. Despite all the pent-up anger of late Edo, there was no violence. A British diplomat traveling in Osaka remarked on the absence of fear or animosity. Everywhere the revelers repeated the same incantatory chant: *Ee ja nai ka!* This elusive term has numerous inexact translations. Its nearest literal meaning is "Isn't it good?" or "Why not? It's all right!" A scholar recently described it as falling somewhere among "Right on! Go for it," "What the hell," and "No more bullshit!"

Odd as it seems, given our image of the Japanese, *ee ja nai ka* was the sound of modern Japan's beginning. The delirious chanting lasted until the spring of 1868. And amid the cacophony of a sexually charged carnival, two samurai clans loyal to the emperor, the Satsuma and the Choshu, found a singular opportunity. During the interim from the autumn of 1867 to the spring of the new year they secured the shogun's resignation and wheeled the new emperor forward as the new ruler of a new Japan.

Ee ja nai ka! The subtext of every shout was an open declaration of liberation, a jack-in-the-box release of pent-up desire. This alone would give *ee ja nai ka* a place in Japan's hidden history, but there is more. What does it mean when people of no great sophistication take to cross-dressing, or to trampling across tatami in muddy shoes, or, in abject poverty, to throwing money away? We cannot be satisfied with the notion that a commoner celebrating sex and gluttony in late Edo Japan saw no farther than the next sake barrel and a free-spirited companion. *Ee ja nai ka* was a shout toward the heavens, a rejection of the reigning order. It was as if people had seen through the roof of the great house of Tokugawa to glimpse an immensity of alternatives in the open sky beyond. Above all, it was an act of public individuality.

Edo's last months were both expectant and subversive. By the end, *ee ja nai ka* took on an explicitly political meaning—it was another inchoate expression of rebellion, like the constant protests of the Edo era. The evident sexuality offers us a clue to understanding this moment as one of undirected individual assertion, desire without an available language. But the formlessness of this rebellion does not obscure its psychological complexity. Speculating, we can wonder whether the shouts of *ee ja nai ka* were the deformed flowers of a Japanese enlightenment ready to sprout but without the ground to grow. More certainly, they reveal that the individual's struggle against the enfolding web was part of modern Japan from the moment it came into existence.

The emperor restored in 1868 was a brisk, intelligent sixteen-year-old named Mutsuhito. Even before he moved in a dazzling procession from Kyoto to the renamed Tokyo, he issued a kind of constitutional preamble called the Charter Oath, an open pledge to his ancestors. Third of its five clauses was this one:

> The common people, no less than the civil and military officials, shall all attain their aspirations, so that the people's minds shall not be made weary.

No number of bearded commodores or imposed treaties can account for such an astonishing proposition. To attain one's goals—even to aspire—was a bracing, revolutionary idea. But the Charter Oath is easily explained. It was issued amid the confusion and anticipation of the *ee ja nai ka* interlude. The oath was intended to calm the nervous, the doubtful, and the impetuous. And to do so the emperor and those around him chose to acknowledge the popular desire for change of the most fundamental kind. In one sentence the young Mutsuhito announced the end of a long, traumatic bondage. All boundaries between the official and ordinary, the high and low, were to be erased. A society of fixed status was to be transformed into one of mobility and striving individuals. When Mutsuhito left Kyoto for Tokyo, for three hundred miles commoners pressed their faces to the earth along the roadside. Mutsuhito may have been a god-king, but let us understand this spectacle properly: He was also

the man who banished the terrorizing shogunate from the life of every Japanese.

But the society the emperor promised never arrived. Meiji freed the Japanese from the feudal castes. They could entertain their individual aspirations. But the modern era did not give them the individual liberty to pursue their aspirations. Meiji turned out to be nothing more than a transition from feudal absolutism to absolutism in nineteenth-century form. Japan remained a communal society—closed instead of open, particular instead of universal, a society of individuals who could cultivate no individual values. The contradiction made modern Japan what it is today—a place of immense but unrealizable dreams, relentless competition, and near-universal frustration. No matter how contemporary we imagine the Japanese to be, the society promised in the Charter Oath is the one they still struggle to attain, whose betrayal they seek to redress.

A period of liberal exploration did ensue after the emperor moved into the shogun's palace. For half a dozen years Japan lived in a state of happy inconsistency. A hundred flowers bloomed. Restlessness replaced the long sleep of Edo, just as it would replace the defeated dictatorship in 1945. There was no fixed way forward. Intellectuals read Rousseau's *Social Contract* and Mill's *On Liberty*, among many other Western works, as quickly as they could be translated. Then the Satsuma and Choshu leadership, known as the Sat-Cho, retreated into conservatism (just as it would in the late 1940s), so making itself an entrenched, undemocratic oligarchy—the worthy successor of the shogunate.

But what was the early idealism made of? And why did it fail? The best answer comes from the educator Yukichi Fukuzawa, he of the ten-thousand-yen note. Fukuzawa was among the foremost exponents of liberalism and later a strident critic of the Meiji oligarchs. In 1876 he collected several years' worth of pamphlets under the title *An Encouragement of Learning*. Rendered in plain Japanese, the book sold more than 3 million copies. In it Fukuzawa invented the very notion of individualism for the Japanese. His term was *dokuritsu*, spirit of independence. The new word, like the book, was beloved for its simplicity, but we should listen carefully to what Fukuzawa meant, for it is a key to the ethos of the era:

> When the people of a nation do not have the spirit of individual independence, the corresponding right of national independence cannot be realized.

> Persons without the spirit of personal independence will not have deep concern for their country.

> Japan must be filled with the spirit of independence

if we are to defend her against foreign threats.

In these passages Fukuzawa defines the intellectual failing of Japan's first foray into liberalism: He took the cultivation of the autonomous individual to be a means, an expedient to a greater goal, instead of an end in itself, the greatest goal of all.

Fukuzawa is ranked today among modern Japan's great *philosophes*. Liberals still claim him for his opposition to the reaction that followed the early period of possibility. The Bank of Japan puts his picture on its bills because his image lends a liberal veneer to early modern history. In his time Fukuzawa had many conservative enemies, men more interested in the Confucian virtues than in the "spirit of independence." But what was this great intellectual clash really about? Only method. Fukuzawa's adversaries wanted a strong state able to resist foreigners and renegotiate the unequal treaties. To them, the road ahead lay not in any notion of individuality but in continued reverence for the hierarchical order. Fukuzawa shared their goal—he never lost sight of it. He differed only over the usefulness of the past.

Meiji Japan became a cauldron of discontent with the defeat even of Fukuzawa's flawed liberalism. Indeed, the new Japan was not much quieter than the Japan of the old shogunate. Crowds gathered as suddenly as summer storms. Popular protests, riots, and resistance movements were features of daily life. Decommissioned samuri, along with intellectuals, small-time factory owners, village landlords, and ambitious rustics of all varieties formed a loose, nationwide group to demand popular rights—an idea so foreign it required an invented word, *kenri*. These were Japan's first politicians. They also introduced the notion of *minshu-shugi*, which meant "people-masterism"—that is, democracy.

By 1881 civil unrest forced the Sat-Cho to promise the Japanese a constitution and a national assembly. These arrived on schedule in 1889 and 1890, respectively. By then there were political parties and a cabinet—as well as a self-appointed peerage modeled (like the constitution) on imperial Germany's. The first elections were held. But having promised the institutions of modern government, the oligarchy then made sure they had no modern meaning. The constitution vested ultimate authority in the emperor—in whose name the oligarchy presided. The imperial Diet, as the legislature was called, was elected by slightly more than 1 percent of the population—and had only an advisory role anyway. The cabinet declared itself to be "transcendental"—that is, beyond politics and party interests. So was modern government imported and rejigged as if it were another new machine.

By century's end Japan was what it would remain until 1945—an ideological state, a nation whose people could understand themselves only as members of the larger community. At the core of Japanese ideology, of course, was worship of the emperor. The emperor was the head of the *kazoku kokka*, the "family state." The family state was unique in the world because it possessed an ineffable quality called *kokutai*, "national essence." Being a family state, having an emperor descended from the gods, and having such a singular thing as national essence made the Japanese a chosen people. These ideas were transmitted in a thousand different ways. Instead of encouraging critical thought, the individual as a shaper of society, the ideologues encouraged conditioned reflexes—the individual as society's object. Ideology is what the Japanese got instead of autonomy and democracy.

Japan's ideological stew was a rich concoction. The Tokyo elite was hardly alone in inventing tradition. Bismarck's new Germany was doing the same thing. Both nations needed legitimacy, some device to make people feel "German" or "Japanese." Being ex-samurai themselves, Japan's leaders turned to their own past to create the new Japanese. Japan would be a nation of noble warriors, all serving the emperor with the old, peculiar notion of loyalty and all the old inflexibility. This feature of the modern era is often missed, but it is essential. While Japan was busy westernizing, it was also busily "samuraizing." The first prime minister, Hirobumi Ito, a former samurai who took up the sword at thirteen, when Perry's ships arrived, explained this point to his colleagues in the 1880s:

> The major task facing us today is inculcating within the entire populace the spirit of loyalty, devotion, and heroism that was formerly associated with the samurai class, and making these values their values. Thus we must teach the common people to work and study hard for the sake of their neighborhoods and villages, and never to waver in matters that would lead to the destruction of their families. Moreover, they must develop a peaceful and obedient character, show respect for the law, and demonstrate an understanding of our noble moral ideals and highly refined national sentiments.

A nation of samurai would be a very different thing from Japan as it had been, a place of conflict between great and little, the elevated and the common. There would be no democracy, but there would be no tension, either. Everyone, however humble his circumstances, would think of himself as part of the great tradition. The old samurai code would become "the beautiful customs." In 1907, five years before the Meiji era ended, a bureaucrat with the benign paternalism of a true imperial subject explained how the beautiful customs were supposed to work. At the time, the nation's new industries were a riot of unrest and violence:

> The old, beautiful customs existing in Japan are concepts of mutual love and respect from employer to employee. This master-servant relationship is not an evil feudal remnant but a benefit gained from feudalism. Will not these beautiful customs, namely compassion from above for those below, and respect from below for those above, be greatly helpful in harmonizing labor-capital relations?

Looking back many decades later, the scholar Masao Maruyama likened ideology to "a many-layered though invisible net over the Japanese people." Another postwar thinker described it as "an enormous black box, into which the Japanese unknowingly walked." Why did this happen? Why were the Japanese so easily led into xenophobia, extreme patriotism—and war? If we understand this about the Japanese we will have understood a great deal about who they were then, who they are now, and who they will become.

The ideological period is a tragic aspect of Japan's past, but it is not incomprehensible. When Japan began to embrace the modern, ordinary Japanese had no notion of what it meant to be part of a modern nation. They knew of nations only what the new oligarchy told them with shrill persistence. And among the most important ways they learned—an essential institution in creating nationality—was military conscription. Neither did they know what it meant to be an individual: The most liberal among them tied the idea to the nation-state. Fukuzawa's mistake, the mistake that said, "To be a person means to be a Japanese person," was repeated many times. And it would be hard to exaggerate the attraction of being "Japanese," and of participating as a recognized part of a modern nation, to people who had been so recently only nameless serfs.

This could not, of course, resolve the problem of public individuality so evident at the restoration. What became of all those shouting individuals? Enveloping though the emperor system was, we deny the Japanese any social or psychological complexity if we assume that, one and all, they became avid followers of emperor ideology. Instead, a kind of con game began in the space between the Meiji ideal and the reality of modern life, a con game played by the concealed individual behind the public mask. Publicly one strove in the new Japan for the emperor and the nation; privately one strove for oneself.

Few Japanese of the Meiji era ever resolved the contradiction their incomplete modernization presented them. What it meant to be Japanese, to say nothing of individualism, was hopelessly fogged. The ideological fanatics were many, selfishness their constant complaint—no surprise, for the con game was extensively played. It is no wonder that Soseki Natsume, the great novelist of the early modern period (and a great writer of any age and nation), was so saddened by the spectacle. The confusion that reigns over the Japanese today has its roots in his time.

Soseki led a troubled life, suffering often to the brink of emotional collapse. In 1900 he traveled to England, where he struggled to learn all he could about Westerners and their literature. Then he made the discovery that was to rule his life: The most profound lesson the Japanese could learn was not to be like anyone else, but to be themselves—to live their own authentic individuality. Soseki spent his life as a writer trying to convey this simple truth. But it never stopped weighing upon him—it was his blessing and his curse—because so few understood it.

In 1914, two years after Meiji ended, two years into the era called Taisho, Soseki gave a lecture titled "My Individualism" to a group of Japanese students. He was almost certainly circumspect in his remarks, for individualism ranked high at that point as a danger to the ideological state. But his message—that one must reject the false coin of Meiji in all its guises—is clear enough today. "You make peace with yourself when the individuality with which you were born arrives where it belongs," he told his young audience at one point. And at another:

> I urge you to accomplish this, *not for the nation's sake*, nor even for the sake of your families, but because it is absolutely necessary for your own personal happiness.

And another:

> Individual liberty is indispensable for the development of [the] individuality that I spoke of earlier.

And finally:

> As I see it, individualism advocates respecting the existence of others at the same time that one respects ones own existence. . . . More simply stated, individualism is a philosophy that replaces cliquism with values based on personal judgment of right and wrong. An individualist is not forever running with the group, forming cliques that thrash around blindly in the interests of power and money. That is why there lurks beneath the surface of his philosophy a loneliness unknown to others. As soon as we deny our little

groups, then I simply go my way and I let the other man go his, unhindered. Sometimes we cannot avoid becoming scattered. That is what is lonely.

Soseki understood loneliness as the mark not only of an authentic individual but of someone isolated by his insight. Few Japanese saw, as he put it, "the distinction between yourself and others." They did not accept that individuality lay finally in rejecting the group and discarding the masks of sameness.

Soseki's Japan, and the Japan that followed, was an unsettled place. The Russian revolution and unrest at home inspired numerous challenges to the status quo I have described. In 1918 a group known as the Association of New Men called for "a rational reconstruction of contemporary Japan." In the 1920s there was a period of party government—a direct affront to the old oligarchy. At this time the Japanese also shifted their focus from institutions to psychology: It was in the twenties that they first began discussing *shutai-sei*, autonomy. But the period of "Taisho democracy," as it is called, was short-lived. There was little social or political framework to support all the new ideas—which were imported ideas, after all. And as intellectuals reacted against the foreignness of the things that inspired them, democrats became nationalists and socialists, national socialists.

It was no long leap to the 1930s, when the military took power in Japan and turned out the lights on such questions as democracy and autonomy. All that had to wait until the end of the coming war—the "total war" against the West.

In December of 1945 an American correspondent named Mark Gayn wandered one day in the Shimbashi district, south of Tokyo Station and the Ginza. Then as now, Shimbashi was a hectic quarter given over to small-time businesses, though all that had survived the war was a bustling black market. Gayn later recorded the excursion in his book *Japan Diary*. "Conductors are having difficulty with men who smoke in street cars, despite 'No Smoking' signs. The men say, 'Do we have democracy, or don't we?'"

Nothing better captures the confusion that greeted the Americans. What was this thing from abroad called (by this time) *demokurashii*? Did it not strip away the past, fulfilling at last the restoration's unmet promise? The promise of the occupation could arrive only as another misunderstood import—precisely what it was. Democracy requires institutions that balance contending political forces. But Japan

had no such institutions. The Meiji oligarchy gave Japan a constitution and a parliament, but neither was democratic. Japan's one try at democracy, in the 1920s, ended with a military takeover. For centuries diversity was simply suppressed—hidden behind masks.

Wasn't the postwar debate over *shutai-sei*, autonomy, which began at the time of Gayn's trolley ride, in some way similar to the shouts of *Ee ja nai ka!* as the shogunate collapsed? Behind the need to achieve individual autonomy and the cries of "Go for it!" was the same desire to be released from the past. Within a year of the surrender more than three hundred political parties appeared. Many of them stood for nothing more than a single person's swollen ambition. Like the men on the trolley, they assumed democracy meant everyone getting what he wanted. These one-man bands are looked upon variously as good or bad measures of the postwar mood. But surely there was something positive in their brief appearance. After all they had been through, the Japanese were eager to take part in public life, even if they had no understanding of a system that mediated between individual desire and the rest of society.

Americans tend to think that it was their example that got the Japanese interested in democracy and the civic self. Certainly their arrival in Japan had something to do with the rise of democratic expectations. But we must be careful, once again, not to misunderstand the role of gaijin. Just as Japan might have been better off without Commodore Perry's black ships, it might have been better off without the occupation—at least as it turned out. Americans opened the door again, as it were, in 1945. But with the reverse course they closed it. Democracy became a showpiece again, for we made it impossible for the Japanese to build a civil society. We gave Japan a new constitution full of liberal freedoms and civil rights, but then we brought back the prewar elite, proven masters at manipulating "the beautiful customs." They made Japan what it is today: a modern example of the corporatist society.

No account of the postwar years captures its essential conflict as thoughtfully as *The Journey*, a novel by Jiro Osaragi written at the end of the 1950s. Osaragi never uses the term, but his real subject was *shutai-sei*. His main characters struggle against all the old conventions. They fight to make their own decisions, to rely upon themselves, to follow their own ideas and passions. These are Japan's heroes, we are told by the aging professor through whom the novelist speaks. In one passage the professor quotes an ancient tea master: "I exhort you to do all those things in the world that are bad." As with the Greeks and their vases, there is in these words an appreciation of the flaws that signal authenticity in things of beauty or worth, for the professor continues:

> The real point is that if a fellow can't do anything bad in this world, he also can't do anything good. Human beings arent meant to consist just of style or appearance. We shouldn't become like mosquito-larvae bred in lukewarm water under the sun. . . . No lukewarm methods! We don't want the sort of fellows who just have conventional civilized educations. We need people with chips and cracks, twisted in ways, but with uncommon characters.

Osaragi ends in ascending chords. People pressed together by well-worn social conventions diverge along separate paths, so embracing society's multiplicity. But *The Journey* is no bedtime story. Other characters, seduced by postwar materialism and superficial notions of American ideals, fail to connect freedom with responsibility and end up submerged in the very morass of self-centered getting and spending that Tokyo encouraged after the anti-AMPO protests of 1960.

Midway in the book a student who once dreamed of blazing scholarly trails by tracing the path of Alexander the Great worries that his ambitions are shrinking to idle fantasies:

> Apart from the process of growing up, the social uneasiness of the post-war period was responsible for this shrinking process. The age of individualism had come to Japan too late. It was an excellent thing, of course, that the dignity of human rights had finally come to be respected. But at exactly the same time Japan had entered the age in which it was considered essential . . . that people suppress their egos and submit themselves to a system of centralized organization.

Osarigi was not a prophet, only a prescient recorder. By the end of the 1950s Japan was becoming a mass society. The old elite had entrenched themselves once again, bringing with them the old notions of what it meant to be Japanese. Under them the era of Japan Inc. began.

The term *shutai-sei* is not much used anymore. In the 1960s it enjoyed a vogue in the student movement. Opposed to the renewed social hierarchies in which they lived, university demonstrators eventually took the issue to be themselves and the edifices erected in their minds: *uchi naru todai*, the Tokyo University within, *uchi naru onnaishiki*, the traditional woman within. Community groups proliferated during this time. They engaged questions ranging from the environment and nuclear power to textbook screening and local political autonomy—each one an indication of a widespread desire to break free of the old constraints. A woman active through this period once put it perfectly: "We wanted to live without always looking from one side to the other, a habit planted deep within all of us." That the question of the public self became explicitly political was no surprise. Public individuality was always a political issue. The community groups eventually disappeared, and the protests of the 1960s went the way of protest elsewhere—into radical adventure and obscurity. But the task before the Japanese has since changed not an iota: It remains to throw away the masks while tearing down the walls within.

The psychiatrist Robert Jay Lifton, who has studied the Japanese for many years, once interviewed a student who came of age in the 1960s. Like most of his generation, the student was profoundly confused about the Japan that confronted him and his true place in it. Before he was twenty-five Lifton's subject had been in succession an ultranationalist patriot, a Westernized democrat, a martial arts devotee, an Amerophile exchange student, a Christian, a leftist radical, and a dissipated idler. To the student these were alternative selves, different ways of being, yet he seems to have entered fully into none of his serial lives. They were roles or—better, perhaps—different brands of modern life to be pulled from the shelf and sampled. In the end he drifted into a desk job at a large corporation.

Lifton exposed a prevalent condition—the propensity of the modern Japanese to dream. And like the dreams of the Meiji era, the dreams of the postwar Japanese were always dreams of escape. *Sararimen* dreamed of striking out on their own. They had a slangy contraction for this: *datsu-sara*, to escape being a *sarariman*. It was usually enough to imagine such a step, so the idea of *datsu-sara* was merely a popular fantasy. In the same way the Japanese were famously obsessed with their entries in the *Guinness Book of Records*. They sustained an elaborate subculture of dreamer-achievers: climbers, trekkers in Africa, arctic explorers, single-handed sailors. Among the best known was a man called Naomi Uemura, who soloed by sled to the North Pole, lived alone in Greenland, and rafted the Amazon by himself. Uemura died alone in the Canadian tundra, which only enhanced his mystique.

Such preoccupations expressed an abiding desire among the Japanese to release their individual selves. But as dreams, of course, they proved only what they were intended to refute. The Japanese were still individuals who could not live as individuals. Autonomy, as the scholar Masao Maruyama would have put it, was still private. People had no public individuality. In public they still wore masks: They assumed roles from which there was no escape. "Many millions of people throughout Japan were sealed up in many millions of separate boxes, or separated by many millions of walls." That was how the educator Yukichi Fukuzawa described Japan just before the restoration. It was also precisely the Japan Maruyama found after the war—and the Japan one found until a decade or so ago.

Even now the Japanese share a profound ambivalence as to the need to escape the web of belonging. But the conflict between freedom and community has heightened dramatically over the past decade. In this Maruyama was something of a prophet, for the best way to describe the Japanese condition today is the way he described it fifty years ago: It requires that same "internal reform of the psychological structure of society" of which he wrote. That is to say, the line between the private and the public must be redrawn so that the individuality that has been for so long furtive can be manifest. As Maruyama understood, this is necessary not only for personal autonomy to take root, but for democracy. Having neither an experience of public individuality nor the mechanisms to express it, Japan is again launched upon a messy experiment. "The underbelly of this exquisite society is beginning to surface," Lifton remarked in the mid-1990s. "The Japanese are seething within." This is a true description. It remains for us only to recognize that Japan has seethed for a very long time.

If the disintegration of the enveloping web is a gradual process—as it is, exceedingly so—it is also unmistakable. One sees it in schools, neighborhoods, offices, in a proliferation of subcultures of all varieties. Less and less do people identify with their old, traditional groups. The corporate samurai—loyal, dedicated, the quintessential Japanese belonger—is already on the way to becoming a figure of the past. One sees evidence of this change especially in the political world. Behind all the apparent chaos—the constantly shifting alliances, the rise and collapse of parties, coalitions, and cabinets—occurs the essential process of building a system able to accommodate the historic emergence of the civic self, "the new democratic human type," as Maruyama's modernists put it after the war—the unmasked, public individual.

We have noted the practical circumstances surrounding this momentous change. Japan has become the West's equal in material terms; the Cold War has ended. But societies do not evolve—not in any fundamental way—because of economic successes or an altered international climate. Like Perry's black ships

a century and a half ago, these are only catalysts at work on agents of change already assembled. Societies change because the people who comprise them want them to. And such is the truth with which the Japanese now grapple, at once daunting and emancipating: People change institutions; in the end it is not the other way around.

The Japanese are much given to distinctions between generations. Each seems to be a point of departure. Each seems to have some assigned task. In recent years it has become impossible to discuss Japan without discussing the ways it will change, but change is seen as the responsibility only of the young. Others may desire it but feel no obligation to effect it. "Change? Can Japan change?" an aging local official in western Japan once said over lunch. "Our generation is haunted by the old. We must wait for the next for change." This is not so, surely. Change cannot be but the consequence of desire and effort accumulated over many generations and transmitted from each to the next.

A decade ago a new generation emerged in Japan: the *shinjinrui*, the "new human species." The term described Japanese who seemed to be a people apart. The new species knew nothing of postwar reconstruction or the turmoil of the 1950s and 1960s. They were the first Japanese to know only affluence. They spent rather than saved, they felt no obligations toward society, they did not care for corporate loyalty or lifetime employment. To their elders their lack of vigor and direction was a source of worry. They seemed to have no point of view, no identity, no political perspective—nothing to distinguish themselves except the blank stare of indifference toward Japan's postwar values. By decade's end the rest of Japan simply shrugged, and the new species became passé. They seemed to reflect something familiar on the Japanese scene: the conformity of sanctioned nonconformity. Corporations reduced the *shinjinrui* to a marketing conundrum. The man who gave the new human species their name, a writer named Tetsuya Chikushi, repudiated it, saying there was nothing new about them after all.

We must wait to see if this is so, for it is not so easy to dismiss the *shinjinrui*. Rather, we must separate what is ephemeral about them from the things that are of lasting importance. Without even meaning to, the new species announced the end of "the modern" in Japan, the modern as the Japanese had understood it for a century and a quarter. Viscerally, they seemed to recognize that the past was somehow over and that they represented a decisive break with it. Their parents had completed the modernization project. It was the new species who, detached from history, could finally see the great price the Japanese paid for material success. This was their paradox: They consumed with abandon, for that was life's only reward—but always, it seemed to me, with a certain bitter contempt for consumption.

Many of the new species are no doubt *sararimen* by now, having drifted into corporate life as indifferently as Lifton's fickle student. But that is not the point. When one spoke with them, the people of this generation almost invariably explained that their primary concern was to reclaim time. What did they mean by this? Certainly it was not a matter of the passing hours and days. It was the way modern life has been divided in Japan. To reclaim time meant to assert control over themselves as individuals, to redraw the line between public and private—to make private life acceptable, not furtive and secret, and to live publicly as authentic, autonomous individuals.

Understood this way, the new species was aptly named. Its members signaled, it seems to me, the start of a fundamental renegotiation of the terms of Japanese life. They repudiated nothing less than the community ethos that has so long bound the Japanese—and so proposed a new way of being an individual that had nothing to do with being Japanese. They would remain members of a group, almost certainly—but members by choice. They made the refusal to wear the Japanese mask the act not of a mountain-climbing hero but of an ordinary person. And they began, in all this, the final chapter of Japan's hidden history. That is why there is scarcely an aspect of Japanese society that is not now in flux.

"It is not true that we refuse to make any effort," one of the new species once explained. "We are dedicated to finding something worth making an effort for." The notion invites a useful comparison with the Association of New Men, the group that pressed, during the 1920s, for a fundamental renovation of modern Japan. Unlike the New Men, the new species has had no apparent political agenda—and certainly it has no organization. But the new species resembles the New Men in its advocacy of alternative ways of thinking and living. The project of the New Men was to partake of a society still in formation. The *shinjinrui*, by contrast, have confronted an altogether fixed society. They have sought not the right to participate in Japan as it has constructed itself but to quit that Japan in favor of one that admits of autonomy and multiplicity.

Let us return briefly to the matter of names. From this story of names, names printed on paper, we learn the point of transition the Japanese have reached—a peculiar place, but one from which there does not seem to be any turning back.

Meishi, business cards, are essential equipment in modern Japan. They tell you not only a person's name and affiliation but—most important—his rank within the hierarchy. Without some indication of status, two Japanese would have a difficult time because they would not know the proper behavior. Who stands above whom? How deep should the bow be? You can fill drawers with *meishi* in the course of a busy year in Japan. Even the most casual encounters require exchanges of cards; the code they supply is essential. Is the *meishi* not in some way analogous to the samurai's dress—the meticulously displayed colors and patterns by which he identified himself?

The most interesting *meishi* I ever received was from a *sarariman* at the Nikken Corporation. Nikken was a going concern in the early 1990s; perhaps it still is. It did a thriving business leasing office equipment and industrial machinery. It had three factories, 160 sales offices, and almost two thousand employees. There were subsidiaries in Chicago and Bangkok and a listing on the Tokyo Stock Exchange. Yearly revenue came to 60 billion yen, about $600 million.

The man from Nikken who handed me his *meishi* was thirtyish, a "new human species." One side of his card read TARO HONMARU, GENERAL MANAGER. On the other it read MY REAL NAME IS KEIICHI NAKAMURA. What did it mean that a young Japanese executive had two names?

The system started naturally enough. After hiring a nephew with the same surname, Nikken's president soon tired of the confusion. So he called his nephew Imafuku-san, after the younger man's hometown. The characters for "Imafuku" happen to translate as "now luck," a fortuitous stroke, for it yielded a lasting nickname. And so the system evolved. The president was called Kane (Turtle), for his tough demeanor. An executive from a mountain village named himself Kodama-san, *kodama* being the echo heard across peaks. There was a sports fan called Rikishi-san (because *rikishi* is another name for a sumo wrestler) and a Hitomi Sakura (Iris Cherry Blossom). The general manager who explained all this was Honmaru-san because he worked in the head office's planning section. *Honmaru* were the central towers in the castles of the feudal daimyo.

Honmaru-san, tall and boyish, was much taken with the curiosities: the confusion at business hotels, the computer directory where real and invented names were matched. He did not seem to have considered what such a system said about Japan and the Japanese, or what it meant that one's real name represented the private, authentic self, and the made-up name the public self, the mask. Then, in his polite, diffident manner, he began to explain. We sat across from each other at a Formica-topped table in a bare conference room.

"One reason we do this—perhaps it's very Japanese—is that a lot of *sararimen* get confused between their private and public selves. They want to separate the two clearly. While at work, you should have the dedication of the professional businessman—the so-called corporate warrior. After five, you should return to your real self and do what you want to do."

Honmaru paused to judge my reaction before drawing his conclusion. "The Japanese are like actors," he said finally. "Actors can't refuse a role. You can't refuse your part in Japan."

Actors cannot refuse roles, but ordinary people can.

The Grasshopper and the Bell Cricket

Yasunari Kawabata

Walking along the tile-roofed wall of the university, I turned aside and approached the upper school. Behind the white board fence of the school playground, from a dusky clump of bushes under the black cherry trees, an insect's voice could be heard. Walking more slowly and listening to that voice, and furthermore reluctant to part with it, I turned right so as not to leave the playground behind. When I turned to the left, the fence gave way to an embankment planted with orange trees. At the corner, I exclaimed with surprise. My eyes gleaming at what they saw up ahead, I hurried forward with short steps.

At the base of the embankment was a bobbing cluster of beautiful varicolored lanterns, such as one might see at a festival in a remote country village. Without going any farther, I knew that it was a group of children on an insect chase among the bushes of the embankment. There were about twenty lanterns. Not only were there crimson, pink, indigo, green, purple, and yellow lanterns, but one lantern glowed with five colors at once. There were even some little red store-bought lanterns. But most of the lanterns were beautiful square ones which the children had made themselves with love and care. The bobbing lanterns, the coming together of children on this lonely slope—surely it was a scene from a fairy tale?

One of the neighborhood children had heard an insect sing on this slope one night. Buying a red lantern, he had come back the next night to find the insect. The night after that, there was another child. This new child could not buy a lantern. Cutting out the back and front of a small carton and papering it, he placed a candle on the bottom and fastened a string to the top. The number of children grew to five, and then to seven. They learned how to color the paper that they stretched over the windows of the cutout cartons, and to draw pictures on it. Then these wise child-artists, cutting out round, three-cornered, and lozenge leaf shapes in the cartons, coloring each little window a different color, with circles and diamonds, red and green, made a single

and whole decorative pattern. The child with the red lantern discarded it as a tasteless object that could be bought at a store. The child who had made his own lantern threw it away because the design was too simple. The pattern of light that one had had in hand the night before was unsatisfying the morning after. Each day, with cardboard, paper, brush, scissors, penknife, and glue, the children made new lanterns out of their hearts and minds. Look at my lantern! Be the most unusually beautiful! And each night, they had gone out on their insect hunts. These were the twenty children and their beautiful lanterns that I now saw before me.

Wide-eyed, I loitered near them. Not only did the square lanterns have old-fashioned patterns and flower shapes, but the names of the children who had made them were cut out in squared letters of the syllabary. Different from the painted-over red lanterns, others (made of thick cutout cardboard) had their designs drawn onto the paper windows, so that the candle's light seemed to emanate from the form and color of the design itself. The lanterns brought out the shadows of the bushes like dark light. The children crouched eagerly on the slope wherever they heard an insect's voice.

"Does a anyone want a grasshopper?" A boy, who had been peering into a bush about thirty feet away front the other children, suddenly straightened up and shouted.

"Yes! Give it to me!" Six or seven children came running up. Crowding behind the boy who had found the grasshopper, they peered into the bush. Brushing away their outstretched hands and spreading out his arms, the boy stood as if guarding the bush where the insect was. Waving the lantern in his right hand, he called again to the other children.

"Does anyone want a grasshopper? A grasshopper!"

"I do! I do!" Four or five more children came running up. It seemed you could not catch a more precious insect than a grasshopper. The boy called out a third time.

"Doesn't anyone want a grasshopper?"

Two or three more children came over.

"Yes. I want it."

It was a girl, who just now had come up behind the boy who'd discovered the insect. Lightly turning his body, the boy gracefully bent forward. Shifting the lantern to his left hand, he reached his right hand into the bush.

"It's a grasshopper."

"Yes. I'd like to have it."

The boy quickly stood up. As if to say "Here!" he thrust out his fist that held the insect at the girl. She, slipping her left wrist under the string of her lantern, enclosed the boy's fist with both hands. The boy quietly opened his fist. The insect was transferred to between the girl's thumb and index finger.

"Oh! It's not a grasshopper. It's a bell cricket." The girl's eyes shone as she looked at the small brown insect.

"It's a bell cricket! It's a bell cricket!" The children echoed in an envious chorus.

"It's a bell cricket. It's a bell cricket."

Glancing with her bright intelligent eyes at the boy who had given her the cricket, the girl opened the little insect cage hanging at her side and released the cricket in it.

"It's a bell cricket."

"Oh, it's a bell cricket," the boy who'd captured it muttered. Holding up the insect cage close to his eyes, he looked inside it. By the light of his beautiful many-colored lantern, also held up at eye level, he glanced at the girl's face.

Oh, I thought. I felt slightly jealous of the boy, and sheepish. How silly of me not to have understood his actions until now! Then I caught my breath in surprise. Look! It was something on the girl's breast which neither the boy who had given her the cricket, nor she who had accepted it, nor the children who were looking at them noticed.

In the faint greenish light that fell on the girl's breast, wasn't the name "Fujio" clearly discernible? The boy's lantern, which he held up alongside the girl's insect cage, inscribed his name, cutout in the green papered aperture, onto her white cotton kimono. The girl's lantern, which dangled loosely from her wrist, did not project its pattern so clearly, but still one could make out, in a trembling patch of red on the boy's waist, the name "Kiyoko." This chance interplay of red and green—if it was chance or play—neither Fujio nor Kiyoko knew about.

Even if they remembered forever that Fujio had given her the cricket and that Kiyoko had accepted it, not even in dreams would Fujio ever know that his name had been written in green on Kiyoko's breast or that Kiyoko's name had been inscribed in red on his waist, nor would Kiyoko ever know that Fujio's name had been inscribed in green on her breast or that her own name had been written in red on Fujio's waist.

Fujio! Even when you have become a young man, laugh with pleasure at a girl's delight when, told that it's a grasshopper, she is given a bell cricket; laugh with affection at a girl's chagrin when, told that it's a bell cricket, she is given a grasshopper.

Even if you have the wit to look by yourself in a bush away from the other children, there are not many bell crickets in the world. Probably you will find a girl like a grasshopper whom you think is a bell cricket.

And finally, to your clouded, wounded heart, even a true bell cricket will seem like a grasshopper. Should that day come, when it seems to you that the world is only full of grasshoppers, I will think it a pity that you have no way to remember tonight's play of light, when your name was written in green by your beautiful lantern on a girl's breast.

Selections on the Bombing of Hiroshima

Hiroshima Observes 55th Anniversary of Bombing

From *The Japan Times*: Aug. 7, 2000

HIROSHIMA (Kyodo) Hiroshima on Sunday commemorated the 55th anniversary of its 1945 atomic bombing in a ceremony attended by the Russian ambassador to Japan, the first envoy from a full-fledged nuclear power to join the annual event.

After a one-minute silent prayer held under the scorching sun at 8:15 A.M., when the atomic bomb was dropped on the city 55 years ago, Mayor Tadatoshi Akiba delivered an annual peace declaration.

"Having called on the world to abolish nuclear weapons, Hiroshima wishes to make a new start as a model city demonstrating the use of science and technology for human purposes," Akiba said in the city's Peace Memorial Park near ground zero.

"We will create a 21st century in which Hiroshima's very existence formulates the substance of peace," he said at the final memorial ceremony this century.

"On the international stage, Hiroshima aspires to serve a mediator actively creating reconciliation by helping to resolve conflict and animosity," he told some 50,000 attendees, including Prime Minister Yoshiro Mori and Russian Ambassador to Japan Alexander Panov.

At the start of the 50-minute ceremony, Akiba and two citizens placed two books listing 5,021 people whom the city office has newly recognized as victims of the bombing over the past year into a room under the arch-shaped cenotaph in the park.

The total number of victims as claimed by the city came to 217,137 as of Sunday, including an estimated 140,000 who died as a direct result of the bombing by the end of 1945.

Mori said in an address, "(Japan) welcomes the May agreement by a U.N. meeting to review the 1968 Nuclear Non-Proliferation Treaty (NPT) to promote the policy of nuclear disarmament."

In that April-May meeting, the world's nuclear powers agreed for the first time to seek an "unequivocal undertaking" to eliminate their nuclear arsenals.

"Furthermore, Japan has just issued a peace message from Okinawa after urging the leaders of the other Group of Eight powers to reach an agreement to promote nuclear disarmament and nonproliferation in the July 21–23 summit, based on the results of the NPT meeting," Mori said. Abdallah Baali, who chaired the NPT meeting, was among the dignitaries attending the ceremony.

But Akiba did not praise or otherwise highly evaluate the agreement of the NPT meeting in the declaration, the 52nd issued since 1947. The city office did not issue a declaration in 1950 and 1951, when it was affected by political disputes over the 1950–1953 Korean War.

Mori later told reporters, "During the ceremony I renewed my belief that this tragedy must not be repeated. Japan is prepared to submit a draft resolution to eliminate nuclear weapons to the U.N. General Assembly session in fall."

Mori also said the government will study if it is possible to help overseas atomic-bomb survivors, particularly those now residing in North Korea.

After the ceremony, Panov said, "The tragedy in Hiroshima was the worst the world has ever seen. I decided to attend today's ceremony since it is the last one in the 20th century."

Speaking at a press conference in Hiroshima, Panov said the process to scrap nuclear arsenals should be accelerated, adding that Russia is prepared to cooperate to reduce the number of strategic nuclear warheads in the world to 1,500.

Health and Welfare Minister Yuji Tsushima, whose ministry handles policies for rehabilitation of atomic-bomb survivors, also was present, as were House of

Representatives Speaker Tamisuke Watanuki and House of Councilors President Juro Saito.

The city has invited the envoys of the five main nuclear powers—Britain, China, France, Russia and the United States—plus India and Pakistan to attend the ceremony since 1998, when New Delhi and Islamabad conducted a series of nuclear tests.

India and Pakistan sent their ambassadors to the ceremony that year, while only Pakistan did so in 1999. Russia is the only country among the seven to send its ambassador this year.

Historian Says Truman's Bomb Orders Unjustified

From *The Japan Times*: Aug. 7, 2000

NEW YORK (Kyodo) The decision by the U.S. President Harry Truman to drop atomic bombs on Hiroshima and Nagasaki in 1945 cannot be justified as a "military necessity," a U.S. writer says in an essay published recently in Internet opinion journal TomPaine.common sense, www.tompaine.com

Philip Nobile, in his essay "Hiroshima Debate: Was Harry Truman a War Criminal?," claims to be the first British or U.S. historian to pursue the "tantalizing criminal angle" over the atomic bombings.

He slams the decision by Truman, saying the United States dropped the bombs on nonmilitary targets without telling Japan about the possibility of the weapons' use.

"Anyone familiar with the literature knows that Japan was in wretched shape by the summer of 1945 and that Truman was aware of both (then Emperor) Hirohito's desire to surrender and his secret peace initiative in Moscow," he says.

"With the invasion delayed until Nov. 1, Truman had ample time and opportunity for a diplomatic conclusion."

Many Americans believe that the dropping of the atomic bombs on the two Japanese cities was indispensable to end World War II.

"I visited Hiroshima two years ago and I gave a talk at the Peace Museum. Just to test my audience—mostly Japanese intellectuals, journalists, professors—I asked them whether they thought Harry Truman was a war criminal. Everybody at the table raised his or her hand," Nobile writes.

"Then I asked a control question. I said, 'Do you think that your leaders, (Hideki) Jojo and his men,

were war criminals?' And everybody raised his or her hand again," he says.

"I promised those people in Japan that when I came back to the United States and found a comparable audience I would ask the same question (about Truman)."

Nobile also points out that Truman discussed with former British Prime Minister Winston Churchill whether the dropping of the atomic bombs was a criminal act, when Churchill visited Washington in January 1953.

"During a state dinner at the White House, the prime minister startled Harry Truman with a provocative question about the fate of their souls. 'Mr. President, I hope you have your answer ready for that hour when you and I stand before St. Peter and he says, "I understand you two are responsible for putting off those atomic bombs. What do you have to say for yourselves?"'"

Hiroshima Debate: We Were Right to Drop the Bomb

From TomPaine.Com[mon Sense] August 6, 2000

Review of Richard Frank's *Downfall*

Hans Koning is a novelist and essayist. His most recent novel is *Pursuit of a Woman on the Hinge of History*. He is a contributing editor at TomPaine.com.

It is rare that a single book shakes one's long-held ideas about a crucial political drama, but such was the case for me by reading *Downfall*, a history of August 1945, the Japanese surrender and the ending of World War II. Its author is Richard B. Frank, whose second book it is. (His first one, *Guadalcanal* was the story of the American capture of that island from the Japanese in the summer of 1942). Frank's writing style isn't particularly inspired, but the book's impact lies in the vast amount of research he has done, going through four years of Japanese military messages deciphered by American Intelligence (the so-called Magic and Ultra decoding), and such hitherto unpublished material as a private journal kept by Emperor Hirohito during the war. It isn't a case of being won over by his arguments, but by his original presentation of new facts.

Like most leftish writers, I have held it proven that Japan was on the verge of surrendering in early August 1945, and that the primary reason for using the atom bomb was "to show" the Russians, to show them that their victory over the Germans had not bought them security and preeminence in Europe—that Hiroshima was a diplomatic, not a military, move.

I, too, believed that if a discussion of the morality of Hiroshima was possible (Truman's "It saved a million American boys"), there was no conceivable justification for the second atom bomb, dropped three days later on Nagasaki.

Frank's data question both concepts. They do not make the use of atomic weapons seem less awesome and less awful, but they throw different light on it.

About the "pending surrender of Japan": the material on the cabinet meetings in Tokyo in early August (of the six men then in control of Japan's fate), mention the discussions of a negotiated peace among the civilian members but show how these led nonetheless to the unanimous rejection, and "with contempt," of the Allied ultimatum issued from Potsdam. The civilian members would have had to fear for their lives if they had acted otherwise. A total military takeover, and martial laws were, around the corner. The Emperor stayed silent.

The military plan, Ketsu-Go, for action after an American invasion of the mainland, foresaw the erasing of the line between soldiers and civilians. Massive suicide attacks, not only from the air but also on land, were planned and some six thousand primitive kamikaze planes were waiting on Kyushu, Japan's most southern island. Ketsu-Go was prepared to sacrifice the lives of twenty million Japanese. The military cast had started the war and losing it through surrender would be an unacceptable blemish on their reputations. One great victorious land battle was needed to maintain their honor; thereafter peace could be negotiated. As for Nagasaki, at the cabinet meeting on that same day (August 9), the military reported that the damage was considerably less than in Hiroshima, and that in all likelihood the U.S. had only one or two more atom bombs.

Actually the American top brass had already increasing doubts about "Operation Olympic," a landing on the island of Kyushu. The next non-atomic move for which there was complete support from the U.S. army, air force, and navy, was a series of bombing raids with planes and ships to knock out Japan's fragile railroad system of which the main lines ran along both coastlines, east and west. With the Japanese merchant fleet already gone, this would have brought almost immediate famine in the cities. (Japan had no road yet for long distance freight. When I drove around there, twenty years later, I still found no asphalted roads outside Tokyo.) Would it then have been more humane to bank on famine as leading to a Japanese surrender?

Frank asks why it would have been more humane to kill Japanese women and children that way, and why Japan's victims were more expendable than the Japanese themselves. He estimates that some one hundred thousand Chinese died each month in the Japanese work camps, and thousands of allied prisoners-of-war and civilian internees. If it is argued that without atom bombs the war would have lasted "only" three months longer, he demonstrates that those three months, plus the ongoing famine, would have killed ten times more people than the two atom bombs. Moreover, without the bombs the Emperor would have had no "alibi" to stop his generals. Frank, who was born in 1947, two years into the atomic era, may lack understanding of the feelings of horror the bombs created. Worldwide it was immediately realized that these were not "just bombs, only more so." Mankind had created the means to destroy itself. Frank doesn't argue this. But he gives a more precise insight into what was going on in the minds of the actors in that deadly August month, and into the options as they saw them.

Hiroshima Debate: Zinn Versus Koning

Was Bombing Necessary?

From TomPaine.Com[mon Sense] August 6, 2000

Howard Zinn is the author of *A People's History of the United States*, and many other books. He is also a columnist with the *Progressive*. Editor's Note: Following the publication earlier this week of Hans Koning's defense of the bombing of Hiroshima Mr. Zinn submitted the following riposte.

I am surprised that my friend Hans Koning, a stalwart protester against the war in Vietnam, seems to have been taken in by the argument of Richard Frank, in his review of Frank's *Downfall*). Yes, we must all be willing to reconsider our most hardened judgments in the light of new evidence. But there is nothing in Frank's argument—however assiduous his research—to make those of us who see the atomic bombings of Hiroshima and Nagasaki as an unspeakable atrocity change our minds.

Frank points to the fact that the discussions of a negotiated peace with the Japanese cabinet "led nonetheless to the unanimous rejection, and 'with contempt' of the Allied ultimatum issued from Potsdam." Yes, unanimous rejection, because the Allied ultimatum was for unconditional surrender, and the

Japanese were ready to surrender, if one condition could be met—the retention of the Emperor. On July 13, 1945, Foreign Minister Togo wired Ambassador Sato, sent to Moscow precisely to find a negotiated way out of the war: "Unconditional surrender is the only obstacle to peace. . . . It is his Majesty's heart's desire to see the swift termination of the war."

The argument has been made before, that the Japanese military were fanatics who would never surrender, and Frank makes it even more dramatic by describing the Japanese military plan, Ketsu-Go, to go into effect upon an Allied invasion, as "prepared to sacrifice the lives of twenty million Japanese." And only after such a massive sacrifice could they, with honor, negotiate a peace.

It is a preposterous argument. If they were such fanatics, requiring twenty million Japanese deaths before they could surrender, why did they, in fact, surrender after hundreds of thousands of deaths in Hiroshima and Nagasaki? Clearly, as was concluded by the U.S. Strategic Bombing Survey, which interviewed the Japanese decision-makers right after the war, Japan was on the verge of surrender, and would have done so even without the bombing of Hiroshima and Nagasaki. Yes, those bombings speeded things up, but so would a U.S. acceptance of the one condition the Japanese asked, the sanctity of the Emperor—and without that horrendous loss of life and prolonged suffering.

If that condition were accepted, none of the horror scenarios conjured up by Frank would need to occur. Without the atomic bombs, Frank postulates, the "next non-atomic move" (Koning's words) would have been a series of bombing raids to destroy Japan's rail system and cause a famine in the cities. "Would it then," Koning asks, "have been more humane to bank on famine as leading to a Japanese surrender?"

We are being given the typical multiple-choice test, in which the tester assumes we are too dumb to think outside the given alternatives. In this case, we are confronted with three options: a) drop the bombs; b) invade Japan; c) starve the Japanese population. And so we are hemmed in to the conclusion (because we seek the humanitarian solution) that dropping the bombs is "more humane." But there is once again, the alternative suggested by Ambassador Joseph Grew, who knew Japan well, that we not insist on "unconditional" surrender, just on "surrender," and agree to keep the emperor.

Why was this not done, if it was by far the most life-saving of the alternatives? Because, simply put, our leaders did not have the humanitarian concerns which I assume motivate Frank, and which I know motivate Hans Koning. They were not looking for

the alternative that would be least costly in human life. Their motives were political and strategic. Yes, as Gar Alperovitz and his team of researchers documented in great detail in *The Decision to Drop the Atomic Bomb*, there is strong evidence that Truman was listening to his closest advisor, James Byrnes, who saw the bomb as showing off American power to the Russians. Byrnes said the bomb "could let us dictate the terms of ending the war."

There was another political motive, this time domestic. In his recent book, *Freedom from Fear*, David Kennedy quotes Secretary of State Cordell Hull advising Byrnes, before the Potsdam Conference which decided on unconditional surrender, that "terrible political repercussions would follow in the U.S." if the unconditional surrender principle would be abandoned. The president would be "crucified" if he did that, Byrnes said. Kennedy writes: "Byrnes accordingly repudiated the suggestions of Leahy, McCloy, Grew and Stimson." (All of whom were willing to relax the "unconditional surrender" demand just enough to permit the Japanese their face-saving requirement for ending the war—the retention of the emperor.)

Can we believe that our political leaders would consign hundreds of thousands of people to death or lifelong suffering because of "political repercussions" at home? The idea is horrifying, yet we can see in recent history a pattern of presidential ambition considered more important than human life. The tapes of John F. Kennedy reveal him weighing withdrawal from Vietnam against the upcoming election. Transcripts of Lyndon Johnson's White House conversations show him deciding against withdrawal from Vietnam, because "They'd impeach a president . . . wouldn't they?"

Just before the Gulf War, President Bush's aide John Sununu was reported "telling people that a short successful war would be pure political gold for the President and would guarantee his election." And is not the Clinton-Gore support for the "Star Wars" anti-missile program (against all scientific evidence or common sense) prompted by their desire to be seen by the voters as tough guys, even if it leads to a dangerous arms race?

Frank starts with the premise that either an invasion or famine would be necessary to bring about a Japanese surrender, and adds to those huge numbers of casualties an estimate as to how many Chinese would die in Japanese work camps if a surrender were delayed. Combining a false premise with a guess, he concludes that the bombing of Hiroshima and Nagasaki was more merciful. He also, according to Koning (and I hope Hans would not go along with this idea, though he reports it without comment) wonders why we would not rather kill Japanese in Hiroshima than Chinese in work camps. The odious implication is that the Japanese civilians of Hiroshima and Nagasaki are "more expendable" than the Chinese prisoners, because, presumably, they bear some degree of guilt for their government's cruelties.

I would conclude with one question to Richard Frank, to Hans Koning, and to any other American who becomes convinced that dropping the atomic bombs on Hiroshima and Nagasaki "saved lives." Imagine a situation in which we were in a brutal war, coming to its end soon but we knew not when, and we were told that by killing 100,000 American children we would "perhaps" or "probably" (none of the evidence produced by Frank can lead us to use the word "certainly") bring the war to an immediate end and save many more lives than that 100,000. Would we agree to it?

And (okay, more questions) if we would react to that suggestion with horror, as I am supposing, does it not mean that the lives of Japanese children are less valuable to us than the lives of American children? And does not the bombing, not only of Hiroshima and Nagasaki, but of any civilian population, anywhere, depend on the same morally unacceptable judgment?

Disaster Beyond Description

Miyoko Watanabe

(then aged 15, 2.3 km from the hypocenter)

I was born in 1930, just the year before the Manchurian Incident. The Second Sino-Japanese War broke out when I was six years old, in my first year of primary school. The Greater East Asia War began on December 8th, 1941, in my fifth year. I started at Hiroshima Municipal Girls' High School in April 1943, and was hit by the atomic bomb in my third year (at 15 years old).

When students moved up to secondary school, they were engaged in labor service in such places as the Japan Tobacco and Salt Public Corporation, the Clothing Depot or the Ordnance Supply Depot. Although the work was voluntary, you couldn't really refuse if you were asked to do it.

In 1944, as the war got worse, the student mobilization order was issued. Students from the third grade and over (14 or 15 years old) of secondary school had to work at a factory in the school or at a military supply factory. Our normal school life was taken over by labor service and we had no classes.

In March 1945, in the third term of our second year, we were enlisted to work at the Nishikaniya plant of the Japan Steel Company. We were engaged in six hour shifts, with four shifts a day—morning, afternoon, night, and dawn. Children of thirteen or fourteen had to work through the night without sleeping. This is how bad things were in Japan. There was almost no iron or anything else left available.

August 6th 1945 was a Monday, and a "no electricity day." If I had been on the dawn shift, I'd have been on the streetcar passing near the hypocenter at around 8:15. On that day the midsummer sun had been shining down since early morning. The fine weather was unfortunate for those who were hit by the bomb, as the heat rays from the atomic bomb were at their most effective on a clear day. Large numbers of civilians were around at that time, so the aim of causing a massacre was easy to achieve. B-29 bombers had visited us every day, but no

bombs had been dropped. We just felt, "Oh, here it comes again."

There was an air-raid alert just after 7:00 A.M. and the all-clear was given at 7:31. Two aircraft had come to survey weather conditions in Hiroshima. They notified the Enola Gay, a B-29 bomber which had taken off from Tenian Island, that the sky was clear over Hiroshima. We humans cannot foresee the future, however, and because the all-clear had been given, we went with relief to our labor service work of breaking down houses and other buildings to make fire prevention lanes.

I'd gone halfway to Miyukibashi Post Office, twenty meters from our house, when I turned back to get a parasol because it was so hot. Just as I came out of the front door and opened the parasol, an intense yellow, orange, and white light overwhelmed me. It was as if a bomb had been dropped on the gas tanks across the river, and the light was thousands of times brighter than a magnesium flash gun. I quickly went back into my house and lay down in a self-defense position. There were strange sounds, crashing noises and jolts, and I kept no track of the time.

I came to myself. Once I realized I'd been saved, I felt an inexpressible fear. I timidly opened my eyes—the house was a wreck and our factory on the west side of our backyard had been flattened. I though that a bomb must have fallen on the factory. Removing pieces of debris that were on my body, I came out of the house. The clear blue sky had turned hazy as if it were evening, and the other side of the river could only just be made out. There was a strange, indescribable smell in the air, like the smell of gunpowder smoke or mud walling.

When I came to, I looked back to see how my mom was. She looked worse than a devilish witch, her hair standing on end and her bleeding lips ripped down like an overripe fig. I was sure that my mom was going to die. Then my little brother, in the sixth year at primary school (11 years old), came tottering out.

The back of his kimono pajamas, with their blue and white splash pattern, was dyed red, dripping with blood. I thought he was badly wounded, but my resilient mom said, "That isn't your brother's blood, it's mine." Then I saw the blood dripping from her right wrist.

When there was an air raid alert or if we went far from home, we'd carry an air raid hood and a first aid bag with us, but because we'd just been given the all clear, we were feeling relieved and didn't have them with us. I stepped back into the house, eventually found the first aid bag, and sprinkled yellow iodoform on my mother's wounds. Her lips and chin stopped bleeding. I sprinkled it on mom's head and the right wrist too, but it didn't stop the bleeding from the vein in her wrist so I finally put a stop to it by using a triangular bandage with a stop-bleeding stick.

Immediately some workers of the factory appeared and offered to take mom to the Red Cross Hospital on a stretcher. In the middle of this disaster it was unimaginable that, only 2 km from where the bomb had exploded, someone would offer to take her to the hospital on a stretcher. Most people were injured and hardly anyone could afford to care about other people.

Mother told me later that they were going to take her to the Red Cross Hospital via Miyuki Bridge, but they were stopped by the fire so she was taken to the Army Welfare Hospital near Ujina. When they were near a post office, a pharmacist rebandaged her bleeding arm.

With glass all over the place and so many things broken at the hospital, there were a lot of injured people when she arrived. Without using anesthetic, an army surgeon stitched up her lips unevenly. Stitches were put in two places on her lips, in two on her chin and in two on her shoulder. There were over a hundred wounds on the upper part of her body, although it wasn't until later that we noticed. Her right wrist, which was where she was most severely wounded, was left untreated. Because of the masses of people, any wound that had received first aid was not given any further treatment.

Someone we knew had a wound on the back of his head so that the skull was visible, but when he arrived at a hospital, it was too late to get operation. They had no thread for stitches. The wound was left open for over a month, festering and dripping pus. It was the same for my mom's wrist. Even forty-five years later, her thumb was still bent, her forefinger numb, and her hand cold even through the summer.

After I saw my mom off to the hospital, I saw that a door of a house on the river bank had started burning and I put out the fire with water pumped from the well. Then I happened to see there was blood sprinkled in my friend's house on the levee there. My friend's mother, who had been nursing her baby, was dead; glass had pierced her carotid artery. However, her three or four month baby was still sucking at her mother's breast as there was still milk. I remember the scene very clearly. Then my friend came back to her home, and picked up the baby, screaming terribly. I don't know what happened after that. If it had been now, I could have done something to help her. At the time we were all busy with our own affairs.

Thinking about my blood-covered brother, I went back home and took refuge in a shelter. I came across middle school students trudging along, only the top part of their hair left, because it had been protected by their battle caps. They seemed to be barefoot, the skin on their cheeks peeled off like the skin off a peach and the skin on their hands coming off like new potatoes. All they said was "It's too hot. Please give me water," instead of "Help," because boys weren't meant to be cowards. The clothes of high school girls had burned into tatters, and the skin from their fingers hung down, still keeping their shape.

Soon my dad came back. He'd been working on the demolition of houses near the Red Cross Hospital. I heard he'd only been wearing a running shirt and not the national uniform, because it was very hot to wear and the alert had been lifted. His face and the top half of his body were badly burned. He had been on top of the shelter at the time, and had looked up and seen a B-29 bomber. He said, "Oh, a B-29! Why is it there when the alert's been lifted? We'd better get in the shelter." At that moment he was exposed to the flash.

Because I'd seen countless badly burned people escaping along the riverbank, I didn't notice how badly my father had been burned. I told him that mom was bleeding so badly that she was going to die. I took some cooking oil from the kitchen and put it on dad's body. Some middle school students and girls' high school students came along and the oil ran out in a moment. Their hair had been burned to a crisp and their skin was charred like charcoal. I could only tell which were girls from their *mompe*, their work pants, hanging down with the rubber waistband left. It pained me so much to see them that I gave them bandages. The skin on their hands looked dry and wrinkled, like *wakame* seaweed. They all kept saying, "Give me water," "It's hot!"

"Help me!" Then I looked up to the center of the city for the first time, and saw plumes of smoke rising in different places. It seemed strange because I'd thought the bomb had fallen near my house.

A soldier told us, "It's dangerous here. Evacuate to Ujina. Don't give water to people who are burned." I went into the shelter again with my brother. It was so full of groaning and a bad, stale smell that I wanted to throw up. In front of me there was a boy of about a year and a half who had died from internal wounds, and another child of about five passed away too.

The area around our house was about 95% destroyed. Three out of about thirty neighbors lost their lives, and countless people had gone somewhere toward where the bomb had gone off or were working at labor service.

Someone we knew who worked for Hiroshima Dentetsu Company (1.9 km from the hypocenter) appeared, his head wrapped in bandages. He'd run the 700 meters or so to his house at Takanobashi (1.1 km from the hypocenter) along the streetcar road. His house had been flattened. He called out his sister's name, and heard "Help me. Call for some of the citizens' defense reserve, please. Please!" Since everyone in Hiroshima had been attacked, the defense reserve outside, too, were burned up like leaves on a tree. We weren't able to help people who had been crushed as their houses were smashed by the blast wind. Although he was taking off roof tiles one by one, flames started springing up all over the place. The flames attracted other flames and got very close. He asked, "Are you injured?" and heard "No. Hurry up and help." She couldn't get out. "I'm sorry. Forgive me." He said to her. He heard a terrible cry from his sister and "My brother, are you leaving me? You're a devil." It was so hot that all he could do was leave her to her fate and escape.

There was one person who was near the center of the city. He was the only person in his family who survived. His child grabbed his ankle, crying "Help me! Help me!" In a tormented voice he told us that all he could do was run away leaving his child behind. It was such a painful story, yet no one who survived lived without experiencing things like this.

I was about two or three kilometers from the explosion and upwind, in an area that was not so badly burned. Because of that, I didn't experience stepping over bodies or shaking off people clinging and begging for help. Those who fled from one or one and a half kilometers from the hypocenter really did have to step over bodies and shake off hands grasping their legs for help. When someone caught hold of their shoes they just had to leave their precious shoes and flee—otherwise they wouldn't survive.

My mom and dad came back around noon. The only medicine my dad used on his body was a little mercurochrome. When I asked why he said, "There were so many people that the medicine soon started running out." The futon mattress on the stretcher which my mom had been carried on was dyed red with her blood. My mom's fingers were stuck together with dried blood and she couldn't move them until we washed them. Her toes were the same. Her *mompe* work pants became stiff with the dried blood, although when we soaked them overnight the blood kept coming out even when we changed the water many times. Mom said she had a prickling feeling, so I checked her body and found lots of slivers of glass stuck into it, which I took out with tweezers.

Numberless people were trudging toward Miyuki Bridge, as if in a procession of ghosts. A soldier gave the announcement, "Please bring the injured to the relief center at Miyuki Bridge." As my dad had been injured, I let him go there to get treatment by himself. I feel bad now, thinking that I let him go alone so badly burned. I suppose the sudden, horrible bomb just made me frightened. "I'll be O.K. I'll go by myself." Leaving us with these words, he strode off.

God alone knows if this incident is what led to my older brother's eventual death from leukemia. When our father didn't come back soon, he went to look for him. Dad had already been taken to Ninoshima Island. We worried about how seriously he was wounded.

One of our factory workers lived at Tanna (at the foot of Ogonzan hill), 4.2 km from the hypocenter. He invited us to come to his house, so I took my mom and younger brother on a cart and we arrived at Miyuki Bridge. The post office there had been totally destroyed and there was a horse there, dead on its back.

People, dead or alive I couldn't tell, were crouched at the foot of the bridge and begging for water in feeble voices. When no one gave them water there, they went into the river with their faces bent into the water because they felt so hot. Because the river was near the sea so many people died when the tide rose. On each of Hiroshima's seven rivers, there were countless people floating on the tide. The railings on Miyuki Bridge had been broken by the blast and had fallen into the river. I didn't feel anything at the time but later I was struck with fear. The broken granite showed how tremendous the blast had been.

When we got near the Welfare Hospital, there was a strange stinking smell. We found it came from soldiers cremating bodies by the roadside. A large number of bodies were piled up. Apparently, expecting to get some help, those people with burns had used up their last gasp of life to get to the Welfare Hospital. If it were now, I couldn't walk past those lined up bodies. But there was no other way for us to go. Because I'd seen so many people die, all I felt was that those people were dead.

It was evening by the time we finally arrived at the worker's house. We were given dinner sitting on *tatami* mat flooring. I was so worried about my mom and dad that I didn't even taste what I ate and I just felt helpless, not knowing what to do. In spite of the blackout, the city of Hiroshima was blazing as brightly as daylight and we could see each other's faces in the light.

On the morning of the 7th, my brother went to search for our father but as only the seriously wounded were allowed to board the ship, he wasn't allowed on.

Early morning on the 8th, we took our mother to the Welfare Hospital on a wagon. A doctor said to me, "Don't bring your mom any more. We've stitched up her wounds so you'll have to take out the stitches." Dispirited, we went back home.

On our way back we saw people who had been burned laid on straw mats on the road, similar to what I'd seen on the 6th. People who were burned on the front of their bodies had been laid on their backs and people whose backs had been burned were laid face down. They looked like lines of fish laid out in the market. Tents had been set up over these people. Some people who were barely keeping alive were begging for water in weak voices. The smell was horrible. Everyone had been living normal lives until the morning of the sixth so it was natural that they needed to go to the toilet. There weren't enough nurses to help so they were just lying in their urine and feces. Flies came and laid eggs. A few days later there were hordes of maggots about a centimeter long. The maggots ate into human flesh and caused indescribable pain. There were some dead bodies left around that were ravaged by them to such an extent that their bones were visible.

Finally, on the afternoon of the 8th, large numbers of soldiers came from Yanai in Yamaguchi Prefecture and Fukuyama in Hiroshima Prefecture. They moved the wounded to schools and other large buildings.

My brother, borrowing a cap and an armband from the Home Guard, went to search for our father on Ninoshima Island, across the sea. He went from barracks to barracks, looking him among men of a similar build. Thinking that he might be dead, my brother looked among the piled up bodies. He met someone he knew there, who told him that our father was in the innermost barracks. Our father was unrecognizable when he brought him home. My brother was also exposed to a lot of secondary radiation.

Fortunately our father didn't have maggots in his body, but the pus mixed with medicine gave off a horrible smell. Father was plagued by annoying flies, and it was my job to keep them at bay. He kept pleading to be given water. We'd been told that if we gave him water he'd die. Although there was good water available, we only gave him a small cup each time. Even now I'm sorry that we didn't give him all the water he wanted.

A week later I cut the stitches which had been used to sew up my mother's chin and shoulder. She said she felt numb in her lower lip. I had a look at it and saw some fragments of glass peeping out and I removed five long shards. "I feel sick, don't do that anymore," my mother said, but another two slivers came out. The wound on her right wrist kept oozing for a couple of months. Part of the nerve system might have been damaged; because it was numb, the tip of her forefinger started decaying and fell off. She refused to have any operations so it was left as it was. Lots of people in Hiroshima still have glass fragments in their bodies. They are afraid that if they are forced to have them removed their nerve system will be damaged.

Japan lost the war on August 15th. My father died, all too quickly, on the evening of the following day. At the time, I was just going to have a look at the dead sister's remains of one of our factory workers. She had been conscripted to the labor service and was working one kilometer away from where the hypocenter was. She was missing, so this brother had gone looking for her many times. Finally he saw an unburned part of his sister's *mompe* work pants under a concrete block wall, and identified his sister's ankle. He brought her leg home, carrying it on his back. Just as I was putting my wooden sandals on to go and look at her remains with two of the worker's children and my little brother, my father's condition got much worse. It was fortunate in a sense that we were able to avoid seeing the horrific sight of her leg: if we had witnessed it, the scene would have haunted us all our lives with feelings of regret.

Seeing and experiencing so many horrific things such as people dying robbed me of all human feeling. I am telling about shameful things because I want you to understand how an atomic bomb not only afflicts people with its massive destructive power, heat rays and radioactivity, but also drives people crazy. We were able to have my father's body cremated at a crematorium. His hard, pure white bones were left.

After the war, the atomic bomb was called "Pika-don," although no one knows who started calling it that. We heard that no plants would grow for seventy-five years. On September 17th, a typhoon and heavy rain struck Hiroshima with enough force to rock heaven and earth. This was followed by another typhoon. These may have been a blessing from heaven, with radioactivity washed away. Grass started to grow on land that had been burned. Because of the information ban of the Press Code, we didn't know the full horror of radioactivity. People said, though, that poison that came out of people's bodies would drive you mad, so nobody wanted to be involved in the disposal of dead bodies. People would get leukemia, which gave them a high fever and stigmata, and they would writhe in agony.

For us, these symptoms started appearing at the end of August. We were struck by diarrhea, passed blood when we defecated, and lost our hair. Medicinal herbs such as *dokudamiso* or *gennoshoko* seemed to help overcome these symptoms.

People said my elder brother was a lucky man. On August 5th he'd been with the volunteer service demolishing houses and other buildings at Zaimoku-cho, near the hypocenter (400 m away). The next day he'd had a headache so he didn't go to work and was at home when the bomb was dropped. His company's office was in what is now the A-bomb Dome. He went to Ninoshima Island to bring back our father. He also went to his office several times to help with the disposal of bodies or to get things which had been buried under the rubble.

After he was told he contracted infiltration of the lungs in 1947 or 1948, he kept going in and out of the Red Cross Hospital. That was the first sign of his having "A-bomb disease." He then developed stomatitis and also lost his sight. People said he was weak and a collector of diseases. Now I know these were symptoms of "A-bomb disease." I think this must have been a very hard time for him. He kept working hard without realizing that he had contracted myelocytic leukemia.

In 1954, in the year the "Lucky Dragon No. 5" fishing boat was sprayed by radioactive ash, my brother's feet and legs swelled up, as a result of the radiation from the A-bomb, so he went to have them massaged. Wearing shoes two sizes bigger, he kept going to work.

In the summer of 1961, he suddenly lost weight and looked like a different person. In December of that year he was told he had diseased testes. They noticed that the number of white corpuscles in his blood was abnormally high and discovered that he had leukemia. This was sixteen years and five months after he was exposed to the radiation of the A-bomb.

It was discovered too late. Without an operation, he would die, and there was only a 50% chance of the operation being successful. As he had two small children he just had to survive. He had the operation and, although there was a lot of bleeding, escaped with his life. A year and three months after going into hospital he was very pleased to hear that he'd be able to leave, as his condition was much improved. Just before leaving he had a splitting headache. His white corpuscle count increased to 90,000. He was transferred to the Radiation Effects Research Foundation, and died in agony there on July 3, 1963. He was nothing but skin and bones. His legs had become thinner than my arms. The disease had gone right to his marrow.

When he was cremated I felt a shock of horror, as if my back had been sprayed with freezing water or as if I'd got an electric shock. His bones looked porous like pumice stone. When I touched or tried to hold a rib bone it just crumbled into sand. When we tried to look for his Adam's apple bone all we found was half of it. Were these bones really those of my 38-year-old brother? It gave me a jolt of realization of the horror of the radioactivity from the atomic bomb. Not only it going through hell to experience the destructive force and the heat rays of the bomb, it was also hell to watch people dying. People rushed all over the place, going from a searing hell to a hell of water.

Every year, at 8:15 A.M. on August 6th tears roll from my eyes as I'm overwhelmed with heartrending sorrow. My son asked me. "Mom, why are you so sad?" People who have grown up at a time of peace, knowing nothing about war, are so fortunate that they take peace for granted.

Everyone in the world knows about 'Hiroshima'—the city destroyed by an A-bomb. Those of us who barely escaped with our lives from this city of death continue to feel uneasy about our health and the aftereffects of the bomb. The struggle with the atomic bomb has continued over fifty years. What gives me the courage to tell of my experience of the A-bomb is my determination that Hiroshima's experience will not be repeated. I'm not conveying my story as a victim of the bomb with hate for the B-29 bomber that dropped the A-bomb, but rather from being aware that if there is a nuclear war, all the people of the world would face possible annihilation.

I don't want to bare my life in public, but I do want the young people entering the 21st century to understand why I'm telling my story. When I think about it, how hot the victims must have felt! There were people not given even a drop of water. There were innocent schoolchildren who worked loyally for their country, in hunger and without freedom, and were sacrificed to the bomb. It is to these victims that we owe the peace we know today. I want it to be known that War is the most terrible of things for us human beings. To keep a lasting, permanent peace, I want to convey the heart of 'Hiroshima,' hoping that what I do will be like small ripples developing into big waves and into a tidal wave. I am determined that, while not wearing myself out, I will tell the real facts of exposure to the Bomb to as many people as I can.

Selected Poems

Kurihara Sadako

Let Us Be Midwives!

—An untold story of the atomic bombing

Night in the basement of a concrete structure now
    in ruins.
Victims of the atomic bomb
jammed the room;
it was dark—not even a single candle.
The smell of fresh blood, the stench of death,
    the closeness of sweaty people, the moans.
From out of all that, lo and behold, a voice:
"The baby's coming!"
In that hellish basement, at that very moment,
a young woman had gone into labor.
In the dark, without a single match, what to do?
People forgot their own pains, worried about her.
And then: I'm a midwife. I'll help with the birth."
The speaker, seriously injured herself,
    had been moaning only moments before.
And so new life was born in the dark of that pit of hell.
And so the midwife died before dawn, still bathed
    in blood.
Let us be midwives!
Let us be midwives!
Even if we lay down our own lives to do so.

              —SEPTEMBER 1945

This poem appeared first in the inaugural issue of
Chūgoku bunka (the special issue on the atomic bomb,
March 1946.) The cellar in the poem was the cellar of the
old post office in Senda-machi.

Once More, the Sun

When in former times
from ramparts high and strong
our ancestors defended the lands they held in common,
the sun shone brightly.

But hellish ideas
gradually became the black smoke of munitions factories
    and threatened to cloud the sun,
to rise on wings, cross the sea,
become fire bombs and set human civilization
    ablaze,
to become bombs and destroy culture,
to become poison gas
and consign fellow human beings to oblivion.

At that very moment new life
ready to emerge from the womb
was about to end in silence on its deathbed.

Thus hellish ideas filled the world,
dense black smoke belched up
day and night,
factory workers—male and female,
    faces pale,
were made to work double-time, as if possessed,
and sitting atop the cauldron of hell,
scholars, artists, educators,
politicians
all extolled hellish ideas.

Is it not time, people,
to bring back once more
the bright, shining sun
our ancestors praised?

              —OCTOBER 1941

The three lines of the third section I deleted from the first
edition because I thought that they lacked polish. Labor
unions were organized into the Patriotic Production Association; workers, into the Production Warriors; writers, into the Writer's Patriotic Association; politicians too
became members of the Imperial Rule Assistance Association and cooperated in the war effort.

War Close Up

—On hearing over the radio a simulation of the sounds of battle

Stirring bugles! Rousing martial music!
Announcers reporting victory as if possessed,
fanning, fanning the passions of battle!
Masters of state magic appearing one after the other,
adroitly spreading poisoned words
to block all recourse to reason!
Artistic expression turned wholly into state magic!

Our army advances, advances, advances toward the
    enemy:
boots, rifles, bombs, cannon.
The rumble of tanks moving forward.
The sudden sinking of enemy ships.
A radio broadcast simulating the sounds of battle.
A hymn to war booming to Heaven,
sung by pious men and women
who worship this cruel idol called war.
Ah, so mysterious that a puff
addles even completely independent spirits—
the narcotic of patriotism!!
the sophistry of race!!

On the beautiful islands and vast continents
that lie scattered over the globe,
great landholders soon appear and draw boundaries:
from here to here—my country.
They fight and increase their holdings or lose them.
Driven by boundless greed, they make war again
    and again.
They instill hatred in the people born there
and drive them into battle.
On high-sounding pretexts tailored to each occasion,
they raise high the banners: Our cause is just;
    our war is holy.

Justice becomes the password of thieves.
They square their shoulders: "Annihilate
    the evil enemy
and secure world peace."
They howl out:
"Fight to the last man, the last woman
even if it takes ten years, a hundred years."
Then the martial music of the magicians
    sounds still louder,
and fanatic bull-headed patriots
roar and revel;
completely bewitched, the people sing as one:
"Let me die by the side of my Sovereign!"

—August 1942

What Is War?

I do not accept war's cruelty.
In every war, no matter how beautifully dressed up,
I detect ugly, demonic intent.
And I abhor those blackhearted people
who, not involved directly themselves,
constantly glorify war and fan its flames.
What is it that takes place
when people say "holy war," "just war"?
Murder. Arson. Rape. Theft.
The women who can't flee take off their skirts
    before the enemy troops
and beg for mercy—do they not?
In fields where the grain rustles in the breeze,
sex-starved soldiers chase the women,
like demons on the loose.
At home they are good fathers, good brothers, good
    sons,
but in the hell of battle,
they lose all humanity
and rampage like wild beasts.

—October 1942

This poem was censored in its entirety.

The Day of the Atomic Bomb

In the field out back,
a bluish-white flash;
thinking to myself,
"A flare,"
I look out.

Uneasy about
the weird blue flash,
I step outside—
something
is very wrong.

The sky is
a strange hue—
hazy;
suddenly
it's almost dusk.

Acting on instinct—
air raid!—
I race to our trench,
and hold
my breath.

Crawling out
of the shelter,

I find doors and shoji
blown off
and ceiling down.

Must have been
a near miss,
and the children at school;
I become anxious,
unbearably so.

Go get them!
Rushing out,
I find children
on the street,
coming home crying.

Some
are all bloody;
in my mind's eye
I keep seeing my own children
injured.

They come home,
the older leading
the younger by the hand;
they run to me,
still crying.

Children! Children!
You're alright!
I take them firmly
by the hand
and squeeze hard.

"I'll never let you
out of my sight!"
My love for them
swells
enormously.

A bizarre stormcloud
rising to a peak:
the children are scared
and stay
close by me.

Thunder rolls
like the roar
of a plane;
the children
are terrified.

(The atomic bomb exploded at 8:30 A.M.; by 10:00 A.M., refugees were fleeing to the suburbs in one continuous stream.)

Frightening
street of hell—
each moment
the number of refugees
grows.

The refugees all
have burns;
clothes
are seared
onto skin.

Uninjured
but utterly naked,
a young girl fleeing—
I give her
my child's underpants.

The road to the aid station
outside of town:
the line of refugees
stretches on
and on.

On the relief trucks,
the bodies of the dead
and the injured,
blistered and
horrible.

The last five *tanka* passed prepublication censorship, but I eliminated them from the first edition. On 5 August, the day before the atomic bomb fell, I had been mobilized to clear firebreaks in Tenjin-chô, ground zero. On the morning of 6 August, I saw my husband off to the Mitsubishi Precision Machine factory in Gion where we lived and the two children off to school. Then, as I was cleaning up in the kitchen, I saw the flash. I was four kilometers (two and a half miles) from ground zero.

Nightmare
—Going to the aid station to bring home a corpse

After searching more than two days
in vain,
now we learn
the girl
is dead.

Consoling her mother,
we go to retrieve
the girl's corpse:
the city
ravaged by war.

Equipped
for air raid,
we make our way
quickly:
war-ravaged streets.

The last fires
smolder on;
war-gutted streets
still hot
from the flames.

Corpses lie at the roadside,
and the injured form
a great throng:
people
keep aloof.

We near the aid station:
so many ambulances
coming and going
and the stench
of blood.

Near the gate
to the aid station,
it's already awful:
a crowd
of the badly injured.

Lying
every which way,
great numbers
of dead and injured
fill the halls.

In the dim halls
of the aid station,
the living
lie groaning
among the dead.

Among the dead bodies,
a young boy
opens his eyes
and pleads
for water.

He nods gratefully
for a palmful of water:
his mother
surely is
looking for him.

We check
rows of corpses in the halls

one by one,
but can't tell
which one is she.

Not even
their own parents
would know them:
their faces
so utterly transformed.

Dusk falls,
and the halls
with their stench of death
become yet more ghastly,
horrific.

Amid this
horrific reality:
strange
I haven't
stopped breathing.

There, at last—
her corpse;
the injured nearby
lie silent,
eyes open.

Smeared with mud
and black blood,
blistered—
her dear face
gone without a trace.

Loading the corpse
onto the cart we brought,
we leave the aid station;
outside, dusk
closes in.

Carried home
on stretchers and carts—
by parents
and relatives:
so many corpses.

Dusk deepens each moment;
a brightness
over there in the city—
fires
still burning.

(Eerily, the hills around the city were still burning
on the third day.)

Evening falls,
fires on the surrounding hills

gather force,
burn bright red—
without end.

We carry the corpse
from the aid station
through streets
bright with
cremation flames.

I look back at the city:
cremation flames
here and there
dye the black night red—
what sorrow!

The atomic catastrophe occurred on 6 August, and a neighbor girl, a freshman at First Prefectural Girls' Higher School, did not come home. Finally, on 9 August, we heard that her corpse was in the primary school in Koi, so three of us—her uncle, her mother, and I—immediately set out at four o'clock to bring her body home. This is a poem about the scene at the aid station, the fires still burning as we came home, and the streets bright with crematory fires. It appeared first in the inaugural issue of *Chūgoku bunka*. I later composed a free-verse poem about this scene, "Sachiko, Dead in the Atomic Bombing."

Hiroshima Notes

Kenzaburo Oe

1995 Introduction

As a child I did not believe the old saying that one's whole life can be decided by the events of a few days. But now, recalling my summertime experiences some thirty-two years ago, I am forced to concede that such a decisive time is surely possible. And I do so with a profound sense of awe.

I was twenty-eight that year, a young novelist who had made a successful debut and was busy building an impressive résumé. Having experienced in boyhood our nation's defeat and then the initial heyday of postwar democracy, I had by that summer of 1963 become a spokesman, through my essays, for the younger generation. Even so, I felt that my career as a writer had already reached a stalemate.

Moreover, in my personal life I faced a real crisis: my first child, a son, had just been born with a severe head abnormality, and would have to undergo emergency surgery. The young doctor, about my age, warned that even if my son's life were saved, he would very likely suffer serious disabilities. So my personal life had clearly reached an impasse.

In these troubled circumstances, I accepted a request to go to Hiroshima that summer to write a report on a large international rally to abolish nuclear weapons—a gathering that, influenced by global trends, was expected to end in serious fragmentation of Japan's peace movement. By the end of my first week in Hiroshima, however, my attitude toward my personal life had been fundamentally changed. The Hiroshima experience also completely altered my literary work. So in a single week a decisive turnabout took place in my life—eschewing all religious connotations, I would still call it a conversion. Today, thirty-two years later, I am even more deeply and surely aware of that determinative shift in my life.

Beginning with that first week, I have since conducted many interviews with survivors of the atomic bombing and with the Hiroshima doctors, themselves survivors, so as to recount their memories, daily lives, and reflections. My essays also depicted the social and political contexts of their lives. But my basic motivation for writing the essays was very personal. Some critics have said that I used bits of Hiroshima's reality as springboards for flights of personal reflection, and in a sense they were right.

Yet today I believe that what I experienced in Hiroshima that summer thirty-two years ago, and the fabric of thought that I personally wove from that experience, contain something distinctly universal. At the very least this experience produced the views of human beings, society, and the world that subsequently shaped my literature. Of this I have been keenly aware during my life and work as a writer ever since that epochal summer. Without that transforming summertime experience, my literary work and my personal life would never have evolved as they did. A few days can indeed determine one's whole life—my experience has led me to believe this 'myth.'

In my Nobel lecture in Stockholm I spoke of things that have evolved from my one-week Hiroshima conversion. I stressed the ambiguities of Japan and the Japanese. But the situation of Hiroshima is even more, and even now, full of ambiguities.

At the time of writing the essays in this book I was sadly lacking in the attitude and ability needed to recast Hiroshima in an Asian perspective. In that respect I reflected the prevailing Japanese outlook on Hiroshima. In response to criticisms from Korea and the Philippines, however, I have since revised my views of Hiroshima. I have focused more on Japan's wars of aggression against Asian peoples, on understanding the atomic bombings of Hiroshima and Nagasaki as one result of those wars, and on the special hardships suffered by the many Koreans who experienced the atomic bombings. These emphases have taken their place alongside the prolonged struggle by Japanese A-bomb survivors for passage of an A-bomb Victims Relief Law.

In the A-bomb survivors' view, Japan's rapid modernization, with its many distortions, led to Japan's wars in Asia, which in turn led to the atomic bombings of Hiroshima and Nagasaki; thus they hold the Japanese state responsible for their sufferings. While they also criticize the United States for dropping the bombs, they have long sought compensation for their suffering from the Japanese government. Last year the A-bomb Victims Relief Law was finally passed, but without any reference to the basic idea of state compensation. This year the national parliament has taken the occasion of the fiftieth postwar anniversary to debate a 'no-war resolution,' but this resolution will surely fail to assume full responsibility for Japanese aggression in Asia. Powerful conservative forces will busy themselves in maneuvers to strip it of any such considerations.

For me, the pressing question today is, Did the Japanese really learn anything from the defeat of 1945? In these essays the reader will find that one young writer cried out, three decades ago, for the nation to learn the lessons of Hiroshima. As the record of that urgent call, this book has a vital message for today. I have tried to live by the lessons I learned during my first summer in Hiroshima, and my writing has been based on those lessons. In the concluding paragraphs of my Stockholm lecture, I traced the evolution of my core feelings and thoughts, then expressed a personal hope that had its beginning in the work that produced these essays. It is appropriate therefore to restate here those concluding thoughts.

In the lecture I recalled that my mentally impaired son Hikari became able to express in music what was not accessible to him in words, and that his earliest efforts were full of fresh splendor and delight. But gradually his music came to express something dark and sorrowful, like the voice of a crying and dark soul. Yet that voice is beautiful, and his ability to express it in music cures him of his dark sorrow in a process of recovery. Moreover, his music has been well received because it heals and restores his contemporary audiences as well. This gives me courage to believe in the wondrous healing power of art.

While I cannot prove this belief, I do rely on it, 'weak person' though I am, to 'suffer dully all the wrongs of man'[1] accumulated throughout the twentieth century's monstrous developments in technology. This I do in the hope that, as one with only a peripheral place in the world, I can find decent and humanistic ways to contribute to the healing and reconciliation of all peoples.

Kenzaburo Oe
David L. Swain, Tr.
April 1995

Chapter Three: The Moralists of Hiroshima

September 1964

In talking with A-bomb victims in various hospitals, in their homes, and on the streets of Hiroshima, and hearing what they have been through and how they feel about things now, I have come to realize that they, one and all, possess unique powers of observation and expression concerning what it means to be human. I have noticed that they understand in very concrete ways such words as courage, hope, sincerity, and even 'miserable death.' The way they use these terms makes them what in Japanese has traditionally been called 'interpreters of human nature,' and what today would translate as 'moralists.' The reason they became moralists is that they experienced the cruelest days in human history and have endured nineteen years since. Whenever I think of the moralists of Hiroshima, I recall first an old woman who is one of the leading members of the Hiroshima Mothers' Group which publishes the splendid small magazine, 'The Rivers of Hiroshima.' She is a woman who speaks her mind boldly, and how attractive her vivid, incisive expression is—especially when describing the life and opinions of a certain local conservative politician who managed to rise to prominence during and after the Second World War.

I hope that readers will take what follows as an episode in a roguish novel about a fictitious person, since my purpose in introducing it here is to present this woman's interesting manner of speaking. Most probably every district of Japan has stories of similar rogue heroes. But those stories may relate to real persons, while this tale from start to finish consists of only rumor. I will therefore call my rogue hero 'Red Blood,' a purely fictitious character. It is said that at the close of the war he had brought dishonor on himself as an unpatriotic person and was arrested by the military police. But he was later released, at which time he said to the people of his town, 'The blood of an unpatriotic person may not be red, but mine is red.'

Well, it is rumored that Red Blood was arrested by the military police during wartime because there were many defective shells among the munitions produced for the army by his factory. One day, when the war was at its height, an old woman (the narrator of this episode) met a farmer as she was on her way to gather mushrooms in the forest. The farmer was so excited that he foamed at the mouth; he was in a hurry to go see the rogue Red Blood executed by a firing squad. The woman, middle-aged at the time, cried out, 'I can gather mushrooms any time, but this is the only chance I'll ever have to see him shot.' She turned from her way and ran after the farmer. Fortunately, the execution was called off, and the rogue Red Blood was released, leaving his famous words.

It was after the war that Red Blood began to play an active social role. As with the rogue hero in every novel, he displayed such sexual prowess that his first nickname was 'Widow Robber.'

He next tried to enter the political arena. For that purpose he stressed that late in the war he had come close to being executed by a firing squad; that is, he tried to present himself as having been a fighter against imperialism. But this rogue was not so simple-minded as to think that he could win a local election through such an abstract tactic alone. So, with the widow who became his collaborator throughout his political career, he cleaned out all the drainage ditches in his electoral district. This clever tactic worked; he was elected and gained influence as a powerful local politician. He soon found favor among more powerful men, especially the conservatives from pre-war days, through whose support he won a seat as a conservative member of the local assembly. In that capacity, he performed well in getting helpful, concrete relief for the A-bomb victims. When various influential groups, including the progressive Japan Council against A- and H-bombs, engaged in the 'religious war of the peace movement,' Red Blood gave some support to the conservatives in Hiroshima. In time, as happens with rogue heroes in novels, Red Blood acquired something of the aura of a saint. Consequently, Red Blood prospered after the war.

On the other hand, the old woman's husband, a doctor, was purged for having been a town assembly leader during the war. The old doctor lamented, 'My reputation is ruined.' He was afflicted with neurosis and, in his disappointment, took to buying all sorts of new medicines and trying them all. For several days following the atomic bombing, the aged doctor had been one of the doctors who worked devotedly to help the people of Hiroshima. As he, too, had been exposed to the atomic bomb, it was not unnatural that he should obtain and himself use sizeable quantities of each new medicine that came out as soon as he heard of it. But he indulged this interest to excess; and, according to his old wife, he died because his internal organs were eroded by the poisons produced by the reaction of all the new medicinal substances in his stomach. The old woman was also an A-bomb victim but had enjoyed good health, so she firmly refused to take any of the new medicines. Instead, she took a traditional herbal medicine, which cost her five thousand yen each month; and she criticized her husband for his indulgence. Herbal medicines are not used by the hospitals in Hiroshima for the treatment of A-bomb diseases; consequently, she could not depend upon the national assistance for medical expenses available to certified A-bomb victims. The old doctor and his old wife had both been healthy before the atomic bombing; that they both grew remarkably weaker after the bombing indicates clearly that they suffered various symptoms due to exposure to the atomic bomb, regardless of the fact that one had an obsession for new medicines and the other a preference for traditional herbals.

The truth is, though, that A-bomb victims cannot obtain certification for government medical assistance unless they have one or more of certain specific symptoms designated by the Ministry of Health and Welfare. How often I have had A-bomb victims tell me confidentially that they had no illness before the bombing and no definite symptoms of A-bomb disease afterward, yet they are certainly not in good health.[2] Thus, for the A-bomb victims, there are two conflicting factors involved: on the one hand, almost any symptom may be related to the massive and multiple impact of heat, blast, and radiation, including long-term after-effects—conditions which the human race, including the medical profession, never before experienced and has yet to comprehend fully; and, on the other hand, they cannot qualify for government protection unless their complaints fall within the rather narrow range of specified symptoms, many of which are fatal.

Now, this old woman has no connection whatsoever with any authoritarian belief or value system. She is a stubborn, independent-minded person who bases her judgments on what she sees with her own eyes and hears with her own ears. She has no use for dogmatic or conventional ideas; she has seen too many people struggle to overcome difficulties which established ideas and norms could not have solved anyway. It is people like this woman whom I call the moralists of Hiroshima. According to her, people who drowned their cares in liquor immediately after exposure to the atomic bomb did not suffer radiation illness, for the radioactivity turned to froth and oozed out of their skin.[3] Hot-bath therapy and moxa cauterization[4] of infected skin areas have been tried, with good effect, by some people. These traditional therapies cannot be simply rejected out of hand. The point is that Dr. Shigeto and others of the A-bomb Hospital staff have recorded everything done in the treatment of A-bomb diseases because they were coping with unprecedented conditions;

they were pioneering in virgin territory. Thus the old woman continued to speak eloquently. But when she came to reporting on fellow bomb victims with whom the Hiroshima Mothers' Group is always in contact, a certain sadness crept into her forceful expression.

A young mother, who is a friend of the old woman's daughter, gave birth to a stillborn, deformed child. The young mother was an A-bomb victim who had suffered burns and consequent keloid scars; she had prepared herself for misfortune, but wanted to have a look at her baby. When the doctor refused to permit it, she asked her husband to look at it. He went to see the baby, only to find that it had already been disposed of. I am told that the young mother lamented, 'If only I could see my baby, I would have courage.' I was astonished by the word 'courage' in her otherwise grief-stricken and hopeless statement. The word belongs among those which have been given a new depth of meaning by the existentialists. The hospital policy of not showing deformed stillborn babies to their mothers is certainly humane. Limits need to be maintained on what we are allowed to see so that we will remain human. But if a mother wants to see her dead deformed child so as to regain her own courage, she is attempting to live at the minimum limit under which a human being can remain human. This may be interpreted as a valiant expression of humanism beyond popular humanism—a new humanism sprouting from the misery of Hiroshima. Who is not moved by the spirit of this young mother, for whom even a deformed stillborn baby would be a sign to which she could cling in order to regain her courage?

Another young mother was obsessed with anxiety throughout her pregnancy at the thought of bearing a deformed child—so much so that her fear disturbed the physical functions necessary to delivery. As a result, when her time came, her labor pains came and went, off and on, for many hours. She finally had a normal baby, but her own body never fully recovered from that time on.

Although many young mothers suffer neurosis, the fact that they reject abortion and choose to go ahead and bear children shows the bravery of these young A-bomb victims. The overall picture, however, is not always so encouraging. Not a few couples among the A-bomb victims have divorced because they could not have children; and some young wives, compelled by those around them to appear brave, must struggle secretly with neuroses.

There are, of course, even sadder stories. One girl, for example, happened to see her hospital chart, on which was written 'myeloid leukemia,' and then hanged herself. Whenever I hear such stories, I feel we are fortunate that ours is not a Christian country. I feel an almost complete relief that a dogmatic Christian sense of guilt did not prevent the girl from taking her own life. None of us survivors can morally blame her. We have only the freedom to remember the existence of 'people who do not kill themselves in spite of their misery.' My personal feeling about myself is that I, as a Japanese, might be the kind of person who, if attacked by cancer, would hang himself without any sense of guilt or fear of hell. At least, I doubt that I am qualified to prevent others from committing suicide. I am, as it were, too corroded by a sort of spiritless mold. Being such a person, I regain courage when I encounter the thoroughly and fundamentally human sense of morality in the Hiroshima people 'who do not kill themselves in spite of their misery.'

Notes

[1] W. H. Auden, 'The Novelist.'

[2] The Council for Investigation and Research into A-bomb Diseases in 1954 reported that 'many victims complained of various vague and obscure subjective [i.e. felt by the victims but not discernible to doctors] symptoms. . . . The complaints of vague suffering without any characteristic disease should be regarded as one kind of chronic A-bomb illness . . . . Specific efficacious therapies for chronic A-bomb illness are not yet known. Indeed, if the main cause of illness is taken to be the after-effects of radiation injury, then there is no known therapy.' *HN*, 541.

[3] This explanation may have been a lay person's guess; but at least one medical specialist reported that drinking alcohol gave rapid relief from radiation symptoms. *HN*, 534.

[4] In moxa therapy, the powdered moxa is burned on the skin surface at one of the invisible (but histologically indistinguishable) sensitive points, traditionally 365 in number, that are also the loci of acupuncture therapy. This traditional therapy was introduced to Japan from China in the 7th century A.D.

Fuji

Sono Ayako

"Is Daddy coming home today?" asked her three-year-old son, Masayoshi, a kindergartener in the younger-age class, and Ona Tamiko answered,

"Yes, he'll be back on the afternoon train." Then she added, "When he comes home, you tell him all about kindergarten."

But as she said this, Tamiko was aware that her words lacked conviction. Her husband, Masami, worked for a prominent steel company. The oldest son in a household that consisted only of his mother and two other siblings, he had not been able to go to college. After completing high school, he had immediately taken the entrance examination for J Company and started to work at its Komatsu plant in Ishikawa prefecture. Tamiko had been working at the bank near J Company and eventually got acquainted with Masami.

They had been married for six years now. Since his youth, her husband had a built-in sense of being the head of a household. In Tamiko's eyes he was so firmly in control of himself that she could not believe there was only two years' difference in their ages. Tamiko used to spend almost all her salary from the bank on skiing trips. Masami was quite different; he sent money back home to his family in Noto and had carefully put aside enough to pay for their wedding ceremony at one of the company's recreational facilities. And although he had set his heart on taking their honeymoon way off in Kagoshima, he had, when his original plan proved impossible, settled quite rationally for a place more within their budget. They took a tour around the Kii Peninsula. Tamiko and her mother both admired Masami's self-control in the way he ordered his existence.

Masami and Tamiko gradually settled into married life in a tiny two-room apartment provided by the company at nominal rent. They made do with amusing examples of accommodation, covering a tea crate with vinyl cloth and using it for a television table. There were comical moments too, as when they found there was no room for a cushion that

had been made from an old blanket, and they ostentatiously placed it on top of the shoe cabinet in the front hall. Nevertheless Tamiko was quite satisfied with the small pleasures which went into establishing her own household. And maybe the extra weight she put on proved how happy she was, as everyone said, although it was a matter of deep anguish to her when she could no longer fit into her clothes.

Shortly after their marriage Tamiko came to see Masami as not merely worldly-wise in his reactions to all that came his way, but also as rather unyielding in his way of thinking. It became apparent that Masami was taken aback when someone—anyone—knew something he did not. If some item of general knowledge was involved, that was understandable, but he was even embarrassed when he did not know the latest snippet of gossip about some entertainer or other.

"It really bothers me when Masami tells me in all seriousness that some actress is probably going to marry so and so," Tamiko grumbled to her mother. "Me, I know about those things because I read the gossip in the weekly magazines, but I've always felt it was totally trivial."

"But you shouldn't criticize him for his eagerness to know. These days a lot of people seem to think that not knowing anything is perfectly normal. When a person stops wanting to learn, that's the end."

Tamiko winced at her mother's words. She had almost no interest in learning. During her last class in high school, some of the students had cried, but Tamiko was so delighted she could barely control herself. All she could think was that this was the end of studying and tests and that she would be able to take it easy for the rest of her life.

Some wives were embarrassed that their husbands had gone no further than high school and even lied to the children about their father's education ("Papa is a college graduate, you know"), but Tamiko did not share those feelings at all. Since she herself hated studying, it didn't seem fair to expect much education in her husband.

When Masayoshi was born, Tamiko felt she was becoming too content for her own good. She was about ten kilograms heavier than she had been as a girl; but this meant that her breasts never ran dry. Even after she had weaned the baby, some milk, enough for a snack, still flowed. Every time Tamiko took a nap, the baby would take her breast, and both mother and child would sleep soundly, deeply content.

"Be careful you don't smother the baby with those breasts of yours," her mother had warned her, but the baby was clever enough to let go of the nipple when he went to sleep.

Around that time, her husband returned home one night with an intense look on his face.

"I wanted to tell you that I'm thinking about going to college. I've submitted an application," he said.

Tamiko looked at him vacantly, but quickly understood what he meant. J Company had a special employee training program which included a college-level curriculum. A worker with a good performance record (in lieu of his high school transcript) and a superior showing on the written entrance exam (in lieu of his college entrance exams) could enter the four-year program.

"I was going to consult with you first, but then I decided that it was my responsibility to make the decision."

"If you get accepted, you'll go to Fuji, won't you?" Tamiko had heard that the training institute was located near the foot of Mt. Fuji.

"Yes. If I make it, I'll only be able to come home once a month. For four years we'll just have to live apart. There won't be any change in my salary or in the company apartment here, so you don't have to worry about any of those things."

"I see. Well, whatever you think is best," Tamiko said, neither consenting nor opposing the plan.

Dimly, a thought had occurred to her at that moment, though she did not say so to her husband, "He'll probably fail, so it's not worth worrying about yet."

There were a great many applicants to the training center from each of the factories throughout Japan and achieving the honor and privilege of acceptance was no easy task. But Masami carried through on plans he set for himself. He was selected from a huge field of competing applicants and it was decided

that he would go to Fuji. There was actually nothing to worry about. Only men lodged together at the training center. Perhaps some women worked in the office there, but the place was in the middle of an out-of-the-way mountain area, and the accommodations were just like a hotel.

Quiet and rather isolated, the center had a 10 p.m. curfew every day. There would be no time to go into town for drinking. He was not being paid a salary to fool around for four years, and he had been advised that only those employees who were willing to endure a monkish existence and apply themselves earnestly to their studies would be given the opportunity to enter the school. All the men accepted these conditions.

"I feel as if I am sending you away to get married," Tamiko had said two years before when she had seen her husband off.

Although he had claimed that he didn't need anything, she had bought him new pajamas and underwear. She also sent him the best bedding they had and a new small pan so he could fix instant noodles at night.

In enthusiastic letters, her husband would write:

"This school really has everything."

"Famous professors from many universities come and the foremost, top-notch technical people in the company give lectures. The lectures are not big, maybe ten in a class. It must be the best university in Japan."

"When I study, I can feel new knowledge seep into me like water sinking into sand. I can't believe that I could actually have lived this long without studying as I am now."

"Men must really be something special," Tamiko thought. As for herself, she could quite easily get through an entire lifetime without studying. Maybe reading the scandal sheets actually was one big waste of time, but she couldn't see what difference it made what she read as long as she read something. Even if she did not read anything, Tamiko did not feel herself at any disadvantage when it came to educating her child or helping out other people.

Her husband came home faithfully once a month. Masayoshi, having completely forgotten his father's face, had run away when Masami tried to hug him, but that quickly passed. Tamiko had some vague inklings that, little by little, her husband was turning into a different person. If someone had asked her what had changed in him, she would have had trouble answering. During their monthly meeting, which took on aspects of a tryst, her husband made ravenous demands on her. In that sense, the two days they spent together had a new, fresh sparkle to them.

But they had nothing to talk about. Tamiko spoke in great detail of all that had happened in her husband's absence, how Mrs. so-and-so had developed gallstones, or that some dog had gotten run over on the street in front, or that she had found a better place to grow parsley than last year's spot. Even before, Masami had not been exactly overjoyed to hear her relate all these stories, but after he had started living in Fuji, the look on his face showed clearly that her talk irritated him.

"Please stop talking about all that nonsense."

"Then what should I talk about?" Tamiko answered back, offended. "I can't make fancy conversation. I don't go to college like you do."

Her husband was silent but Tamiko felt deeply wounded. She accepted whatever life meted out to her. Her life might be foolish, but life was life.

In addition, her husband had only complaints about the inconvenience of their living accommodations.

"When I get up in the morning, the bathroom is freezing. I can't stand it," her husband said, having become accustomed to central heating. "At least you could put a hot-water heater in the kitchen and bathroom. In the morning, shaving with cold water, I feel so miserable."

"It's nothing to get excited about. There's always a kettle on the heater. Why don't you use that hot water?"

Today her husband was due to return home. The young Masayoshi was getting bigger day by day and had learned to wait for his father's arrival. But for Tamiko, the return of her husband was agony. She waited for him with a sense of obligation, just as he too was probably only coming home out of duty, she thought.

When her husband came home, he longed to eat Tamiko's pickles, although he never once told her directly how much he liked them. He ate a whole bowlful of her pickled cabbage, radishes, and turnips.

"Education does strange things to people," Tamiko muttered, carrying a basket and going out to get some pickles from the small cement-block shed in the back of their apartment. The cabbage and the radishes were all marinating to a natural amber color.

"What is this damn Fuji anyway," she muttered again. Before she knew it, tears welled up and fell into the pickling vat.

The Nobel Prize in Literature 1968
Presentation Speech

Anders Österling, Ph.D.

The recipient of this year's Nobel Prize for Literature, the Japanese Yasunari Kawabata, was born in 1899 in the big industrial town of Osaka, where his father was a highly-cultured doctor with literary interests. At an early age, however, he was deprived of this favourable growing-up environment on the sudden death of his parents, and, as an only child, was sent to his blind and ailing grandfather in a remote part of the country. These tragic losses, doubly significant in view of the Japanese people's intense feeling for blood ties, have undoubtedly affected Kawabata's whole outlook on life and has been one of the reasons for his later study of Buddhist philosophy.

As a student at the imperial university in Tokyo, he decided early on a writing career, and he is an example of the kind of restless absorption that is always a condition of the literary calling. In a youthful short story, which first drew attention to him at the age of twenty-seven, he tells of a student who, during lonely autumn walks on the peninsula of Izu, comes across a poor, despised dancing girl, with whom he has a touching love affair; she opens her pure heart and shows the young man a way to deep and genuine feeling. Like a sad refrain in a folksong the theme recurs with many variations in his following works; he presents his own scale of values, and with the years, he has won renown far beyond the borders of Japan. True, of his production only three novels and a few short stories have so far been translated into different languages, evidently because translation in this case offers especially great difficulties and is apt to be far too coarse a filter, in which many finer shades of meaning in his richly expressive language must be lost. But the translated works do give us a sufficiently representative picture of his personality.

In common with his older countryman, Tanizaki, now deceased, he has admittedly been influenced by modern western realism, but, at the same time, he has, with greater fidelity, retained his footing in Japan's classical literature and therefore represents a clear tendency to cherish and preserve a genuinely national tradition of style. In Kawabata's narrative art it is still possible to find a sensitively shaded situation poetry which traces its origin back to Murasaki's vast canvas of life and manners in Japan about the year 1000.

Kawabata has been especially praised as a subtle psychologist of women. He has shown his mastery as such in the two short novels, "The Snow Kingdom" and "A Thousand Cranes," to use the Swedish titles. In these we see a brilliant capacity to illuminate the erotic episode, an exquisite keenness of observation, a whole network of small, mysterious values, which often put the European narrative technique in the shade. Kawabata's writing is reminiscent of Japanese painting; he is a worshipper of the fragile beauty and melancholy picture language of existence in the life of nature and in man's destiny. If the transience of all outward action can be likened to drifting tufts of grass on the surface of the water, then it is the genuinely Japanese miniature art of haiku poetry which is reflected in Kawabata's prose style.

Even if we feel excluded, as it were, from his writing by a root system, more or less foreign to us, of ancient Japanese ideas and instincts, we may find it tempting in Kawabata to notice certain similarities of temperament with European writers from our own time. Turgeniev is the first to spring to mind, he, too, is a deeply sensitive storyteller and a broad-minded painter of the social scene, with pessimistically coloured sympathies within a time of transition between old and new.

Kawabata's most recent work is also his most outstanding, the novel, "The Old Capital," completed six years ago, and now available in Swedish translation. The story is about the young girl, Chiëko, a foundling exposed by her poverty-stricken parents and adopted into the house of the merchant Takichiro, where she is brought up according to old Japanese principles. She is a sensitive, loyal being, who, only in secret, broods on the riddle of her origin. Popular Japanese belief has it that an exposed child is afflicted with a lifelong curse, in addition to which the condition of being a twin, according to the strange Japanese viewpoint, bears the stigma of shame. One day it happens that she meets a pretty young working girl from a cedar forest near the city and finds that she is her twin sister. They are intimately united beyond the social pale of class—the robust, work-hardened Naëko, and the delicate, anxiously guarded Chiëko, but their bewildering likeness soon gives rise to complications and confusion. The whole story is set against the background of the religious festival year in Kyoto from the cherry-blossom spring to the snow-glittering winter.

The city itself is really the leading character, the capital of the old kingdom, once the seat of the mikado and his court, still a romantic sanctuary after a thousand years, the home of the fine arts and elegant handicraft, nowadays exploited by tourism but still a loved place of pilgrimage. With its Shinto and Buddha temples, its old artisan quarters and botanical gardens, the place possesses a poetry which Kawabata expresses in a tender, courteous manner, with no sentimental overtones, but, naturally, as a moving appeal. He has experienced his country's crushing defeat and no doubt realizes what the future demands in the way of industrial go-ahead spirit, tempo and vitality. But in the postwar wave of violent Americanization, his novel is a gentle reminder of the necessity of trying to save something of the old Japan's beauty and individuality for the new. He describes the religious ceremonies in Kyoto with the same meticulous care as he does the textile trade's choice of patterns in the traditional sashes belonging to the women's dresses. These aspects of the novel may have their documentary worth, but the reader prefers to dwell on such a deeply characteristic passage as when the party of middle-class people from the city visits the botanical garden—which has been closed for a long time because the American occupation troops have had their barracks there—in order to see whether the lovely avenue of camphor trees is still intact and able to delight the connoisseur's eye.

With Kawabata, Japan enters the circle of literary Nobel Prize-winners for the first time. Essential to the forming of the decision is the fact that, as a writer, he imparts a moral-esthetic cultural awareness with unique artistry, thereby, in his way, contributing to the spiritual bridge-building between East and West.

Mr. Kawabata,

The citation speaks of your narrative mastery, which, with great sensibility, expresses the essence of the Japanese mind. With great satisfaction we greet you here in our midst today, an honoured guest from afar, on this platform. On behalf of the Swedish Academy, I beg to express our hearty congratulations, and, at the same time, ask you now to receive this year's Nobel Prize for Literature from the hands of His Majesty, the King.

Japan, the Beautiful and Myself

Yasunari Kawabata

In the spring, cherry blossoms, in the summer the
    cuckoo.
In autumn the moon, and in winter the snow, clear,
    cold.

The winter moon comes from the clouds to keep
    me company.
The wind is piercing, the snow is cold.

The first of these poems is by the priest Dogen
(1200–1253) and bears the title "Innate Spirit."
The second is by the priest Myoe (1173–1232). When
I am asked for specimens of calligraphy, it is these
poems that I often choose.

The second poem bears an unusually detailed account of its origins, such as to be an explanation of
the heart of its meaning: "On the night of the twelfth
day of the twelfth month of the year 1224, the moon
was behind clouds. I sat in Zen meditation in the
Kakyu Hall. When the hour of the midnight vigil
came, I ceased meditation and descended from the
hall on the peak to the lower quarters, and as I did
so the moon came from the clouds and set the snow
to glowing. The moon was my companion, and not
even the wolf howling in the valley brought fear.
When, presently, I came out of the lower quarters
again, the moon was again behind clouds. As the
bell was signalling the late-night vigil, I made my
way once more to the peak, and the moon saw me
on the way. I entered the meditation hall, and the
moon, chasing the clouds, was about to sink behind
the peak beyond, and it seemed to me that it was
keeping me secret company."

There follows the poem I have quoted, and with the
explanation that it was composed as Myoe entered
the meditation hall after seeing the moon behind
the mountain, there comes yet another poem:

I shall go behind the mountain. Go there too, O
    moon.
Night after night we shall keep each other
    company.

Here is the setting for another poem, after Myoe had
spent the rest of the night in the meditation hall, or
perhaps gone there again before dawn:

"Opening my eyes from my meditations, I saw the
moon in the dawn, lighting the window. In a dark
place myself, I felt as if my own heart were glowing
with light which seemed to be that of the moon:

My heart shines, a pure expanse of light;
And no doubt the moon will think the light its
    own."

Because of such a spontaneous and innocent stringing together of mere ejaculations as the following,
Myoe has been called the poet of the moon:

Bright, bright, and bright, bright, bright, and
    bright, bright.
Bright and bright, bright, and bright, bright moon.

In his three poems on the winter moon, from late
night into the dawn, Myoe follows entirely the bent
of Saigyo, another poet-priest, who lived from 1118
to 1190: "Though I compose poetry, I do not think
of it as composed poetry." The thirty-one syllables
of each poem, honest and straightforward as if he
were addressing the moon, are not merely to "the
moon as my companion." Seeing the moon, he becomes the moon, the moon seen by him becomes
him. He sinks into nature, becomes one with nature.
The light of the "clear heart" of the priest, seated in
the meditation hall in the darkness before the dawn,
becomes for the dawn moon its own light.

As we see from the long introduction to the first of
Myoe's poems quoted above, in which the winter
moon becomes a companion, the heart of the priest,
sunk in meditation upon religion and philosophy,
there in the mountain hall, is engaged in a delicate
interplay and exchange with the moon; and it is this
of which the poet sings. My reason for choosing that
first poem when asked for a specimen of my calligraphy has to do with its remarkable gentleness and
compassion. Winter moon, going behind the clouds

and coming forth again, making bright my footsteps as I go to the meditation hall and descend again, making me unafraid of the wolf: does not the wind sink into you, does not the snow, are you not cold? I choose the poem as a poem of warm, deep, delicate compassion, a poem that has in it the deep quiet of the Japanese spirit. Dr. Yashiro Yukio, internationally known as a scholar of Botticelli, a man of great learning in the art of the past and the present, of the East and the West, has summed up one of the special characteristics of Japanese art in a single poetic sentence: "The time of the snows, of the moon, of the blossoms—then more than ever we think of our comrades." When we see the beauty of the snow, when we see the beauty of the full moon, when we see the beauty of the cherries in bloom, when in short we brush against and are awakened by the beauty of the four seasons, it is then that we think most of those close to us, and want them to share the pleasure. The excitement of beauty calls forth strong fellow feelings, yearnings for companionship, and the word "comrade" can be taken to mean "human being." The snow, the moon, the blossoms, words expressive of the seasons as they move one into another, include in the Japanese tradition the beauty of mountains and rivers and grasses and trees, of all the myriad manifestations of nature, of human feelings as well.

That spirit, that feeling for one's comrades in the snow, the moonlight, under the blossoms, is also basic to the tea ceremony. A tea ceremony is a coming together in feeling, a meeting of good comrades in a good season. I may say in passing, that to see my novel *Thousand Cranes* as an evocation of the formal and spiritual beauty of the tea ceremony is a misreading. It is a negative work, and expression of doubt about and warning against the vulgarity into which the tea ceremony has fallen.

> In the spring, cherry blossoms, in the summer the cuckoo.
> In autumn the full moon, in winter the snow, clear, cold.

One can, if one chooses, see in Dogen's poem the beauty of the four seasons no more than a conventional, ordinary, mediocre stringing together, in a most awkward form of representative images from the four seasons. One can see it as a poem that is not really a poem at all. And yet very similar is the deathbed poem of the priest Ryokan (1758–1831):

> What shall be my legacy? The blossoms of spring,
> The cuckoo in the hills, the leaves of autumn.

In this poem, as in Dogen's, the commonest of figures and the commonest of words are strung together without hesitation—no, to particular effect,

rather—and so they transmit the very essence of Japan. And it is Ryokan's last poem that I have quoted.

> A long, misty day in spring:
>   I saw it to a close, playing ball with the children.
> The breeze is fresh, the moon is clear.
> Together let us dance the night away, in what is left of old age.
> It is not that I wish to have none of the world,
> It is that I am better at the pleasure enjoyed alone.

Ryokan, who shook off the modern vulgarity of his day, who was immersed in the elegance of earlier centuries, and whose poetry and calligraphy are much admired in Japan today—he lived in the spirit of these poems, a wanderer down country paths, a grass hut for shelter, rags for clothes, farmers to talk to. The profundity of religion and literature was not, for him, in the abstruse. He rather pursued literature and belief in the benign spirit summarized in the Buddhist phrase "a smiling face and gentle words." In his last poem he offered nothing as a legacy. He but hoped that after his death nature would remain beautiful. That could be his bequest. One feels in the poem the emotions of old Japan, and the heart of a religious faith as well.

> I wondered and wondered when she would come.
>   And now we are together. What thoughts need I have?

Ryokan wrote love poetry too. This is an example of which I am fond. An old man of sixty-nine (I might point out that at the same age I am the recipient of the Nobel Prize), Ryokan met a twenty-nine-year old nun named Teishin, and was blessed with love. The poem can be seen as one of happiness at having met the ageless woman, of happiness at having met the one for whom the wait was so long. The last line is simplicity itself.

Ryokan died at the age of seventy-three. He was born in the province of Echigo, the present Niigata Prefecture and the setting of my novel *Snow Country*, a northerly region on what is known as the reverse side of Japan, where cold winds come down across the Japan Sea from Siberia. He lived his whole life in the snow country, and to his "eyes in their last extremity," when he was old and tired and knew that death was near, and had attained enlightenment, the snow country, as we see in his last poem, was yet more beautiful, I should imagine. I have an essay with the title "Eyes in their Last Extremity."

The title comes from the suicide note of the short-story writer Akutagawa Ryunosuke (1892–1927). It is the phrase that pulls at me with the greatest strength. Akutagawa said that he seemed to be gradually losing the animal something known as the strength to live, and continued:

"I am living in a world of morbid nerves, clear and cold as ice . . . I do not know when I will summon up the resolve to kill myself. But nature is for me more beautiful than it has ever been before. I have no doubt that you will laugh at the contradiction, for here I love nature even when I am contemplating suicide. But nature is beautiful because it comes to my eyes in their last extremity."

Akutagawa committed suicide in 1927, at the age of thirty-five.

In my essay, "Eyes in their Last Extremity," I had to say: "However alienated one may be from the world, suicide is not a form of enlightenment. However admirable he may be, the man who commits suicide is far from the realm of the saint." I neither admire nor am in sympathy with suicide. I had another friend who died young, an avant-garde painter. He too thought of suicide over the years, and of him I wrote in this same essay: "He seems to have said over and over that there is no art superior to death, that to die is to live," I could see, however, that for him, born in a Buddhist temple and educated in a Buddhist school, the concept of death was very different from that in the West. "Among those who give thoughts to things, is there one who does not think of suicide?" With me was the knowledge that that fellow Ikkyu (1394–1481) twice contemplated suicide. I have "that fellow," because the priest Ikkyu is known even to children as a most amusing person, and because anecdotes about his limitlessly eccentric behavior have come down to us in ample numbers. It is said of him that children climbed his knee to stroke his beard, that wild birds took feed from his hand. It would seem from all this that he was the ultimate in mindlessness, that he was an approachable and gentle sort of priest. As a matter of fact he was the most severe and profound of Zen priests. Said to have been the son of an emperor, he entered a temple at the age of six, and early showed his genius as a poetic prodigy. At the same time he was troubled with the deepest of doubts about religion and life. "If there is a god, let him help me. If there is none, let me throw myself to the bottom of the lake and become food for fishes." Leaving behind these words he sought to throw himself into a lake, but was held back. On another occasion, numbers of his fellows were incriminated when a priest in his Daitokuji Temple committed suicide. Ikkyu went back to the temple, "the burden heavy on my shoulders," and sought to starve himself to death. He gave his collected poetry the title "Collection of the Roiling Clouds," and himself used the expression "Roiling Clouds" as a pen name. In his collection and its successor are poems quite without parallel in the Chinese and especially the Zen poetry of the Japanese middle ages, erotic poems and poems about the secrets of the bedchamber that leave one in utter astonishment. He sought, by eating fish and drinking spirits and having commerce with women, to go beyond the rules and proscriptions of the Zen of his day, and to seek liberation from them, and thus, turning against established religious forms, he sought in the pursuit of Zen the revival and affirmation of the essence of life, of human existence, in a day of civil war and moral collapse.

His temple, the Daitokuji at Murasakino in Kyoto, remains a center of the tea ceremony, and specimens of his calligraphy are greatly admired as hangings in alcoves of tea rooms.

I myself have two specimens of Ikkyu's calligraphy. One of them is a single line: "It is easy to enter the world of the Buddha, it is hard to enter the world of the devil." Much drawn to these words, I frequently make use of them when asked for a specimen of my own calligraphy. They can be read in any number of ways, as difficult as one chooses, but in that world of the devil added to the world of the Buddha, Ikkyu of Zen comes home to me with great immediacy. The fact that for an artist, seeking truth, good, and beauty, the fear and petition even as a prayer in those words about the world of the devil— the fact that it should be there apparent on the surface, hidden behind, perhaps speaks with the inevitability of fate. There can be no world of the Buddha without the world of the devil. And the world of the devil is the world difficult of entry. It is not for the weak of heart.

"If you meet a Buddha, kill him. If you meet a patriarch of the law, kill him."

This is a well-known Zen motto. If Buddhism is divided generally into the sects that believe in salvation by faith and those that believe in salvation by one's own efforts, then of course there must be such violent utterances in Zen, which insists upon salvation by one's own efforts. On the other side, the side of salvation by faith, Shinran (1173–1262), the founder of the Shin sect, once said: "The good shall be reborn in paradise, and how much more shall it be so with the bad." This view of things has something in common with Ikkyu's world of the Buddha and world of the devil, and yet at heart the two have their different inclinations. Shinran also said: "I shall not take a single disciple."

"If you meet a Buddha, kill him. If you meet a patriarch of the law, kill him." "I shall not take a single disciple." In these two statements, perhaps, is the rigorous fate of art.

In Zen there is no worship of images. Zen does have images, but in the hall where the regimen of meditation is pursued, there are neither images nor pictures of Buddhas, nor are there scriptures. The Zen disciple sits for long hours silent and motionless, with his eyes closed. Presently he enters a state of impassivity, free from all ideas and all thoughts. He departs from the self and enters the realm of nothingness. This is not the nothingness or the emptiness of the West. It is rather the reverse, a universe of the spirit in which everything communicates freely with everything, transcending bounds, limitless. There are of course masters of Zen, and the disciple is brought toward enlightenment by exchanging questions and answers with his master, and he studies the scriptures. The disciple must, however, always be lord of his own thoughts, and must attain enlightenment through his own efforts. And the emphasis is less upon reason and argument than upon intuition, immediate feeling. Enlightenment comes not from teaching but through the eye awakened inwardly. Truth is in "the discarding of words," it lies "outside words." And so we have the extreme of "silence like thunder," in the Vimalakirti Nirdesa Sutra. Tradition has it that Bodhidharma, a southern Indian prince who lived in about the sixth century and was the founder of Zen in China, sat for nine years in silence facing the wall of a cave, and finally attained enlightenment. The Zen practice of silent meditation in a seated posture derives from Bodhidharma.

Here are two religious poems by Ikkyu:

> Then I ask you answer. When I do not you do not.
> What is there then on your heart, O Lord
> Bodhidharma?

> And what is it, the heart?
> It is the sound of the pine breeze in the ink painting.

Here we have the spirit of Zen in Oriental painting. The heart of the ink painting is in space, abbreviation, what is left undrawn. In the words of the Chinese painter Chin Nung: "You paint the branch well, and you hear the sound of the wind." And the priest Dogen once more: "Are there not these cases? Enlightenment in the voice of the bamboo. Radiance of heart in the peach blossom."

Ikenobo Sen'o, a master of flower arranging, once said (the remark is to be found in his *Sayings*): "With a spray of flowers, a bit of water, one evokes the vastness of rivers and mountains." The Japanese garden too, of course symbolizes the vastness of nature. The Western garden tends to be symmetrical, the Japanese garden asymmetrical, and this is because the asymmetrical has the greater power to symbolize multiplicity and vastness. The asymmetry, of course, rests upon a balance imposed by delicate sensibilities. Nothing is more complicated, varied, attentive to detail, than the Japanese art of landscape gardening. Thus there is the form called the dry landscape, composed entirely of rocks, in which the arrangement of stones gives expression to mountains and rivers that are not present, and even suggests the waves of the great ocean breaking in upon cliffs. Compressed to the ultimate, the Japanese garden becomes the *bonsai* dwarf garden, or the *bonseki*, its dry version.

In the Oriental word for landscape, literally "mountain-water," with its related implications in landscape painting and landscape gardening, there is contained the concept of the sere and wasted, and even of the sad and the threadbare. Yet in the sad, austere, autumnal qualities so valued by the tea ceremony, itself summarized in the expression "gently respectful, cleanly quiet," there lies concealed a great richness of spirit; and the tea room, so rigidly confined and simple, contains boundless space and unlimited elegance. The single flower contains more brightness than a hundred flowers. The great sixteenth-century master of the tea ceremony and flower arranging, Rikyu, taught that it was wrong to use fully opened flowers. Even in the tea ceremony today the general practice is to have in the alcove of the tea room but a single flower, and that a flower in bud. In winter a special flower of winter, let us say a camellia, bearing some such name as White Jewel or Wabisuke, which might be translated literally as "Helpmate in Solitude", is chosen, a camellia remarkable among camellias for its whiteness and the smallness of its blossoms; and but a single bud is set out in the alcove. White is the cleanest of colors, it contains in itself all the other colors. And there must always be dew on the bud. The bud is moistened with a few drops of water. The most splendid of arrangements for the tea ceremony comes in May, when a peony is put out in a celadon vase; but here again there is but a single bud, always with dew upon it. Not only are there drops of water upon the flower, the vase too is frequently moistured.

Among flower vases, the ware that is given the highest rank is old Iga, from the sixteenth and seventeenth centuries, and it commands the highest price. When old Iga has been dampened, its colors and its glow take on a beauty such as to awaken on afresh. Iga was fired at very high temperatures. The straw ash and the smoke from the fuel fell and flowed against the surface, and as the temperature dropped, became a sort of glaze. Because the colors were not fabricated but were rather the result of nature at work in the kiln, color patterns emerged in such varieties as to be called quirks and freaks of the kiln. The rough, austere, strong surfaces of old Iga take on a voluptuous glow when dampened. It breathes to the rhythm of the dew of the flowers.

The taste of the tea ceremony also asks that the tea bowl be moistened before using, to give it its own soft glow.

Ikenobo Sen'o remarked on another occasion (this too is in his *Sayings*) that "the mountains and strands should appear in their own forms." Bringing a new spirit into his school of flower arranging, therefore, he found "flowers" in broken vessels and withered branches, and in them too the enlightenment that comes from flowers. "The ancients arranged flowers and pursued enlightenment." Here we see awakening to the heart of the Japanese spirit, under the influence of Zen. And in it too, perhaps, is the heart of a man living in the devastation of long civil wars.

The Tales of Ise, compiled in the tenth century, is the oldest Japanese collection of lyrical episodes, numbers of which might be called short stories. In one of them we learn that the poet Ariwara no Yukihira, having invited guests, put in flowers:

"Being a man of feeling, he had in a large jar a most unusual wistaria. The trailing spray of flowers was upwards of three and a half feet long."

A spray of wistaria of such length is indeed so unusual as to make one have doubts about the credibility of the writer; and yet I can feel in this great spray a symbol of Heian culture. The wistaria is a very Japanese flower, and it has a feminine elegance. Wistaria sprays, as they trail in the breeze, suggest softness, gentleness, reticence. Disappearing and then appearing again in the early summer greenery, they have in them that feeling for the poignant beauty of things long characterized by the Japanese as *mono no aware*. No doubt there was a particular splendor in that spray upwards of three and a half feet long. The splendors of Heian culture a millennium ago and the emergence of a peculiarly Japanese beauty were as wondrous as this "most unusual wistaria," for the culture of T'ang China had at length been absorbed and Japanized. In poetry there came, early in the tenth century, the first of the imperially commissioned anthologies, the Kokinshu, and in fiction, the *Tales of Ise*, followed by the supreme masterpieces of classical Japanese prose, the *Tale of Genji* of Lady Murasaki and the *Pillow Book* of Sei Shonagon, both of whom lived from the late tenth century into the early eleventh. So was established a tradition which influenced and even controlled Japanese literature for eight hundred years. *The Tale of Genji* in particular is the highest pinnacle of Japanese literature. Even down to our day there has not been a piece of fiction to compare with it. That such a modern work should have been written in the eleventh century is a miracle, and as a miracle the work is widely known abroad. Although my grasp of classical Japanese was uncertain, the Heian classics were my principal boyhood reading, and it is the *Genji*, I think, that has meant the most to me. For centuries after it was written, fascination with the *Genji* persisted, and imitations and reworkings did homage to it. The *Genji* was a wide and deep source of nourishment for poetry, of course, and for the fine arts and handicrafts as well, and even for landscape gardening.

Murasaki and Sei Shonagon, and such famous poets as Izumi Shikibu, who probably died early in the eleventh century, and Akazome Emon, who probably died in the mid-eleventh century, were all ladies-in-waiting in the imperial court. Japanese culture was court culture, and court culture was feminine. The day of the *Genji* and the *Pillow Book* was its finest, when ripeness was moving into decay. One feels in it the sadness at the end of glory, the high tide of Japanese court culture. The court went into its decline, power moved from the court nobility to the military aristocracy, in whose hands it remained through almost seven centuries from the founding of the Kamakura Shogunate in 1192 to the Meiji Restoration in 1867 and 1868. It is not to be thought, however, that either the imperial institution or court culture vanished. In the eighth of the imperial anthologies, the *Shinkokinshū* of the early thirteenth century, the technical dexterity of the *Kokinshu* was pushed yet a step further, and sometimes fell into mere verbal dalliance; but there were added elements of the mysterious, the suggestive, the evocative and inferential elements of sensuous fantasy that have something in common with modern symbolist poetry. Saigyo, who has been mentioned earlier, was a representative poet spanning the two ages, Heian and Kamakura.

> I dreamt of him because I was thinking of him.
> Had I known it was a dream, I should not have
> wished to awaken.
> In my dreams I go to him each night without fail.
> But this is less than a single glimpse in the waking.

These are by Ono no Komachi, the leading poetess of the *Kokinshu*, who sings of dreams, even, with a straightforward realism. But when we come to the following poems of the Empress Eifuku, who lived at about the same time as Ikkyu, in the Muromachi Period, somewhat later than the *Shinkokinshu*, we have a subtle realism that becomes a melancholy symbolism, delicately Japanese, and seems to me more modern:

Shining upon the bamboo thicket where the
    sparrows twitter,
The sunlight takes on the color of the autumn.
The autumn wind, scattering the bush clover in
    the garden,
        sinks into one's bones.
Upon the wall, the evening sun disappears.

Dogen, whose poem about the clear, cold snow I have quoted, and Myoe, who wrote of the winter moon as his companion, were of generally the Shinkokinshu period. Myoe exchanged poems with Saigyo and the two discussed poetry together. The following is from the biography of Myoe by his disciple Kikai:

"Saigyo frequently came and talked of poetry. His own attitude towards poetry, he said, was far from the ordinary. Cherry blossoms, the cuckoo, the moon, snow: confronted with all the manifold forms of nature, his eyes and his ears were filled with emptiness. And were not all the words that came forth true words? When he sang of the blossoms the blossoms were not on his mind, when he sang of the moon he did not think of the moon. As the occasion presented itself, as the urge arose, he wrote poetry. The red rainbow across the sky was as the sky taking on color. The white sunlight was as the sky growing bright. Yet the empty sky, by its nature, was not something to become bright. It was not something to take on color. With a spirit like the empty sky he gives color to all the manifold scenes but not a trace remained. In such poetry was the Buddha, the manifestation of the ultimate truth."

Here we have the emptiness, the nothingness, of the Orient. My own works have been described as works of emptiness, but it is not to be taken for the nihilism of the West. The spiritual foundation would seem to be quite different. Dogen entitled his poem about the seasons, "Innate Reality," and even as he sang of the beauty of the seasons he was deeply immersed in Zen.

The Nobel Prize in Literature 1994
Presentation Speech

Kjell Espmark

Your Majesties, Your Royal Highnesses, Ladies and Gentlemen,

In his novel *The Silent Cry*, Kenzaburo Oe describes a scene which casts light over his entire œuvre. The narrator, Mitsu, living in a marriage which has not survived the birth of a child with serious brain damage, has returned to the Shikoku of his childhood with his younger brother, Takashi, a hardline activist, who dreams of a martyr's death. They are back in the isolated valley in which their ancestors once found refuge in a critical situation. One night Mitsu witnesses how his brother, stark naked, runs round in circles in the newly-fallen snow, and then rolls over and over in the snow-drifts with obvious signs of sexual excitement. Takashi is at one and the same time both the narrator's great-grandfather's brother, and also his own; he is both the leader of a rebellion which took place a century earlier, and the instigator of present-day riots: "every moment of those hundred years was crowded into this one instant in time."

From one point of view the scene allows us a glimpse of Oe's narrative mastery: unerringly he carries a series of events in two time planes to its tragic culmination. From another point of view, the passage is an example of the past breaking into the present, making the figures resume and vary an earlier line of action. In Oe's work, a number of such challenges from the past again and again evoke new answers. We have just been reminded of the escape of the ancestors to the secluded valley, the rebellion of a century earlier, the tension between the mismatched brothers, and the shock caused by the child's deformity. Nuclear catastrophe is another such theme, readily linked to the theme of the brain-damaged son. Certain philosophical elements persist as well, coloured by Oe's early readings of Sartre, such as the absurdity of life, the inescapability of responsibility, and human dignity. But Oe also insists on another point: undefined and inaccessible reality demands a "model" if it is to be perceived by the senses.

The incessant re-emergences are, however, linked to a great project, whose features and dimensions have gradually taken form. Books like *A Personal Matter, The Silent Cry* as well as *M/T and the Tale of the Wonders of the Forest* are, together with the short stories, works that fall into their proper places when we read the novel that was published in French last year under the title *Lettres aux Années de Nostalgic*. Here Oe exploits the device of the Japanese first-person novel to create the illusion of an autobiography. In reality the book—we are told in an interview—is 80 percent fiction. Brother Gii, who is presented to us as the dominant figure in the narrator's life, is thus a literary invention, a counter-figure who embodies the latter's dream of remaining in the woodland of his ancestors, reading Dante. The earlier books now assume their rightful places in this new context which reveals them in a new light. In *The Silent Cry*, for example, occurs a transformation of the crime which once gave Gii ten years in prison, but also a revision of his material about the life of their ancestors.

In Oe's work, therefore, we are dealing with more than persistent leitmotifs. The books re-echo and vary each other in a great ingenious project. Here, if ever, it is justifiable to talk about a writer who is not writing books but "building" an œuvre. And we can add that once again Oe inverts his material in a new novel in which the symbiosis between a father and his spiritually clouded son is focused on anew—a book that paradoxically ends with the word "Rejoice!"

This may sound like a rigidly planned structure but that is not at all what the text looks like. It rather seems as if this stubborn enterprise is the outcome of a poetic obsession. Oe himself has described his writing as a way of exorcising his demons. Hopefully, he will never succeed. But from his incessant wrestling with these risky beings derives an œuvre which succeeds in another way—in escaping the bounds of the author's intentions. Oe has declared that he addresses only his Japanese readers, without glancing at his worldwide audience. But there is in his "grotesque realism" a powerful poetry which communicates across the boundaries of languages and cultures, a poetry full of fresh observations and concise images. The furious persistence, as well, with which he returns to his motifs erases these barriers: eventually we become familiar with his figures, marvel at their transformations, and are enticed into sharing the author's view that no truth, no picture is valid once and for all. Validity exists on another level. Out of this multitude of people and events in ever-changing shapes there rises in the end the vision of a genuine humanist, a poignant picture of that which concerns us all.

Dear Mr. Oe,

You have claimed that reality demands a "model" if it is to be grasped by our senses. Your books offer, indeed, such a "model," enabling us to see the interaction of time present and time past, of relentless change and persistent myth, and to distinguish man's delicate position in the context. It is my pleasure, on behalf of the Swedish Academy, to convey to you our warmest congratulations on the Nobel Prize in Literature for 1994, and to invite you to receive the Prize from the hands of His Majesty the King.

Japan, the Ambiguous, and Myself

Kenzaburo Oe

During the last catastrophic World War, I was a little boy and lived in a remote, wooded valley on Shikoku Island in the Japanese Archipelago, thousands of miles away from here. At that time there were two books by which I was really fascinated: *The Adventures of Huckleberry Finn* and *The Wonderful Adventures of Nils*. The whole world was then engulfed by waves of horror. By reading *Huckleberry Finn* I felt I was able to justify my act of going into the mountain forest at night and sleeping among the trees with a sense of security which I could never find indoors. The protagonist of *The Adventures of Nils* is transformed into a little creature, understands birds' language and makes an adventurous journey. I derived from the story sensuous pleasures of various kinds. Firstly, living as I was in a deep wood on the Island of Shikoku just as my ancestors had done long ago, I had a revelation that this world and this way of life there were truly liberating. Secondly, I felt sympathetic and identified myself with Nils, a naughty little boy, who while traversing Sweden, collaborating with and fighting for the wild geese, transforms himself into a boy, still innocent, yet full of confidence as well as modesty. On coming home at last, Nils speaks to his parents. I think that the pleasure I derived from the story at its highest level lies in the language, because I felt purified and uplifted by speaking along with Nils. His worlds run as follows (in French and English translation):

"Maman, Papa! Je suis grand, je suis de nouveau un homme!" cria-t-il.

"Mother and father!" he cried. "I'm a big boy. I'm a human being again!"

I was fascinated by the phrase 'je suis de nouveau un homme!' in particular. As I grew up, I was continually to suffer hardships in different realms of life—in my family, in my relationship to Japanese society and in my way of living at large in the latter half of the twentieth century. I have survived by representing these sufferings of mine in the form of

the novel. In that process I have found myself repeating, almost sighing, 'je suis de nouveau un homme!' Speaking like this as regards myself is perhaps inappropriate to this place and to this occasion. However, please allow me to say that the fundamental style of my writing has been to start from my personal matters and then to link it up with society, the state and the world. I hope you will forgive me for talking about my personal matters a little further.

Half a century ago, while living in the depth of that forest, I read *The Adventures of Nils* and felt within it two prophecies. One was that I might one day become able to understand the language of birds. The other was that I might one day fly off with my beloved wild geese—preferably to Scandinavia.

After I got married, the first child born to us was mentally handicapped. We named him *Hikari*, meaning 'Light' in Japanese. As a baby he responded only to the chirps of wild birds and never to human voices. One summer when he was six years old we were staying at our country cottage. He heard a pair of water rails (*Rallus aquaticus*) warbling from the lake beyond a grove, and he said with the voice of a commentator on a recording of wild birds: "They are water rails." This was the first moment my son ever uttered human words. It was from then on that my wife and I began having verbal communication with our son.

Hikari now works at a vocational training centre for the handicapped, an institution based on ideas we learnt from Sweden. In the meantime he has been composing works of music. Birds were the originators that occasioned and mediated his composition of human music. On my behalf *Hikari* has thus accomplished the prophecy that I might one day understand the language of birds. I must say also that my life would have been impossible but for my wife with her abundant female force and wisdom. She has been the very incarnation of Akka, the leader of Nils's wild geese. Together with her I have flown to

Stockholm and the second of the prophecies has also, to my utmost delight, now been realised.

Kawabata Yasunari, the first Japanese writer who stood on this platform as a winner of the Nobel Prize for Literature, delivered a lecture entitled *Japan, the Beautiful, and Myself*. It was at once very beautiful and *vague*. I have used the English word *vague* as an equivalent of that word in Japanese *aimaina*. This Japanese adjective could have several alternatives for its English translation. The kind of vagueness that Kawabata adopted deliberately is implied in the title itself of his lecture. It can be transliterated as 'myself *of* beautiful Japan.' The vagueness of the whole title derives from the Japanese particle 'no' (literally 'of') linking 'Myself' and 'Beautiful Japan.'

The vagueness of the title leaves room for various interpretations of its implications. It can imply 'myself as a part of beautiful Japan,' the particle 'no' indicating the relationship of the noun following it to the noun preceding it as one of possession, belonging or attachment. It can also imply 'beautiful Japan and myself,' the particle in this case linking the two nouns in apposition, as indeed they are in the English title of Kawabata's lecture translated by one of the most eminent American specialists of Japanese literature. He translates 'Japan, the beautiful *and* myself.' In this expert translation the *traduttore* (translator) is not in the least a *traditore* (betrayer).

Under that title Kawabata talked about a unique kind of mysticism which is found not only in Japanese thought but also more widely Oriental thought. By 'unique' I mean here a tendency towards Zen Buddhism. Even as a twentieth-century writer Kawabata depicts his state of mind in terms of the poems written by medieval Zen monks. Most of these poems are concerned with the linguistic impossibility of telling truth. According to such poems words are confined within their closed shells. The readers can not expect that words will ever come out of these poems and get through to us. One can never understand or feel sympathetic towards these Zen poems except by giving oneself up and willingly penetrating into the closed shells of those words.

Why did Kawabata boldly decide to read those extremely esoteric poems in Japanese before the audience in Stockholm? I look back almost with nostalgia upon the straightforward bravery which he attained towards the end of his distinguished career and with which he made such a confession of his faith. Kawabata had been an artistic pilgrim for decades during which he produced a host of masterpieces. After those years of his pilgrimage, only by making a confession as to how he was fascinated by such inaccessible Japanese poems that baffle any attempt fully to understand them, was he able to talk about 'Japan, the Beautiful, and Myself,' that is, about the world in which he lived and the literature which he created.

It is noteworthy, furthermore, that Kawabata concluded his lecture as follows:

> My works have been described as works of emptiness, but it is not to be taken for the nihilism of the West. The spiritual foundation would seem to be quite different. Dogen entitled his poem about the seasons 'Innate Reality,' and even as he sang of the beauty of the seasons he was deeply immersed in Zen. (*Translation by Edward Seidensticker*)

Here also I detect a brave and straightforward self-assertion. On the one hand Kawabata identifies himself as belonging essentially to the tradition of Zen philosophy and aesthetic sensibilities pervading the classical literature of the Orient. Yet on the other he goes out of his way to differentiate emptiness as an attribute of his works from the nihilism of the West. By doing so he was whole-heartedly addressing the coming generations of mankind with whom Alfred Nobel entrusted his hope and faith.

To tell you the truth, rather than with Kawabata my compatriot who stood here twenty-six years ago, I feel more spiritual affinity with the Irish poet William Butler Yeats, who was awarded a Nobel Prize for Literature seventy one years ago when he was at about the same age as me. Of course I would not presume to rank myself with the poetic genius Yeats. I am merely a humble follower living in a country far removed from his. As William Blake, whose work Yeats revalued and restored to the high place it holds in this century, once wrote: 'Across Europe & Asia to China & Japan like lightnings.'

During the last few years I have been engaged in writing a trilogy which I wish to be the culmination of my literary activities. So far the first two parts have been published and I have recently finished writing the third and final part. It is entitled in Japanese *A Flaming Green Tree*. I am indebted for this title to a stanza from Yeats's poem *Vacillation*:

> A tree there is that from its topmost bough
> Is half all glittering flame and half all green
> Abounding foliage moistened with the dew . . .
> ("Vacillation," 11–13)

In fact my trilogy is so soaked in the overflowing influence of Yeats's poems as a whole. On the occasion of Yeat's winning the Nobel Prize the Irish Senate proposed a motion to congratulate him, which contained the following sentences:

. . . the recognition which the nation has gained, as a prominent contributor to the world's culture, through his success."
. . . a race that hitherto had not been accepted into the comity of nations.
. . . Our civilization will be assesed on the name of Senator Yeats.
. . . there will always be the danger that there may be a stampeding of people who are sufficiently removed from insanity in enthusiasm for destruction. (The Nobel Prize: Congratulations to Senator Yeats)

Yeats is the writer in whose wake I would like to follow. I would like to do so for the sake of another nation that has now been 'accepted into the comity of nations' but rather on account of the technology in electrical engineering and its manufacture of automobiles. Also I would like to do so as a citizen of such a nation which was stamped into 'insanity in enthusiasm of destruction' both on its own soil and on that of the neighbouring nations.

As someone living in the present would such as this one and sharing bitter memories of the past imprinted on my mind, I cannot utter in unison with Kawabata the phrase 'Japan, the Beautiful and Myself.' A moment ago I touched upon the 'vagueness' of the title and content of Kawabata's lecture. In the rest of my lecture I would like to use the word 'ambiguous' in accordance with the distinction made by the eminent British poet Kathleen Raine; she once said of William Blake that he was not so much vague as ambiguous. I cannot talk about myself otherwise than by saying 'Japan, the Ambiguous, and Myself.'

My observation is that after one hundred and twenty years of modernisation since the opening of the country, present-day Japan is split between two opposite poles of ambiguity. I too am living as a writer with this polarisation imprinted on me like a deep scar.

This ambiguity which is so powerful and penetrating that it splits both the state and its people is evident in various ways. The modernisation of Japan has been orientated toward learning from and imitating the West. Yet Japan is situated in Asia and has firmly maintained its traditional culture. The ambiguous orientation of Japan drove the country into the position of an invader in Asia. On the other hand, the culture of modern Japan, which implied being thoroughly open to the West or at least that impeded understanding by the West. What was more, Japan was driven into isolation from other Asian countries, not only politically but also socially and culturally.

In the history of modern Japan literature the writers most sincere and aware of their mission were those 'post-war writers' who came onto the literary scene immediately after the last War, deeply wounded by the catastrophe yet full of hope for a rebirth. They tried with great pains to make up for the inhuman atrocities committed by Japanese military forces in Asian countries, as well as to bridge the profound gaps that existed not only between the developed countries of the West and Japan but also between African and Latin American countries and Japan. Only by doing so did they think that they could seek with some humility reconciliation with the rest of the world. It has always been my aspiration to cling to the very end of the line of that literary tradition inherited from those writers.

The contemporary state of Japan and its people in their post-modern phase cannot but be ambivalent. Right in the middle of the history of Japan's modernisation came the Second World War, a war which was brought about by the very aberration of the modernisation itself. The defeat in this War fifty years ago occasioned an opportunity for Japan and the Japanese as the very agent of the War to attempt a rebirth out of the great misery and sufferings that were depicted by the 'Post-war School' of Japanese writers. The moral props for Japanese aspiring to such a rebirth were the idea of democracy and their determination never to wage a war again. Paradoxically, the people and state of Japan living on such moral props were not innocent but had been stained by their own past history of invading other Asian countries. Those moral props mattered also to the deceased victims of the nuclear weapons that were used for the first time in Hiroshima and Nagasaki, and for the survivors and their off-spring affected by radioactivity (including tens of thousands of those whose mother tongue is Korean).

In the recent years there have been criticisms levelled against Japan suggesting that she should offer more military forces to the United Nations forces and thereby play a more active role in the keeping and restoration of peace in various parts of the world. Our heart sinks whenever we hear these criticisms. After the end of the Second World War it was a categorical imperative for us to declare that we renounced war forever in a central article of the new Constitution. The Japanese chose the principle of eternal peace as the basis of morality for our rebirth after the War.

I trust that the principle can best be understood in the West with its long tradition of tolerance for conscientious rejection of military service. In Japan itself there have all along been attempts by some to obliterate the article about renunciation of war from the Constitution and for this purpose they have taken every opportunity to make use of pressures from abroad. But to obliterate from the Constitution the principle of eternal peace will be nothing but an act of betrayal against the peoples of Asia and the victims of the Atom Bombs in Hiroshima and Nagasaki. It is not difficult for me as a writer to imagine what would be the outcome of that betrayal.

The pre-war Japanese Constitution that posited an absolute power transcending the principle of democracy had sustained some support from the populace. Even though we now have the half-century-old new Constitution, there is a popular sentiment of support for the old one that lives on in reality in some quarters. If Japan were to institutionalise a principle other than the one to which we have adhered for the last fifty years, the determination we made in the post-war ruins of our collapsed effort at modernisation—that determination of ours to establish the concept of universal humanity would come to nothing. This is the spectre that rises before me, speaking as an ordinary individual.

What I call Japan's 'ambiguity' in my lecture is a kind of chronic disease that has been prevalent throughout the modern age. Japan's economic prosperity is not free from it either, accompanied as it is by all kinds of potential dangers in the light of the structure of world economy and environmental conservation. The 'ambiguity' in this respect seems to be accelerating. It may be more obvious to the critical eyes of the world at large than to us within the country. At the nadir of the post-war economic poverty we found a resilience to endure it, never losing our hope for recovery. It may sound curious to say so, but we seem to have no less resilience to endure our anxiety about the ominous consequence emerging out of the present prosperity. From another point of view, a new situation now seems to be arising in which Japan's prosperity is going to be incorporated into the expanding potential power of both production and consumption in Asia at large.

I am one of the writers who wish to create serious works of literature which dissociate themselves from those novels which are mere reflections of the vast consumer cultures of Tokyo and the subcultures of the world at large. What kind of identity as a Japanese should I seek? W.H. Auden once defined the novelist as follows:

> . . . , among the dust
> Be just, among the Filthy filthy too,
> And in his own weak person, if he can,
> Must suffer dully all the wrongs of Man.
> ('The Novelist,' 11–14)

This is what has become my "habit of life" (in Flannery O'Connor's words) through being a writer as my profession.

To define a desirable Japanese identity I would like to pick out the word 'decent' which is among the adjectives that George Orwell often used, along with words like 'humane,' 'sane' and 'comely,' for the character types that he favoured. This deceptively simple epithet may starkly set off and contrast with the word 'ambiguous' used for my identification in 'Japan, the Ambiguous, and Myself.' There is a wide and ironical discrepancy between what the Japanese seem like when viewed from outside and what they wish to look like.

I hope Orwell would not raise an objection if I used the word 'decent' as a synonym of 'humanist' or 'humaniste' in French, because both words share in common qualities such as tolerance and humanity. Among our ancestors were some pioneers who made painstaking efforts to build up the Japanese identity as 'decent' or 'humanist.'

One such person was the late Professor Kazuo Watanabe, a scholar of French Renaissance literature and thought. Surrounded by the insane ardour of patriotism on the eve and in the middle of the Second World War, Watanabe had a lonely dream of grafting the humanist view of man on to the traditional Japanese sense of beauty and sensitivity to Nature, which fortunately had not been entirely eradicated. I must hasten to add that Professor Watanabe had a conception of beauty and Nature different from that conceived of by Kawabata in his 'Japan, the Beautiful, and Myself.'

The way Japan had tried to build up a modern state modelled on the West was cataclysmic. In ways different from, yet partly corresponding to, that process Japanese intellectuals had tried to bridge the gap between the West and their own country at its deepest level. It must have been a laborious task or *travail* but it was also one that brimmed with joy. Professor Watanabe's study of François Rabelais was thus one of the most distinguished and rewarding scholarly achievements of the Japanese intellectual world.

Watanabe studied in Paris before the Second World War. When he told his academic supervisor about his ambition to translate Rabelais into Japanese, the eminent elderly French scholar answered the aspiring young Japanese student with the phrase: "L'entreprise inouïe de la traduction de l'intraduisible Rabelais" (the unprecedented enterprise of translating into Japanese untranslatable Rabelais). Another French scholar answered with blunt astonishment: "Belle entreprise Pantagruélique" (an admirably Pantagruel-like enterprise). In spite of all this not only did Watanabe accomplish his great enterprise in a poverty-stricken environment during the War and the American Occupation, but he also did his best to transplant into the confused and disorientated Japan of that time the life and thought of those French humanists who were the forerunners, contemporaries and followers of François Rabelais.

In both my life and writing I have been a pupil of Professor Watanabe's. I was influenced by him in two crucial ways. One was in my method of writing novels. I learnt concretely from his translation of Rabelais what Mikhail Bakhtin formulated as 'the image system of grotesque realism or the culture of popular laughter'; the importance of material and physical principles; the correspondence between the cosmic, social and physical elements; the overlapping of death and passions for rebirth; and the laughter that subverts hierarchical relationships.

The image system made it possible to seek literary methods of attaining the universal for someone like me born and brought up in a peripheral, marginal, off-centre region of the peripheral, marginal, off-centre country, Japan. Starting from such a background I do not represent Asia as a new economic power but an Asia impregnated with ever-lasting poverty and a mixed-up fertility. By sharing old, familiar yet living metaphors I align myself with writers like Kim Ji-ha of Korea, Chon I and Mu Jen, both of China. For me the brotherhood of world literature consists in such relationships in concrete terms. I once took part in a hunger strike for the political freedom of a gifted Korean poet. I am now deeply worried about the destiny of those gifted Chinese novelists who have been deprived of their freedom since the Tienanmen Square incident.

Another way in which Professor Watanabe has influenced me is in his idea of humanism. I take it to be the quintessence of Europe as a living totality. It is an idea which is also perceptible in Milan Kundera's definition of the spirit of the novel. Based on his accurate reading of historical sources Watanabe wrote critical biographies, with Rabelais at their centre, of people from Erasmus to Sébastien Castellion, and of women connected with Henri IV from Queen Marguerite to Gabrielle Destré. By doing so Watanabe intended to teach the Japanese about humanism, about the importance of tolerance, about man's vulnerability to his preconceptions or machines of his own making. His sincerity led him to quote the remark by the Danish philologist Kristoffer Nyrop: "Those who do not protest against war are accomplices of war." In his attempt to transplant into Japan humanism as the very basis of Western thought Watanabe was bravely venturing on both "l'entreprise inouïe" and the "belle entreprise Pantagruélique."

As someone influenced by Watanabe's humanism I wish my task as a novelist to enable both those who express themselves with words and their readers to recover from their own sufferings and the sufferings of their time, and to cure their souls of the wounds. I have said I am split between the opposite poles of ambiguity characteristic of the Japanese. I have been making efforts to be cured of and restored from those pains and wounds by means of literature. I have made my efforts also to pray for the cure and recovery of my fellow Japanese.

If you will allow me to mention him again, my mentally handicapped son Hikari was awakened by the voices of birds to the music of Bach and Mozart, eventually composing his own works. The little pieces that he first composed were full of fresh splendour and delight. They seemed like dew glittering on grass leaves. The word *innocence* is composed of *in*—"not" and *nocere*—"hurt", that is, "not to hurt." Hikari's music was in this sense a natural effusion of the composer's own innocence.

As Hikari went on to compose more works, I could not but hear in his music also 'the voice of a crying and dark soul.' Mentally handicapped as he was, his strenuous effort furnished his act of composing or his 'habit of life' with the growth of compositional techniques and a deepening of his conception. That in turn enabled him to discover in the depth of his heart a mass of dark sorrow which he had hitherto been unable to identify with words.

'The voice of a crying and dark soul' is beautiful, and his act of expressing it in music cures him of his dark sorrow in an act of recovery. Furthermore, his music has been accepted as one that cures and restores his contemporary listeners as well. Herein I find the grounds for believing in the exquisite healing power of art.

This belief of mine has not been fully proved. 'Weak person' though I am, with the aid of this unverifiable belief, I would like to 'suffer dully all the wrongs' accumulated throughout the twentieth century as a result of the monstrous development of technology and transport. As one with a peripheral, marginal and off-centre existence in the world I would like to seek how—with what I hope is a modest decent and humanist contribution—I can be of some use in a cure and reconciliation of mankind.